D1633041

# Preparing Teachers to Teach English as an International Language

WITHDRAWN

0 7 MAY 2022

MIX
Paper from
responsible sources
FSC® C014540
www.fsc.org

York St John University

3 8025 00629213 3

## NEW PERSPECTIVES ON LANGUAGE AND EDUCATION

**Series Editor**: Professor Viv Edwards, *University of Reading, Reading, UK* and Professor Phan Le Ha, *University of Hawaii at Manoa, USA*

Two decades of research and development in language and literacy education have yielded a broad, multidisciplinary focus. Yet education systems face constant economic and technological change, with attendant issues of identity and power, community and culture. This series will feature critical and interpretive, disciplinary and multidisciplinary perspectives on teaching and learning, language and literacy in new times.

Full details of all the books in this series and of all our other publications can be found on http://www.multilingual-matters.com, or by writing to Multilingual Matters, St Nicholas House, 31-34 High Street, Bristol BS1 2AW, UK.

NEW PERSPECTIVES ON LANGUAGE AND EDUCATION: 53

# Preparing Teachers to Teach English as an International Language

Edited by
**Aya Matsuda**

YORK ST. JOHN
LIBRARY & INFORMATION
SERVICES

**MULTILINGUAL MATTERS**
Bristol • Blue Ridge Summit

**Library of Congress Cataloging in Publication Data**
A catalog record for this book is available from the Library of Congress.
Matsuda, Aya, editor.
Preparing Teachers to Teach English as an International Language/Edited by Aya Matsuda.
Bristol: Multilingual Matters, [2017]
Includes bibliographical references and index.
LCCN 2016040543| ISBN 9781783097029 (hbk : alk. paper) | ISBN 9781783097012 (pbk : alk. paper) | ISBN 9781783097050 (kindle)
LCSH: English language–Study and teaching–Foreign speakers–Methods. | English teachers–Training of. | Teachers–Training of–Curricula. | English language–Globalization. | Communication, International. | English language–Foreign countries–Discourse analysis. | Intercultural education.
LCC PE1128.A2 P6983 2017 | DDC 428.0071–dc23 LC record available at https://lccn.loc.gov/2016040543

**British Library Cataloguing in Publication Data**
A catalogue entry for this book is available from the British Library.

ISBN-13: 978-1-78309-702-9 (hbk)
ISBN-13: 978-1-78309-701-2 (pbk)

**Multilingual Matters**
UK: St Nicholas House, 31-34 High Street, Bristol BS1 2AW, UK.
USA: NBN, Blue Ridge Summit, PA, USA.

Website: www.multilingual-matters.com
Twitter: Multi_Ling_Mat
Facebook: https://www.facebook.com/multilingualmatters
Blog: www.channelviewpublications.wordpress.com

Copyright © 2017 Aya Matsuda and the authors of individual chapters.

All rights reserved. No part of this work may be reproduced in any form or by any means without permission in writing from the publisher.

The policy of Multilingual Matters/Channel View Publications is to use papers that are natural, renewable and recyclable products, made from wood grown in sustainable forests. In the manufacturing process of our books, and to further support our policy, preference is given to printers that have FSC and PEFC Chain of Custody certification. The FSC and/or PEFC logos will appear on those books where full certification has been granted to the printer concerned.

Typeset by Deanta Global Publishing Services Limited.
Printed and bound in the UK by Short Run Press Ltd.
Printed and bound in the US by Edwards Brothers Malloy, Inc.

# Contents

# Contributors

**Yasemin Bayyurt** (PhD) is a Professor of Applied Linguistics in the Department of Foreign Language Education at Bogazici University, Turkey. She holds a PhD degree in Linguistics and Modern English Language from Lancaster University, UK. Her research focuses on World Englishes/EIL/ELF-based pedagogy, intercultural communication, telecollaboration, ELF/EIL-aware teacher education, mobile learning and corpus linguistics. She has published articles in international refereed/indexed journals. She has also published book chapters and edited books by well-known international publishers (e.g. Springer, Multilingual Matters). Her most recent co-edited book is *Current Perspectives on Pedagogy for ELF* (2015) published by De Gruyter.

**Luciana Cabrini Simões Calvo** is a Professor in the Foreign Language Department at the State University of Maringa, Brazil, and holds a PhD in Language Studies from the State University of Londrina, Brazil. Her research interests include teacher education, foreign language teaching and learning, communities of practice and English as a lingua franca. She co-edited the book *English as a Lingua Franca: Teaching, Learning and Teacher Education*, published in Portuguese by Pontes Editores.

**Thuy Ngoc Dinh** (PhD, Monash University) is currently an Adjunct Lecturer and Research Fellow at the School of Languages, Literatures, Cultures and Linguistics, Monash University, Australia. She has lectured and tutored in the English as an International Language program at Monash University since 2013 and has been a lecturer of English in Vietnam since 2007. Her research interests include EIL, Cultural Linguistics, Vietnamese English, curriculum development and intercultural communication. She has publications in the *Springer Cultural Linguistics book series*, *English Australia*, *International Journal of Language and Culture* and *English as lingua franca* journals.

**Eduardo H. Diniz de Figueiredo** is a tenure-track Professor of English at Universidade Federal do Paraná in Curitiba, Brazil. He holds a PhD in

Applied Linguistics from Arizona State University and an MA in English from Universidade Federal de Santa Catarina. His work has appeared in such publications as *The Encyclopedia of Applied Linguistics, World Englishes, Language and Education, English Today, The Civil Rights Project from UCLA* and *Teachers College Record*. His research interests lie in the areas of sociolinguistics, language and globalization, discourse analysis, critical applied linguistics and second/foreign language teaching.

**Seran Dogancay-Aktuna** (PhD, University of Pennsylvania) is a Professor of English in the Department of English Language and Literature at Southern Illinois University Edwardsville, Illinois, USA. Her research focuses on the global spread of English, its use as an international language and the implications of these developments for English language teaching and teacher education. In addition to her book *Global English Teaching and Teacher Education: Praxis and Possibility*, co-edited with Joel Hardman, she has published chapters in edited volumes and articles in journals including *Language Awareness, ELT Journal, Language, Culture and Curriculum, World Englishes, International Journal of the Sociology of Language* and *Journal of Multilingual and Multicultural Development*.

**Michele Salles El Kadri** is a Professor in the Foreign Language Department at the State University of Londrina, Brazil and holds a PhD and an MA in Language Studies. Her research interests include teacher education, English as a lingua franca, co-teaching/cogenerative dialogue and identities. She co-edited the book *English as a Lingua Franca: Teaching, Learning and Teacher Education*, published in Portuguese by Pontes Editores. Her work has appeared in such publications as *Teacher Development, Teaching Education, The Australian Journal of Teacher Education* and *Revista Brasileira de Línguistica Aplicada*.

**Nicola Galloway** (PhD, MA, MSc) was an English language teacher in Japan for 10 years. She is currently a lecturer in Education (TESOL) at The University of Edinburgh, where she teaches on the MSc TESOL program, including a course on Global Englishes for Language Teaching. Nicola holds a PhD from the University of Southampton and is co-author of an academic text on global Englishes with Routledge.

**Telma Gimenez** (PhD, Lancaster University) is an Associate Professor in the Department of Modern Foreign Languages at the State University of Londrina, Brazil. She supervises research at postgraduate level and facilitates preservice teachers' courses. Her primary research focus is on educational policies and their impact on the lives of teachers and students in schools. Her current research examines ways in which the developments in the field of English as a global language can be incorporated into teacher education programs.

Dr Gimenez is a researcher funded by CNPq (Science and Technology Agency) and was a member of the Advisory Board of ALAB – Brazilian Association of Applied Linguistics (2014–2015). She co-edited the book *English as a Lingua Franca: Teaching, Learning and Teacher Education,* published in Portuguese by Pontes Editores.

**Polina Golovátina-Mora** (PhD, Ural Federal University, Russia) is an Associate Professor (on tenure-track) at the School of Social Sciences, Universidad Pontificia Boliviariana (UPB-Medellín, Colombia. At UPB, she teaches undergraduate-level courses on introduction to epistemology and serves as an adviser in the PhD program in Social Sciences. She is also a Faculty Affiliate for the MA program in Learning and Teaching Processes in Second Languages and the Literacies in Second Languages Project (LSLP). Her current research intersects issues of aesthetics in the city, monstrous theory in popular culture and the use of transmedial discourse in sociocultural studies.

**Joel Hardman** (PhD Educational Linguistics, University of Pennsylvania) is a Professor in the Department of English Language and Literature, Southern Illinois University Edwardsville, Illinois. His scholarly interests include language and literacy acquisition, language teaching pedagogy, sociolinguistics, teacher development and the schooling of language-minority children in the United States. He has published numerous articles and book chapters on family literacy development in multilingual environments, English teacher education and second language writing, and has published one book (with Seran Dogancay-Aktuna) on global English teaching and teacher education. He teaches courses in ESL methods, language assessment, language and culture and ESL teacher development.

**Nobuyuki Hino** (PhD in Language and Culture, Osaka University) is Professor in the Graduate School of Language and Culture, Osaka University, Japan. He is a former director of the International Association for World Englishes, and currently serves on the editorial advisory board for the journal *World Englishes.* His publications include chapters in books such as *Principles and Practices of Teaching English as an International Language* (Multilingual Matters), *English as an International Language in Asia* (Springer), *Communicating with Asia* (Cambridge University Press) and *Current Perspectives on Pedagogy for English as a Lingua Franca* (De Gruyter Mouton) along with articles in journals such as *AILA Review* and *World Englishes.*

**Seong-Yoon Kang** (PhD, Indiana State University) is a Director of Global Education and Government Programs and Curriculum Specialist at Bloomfield College, New Jersey, USA, where he is in charge of Total Immersion Courses for Korean English Teachers, the Math and Science

Teacher Education Program and intensive English programs. His research focuses on L2 learners' individual differences in language acquisition, world Englishes, sociolinguistic influences on speech acts and curriculum/instructional design for in-service English teacher education. Previously he designed, developed and taught intensive English courses in South Korea.

**Lucilla Lopriore**, Associate Professor, Roma Tre University. MA TEFL, Reading University; PhD Italian as a Foreign Language, Siena University. Teacher educator and course book writer, her fields of interest are ELF (teacher education and material development), assessment and evaluation, early language learning and CLIL. Most recent publications: Lopriore, L. (2016) ELF in Teacher Education. A Way and Ways. In Lopriore, L. & Grazzi, E. *Intercultural Communication. New Perspectives from ELF.* RomaTrE-Press; Lopriore (2015) ELF and early language learning, in Y. Bayyurt and S. Akcan (eds) *Current Perspectives on Pedagogy for English as a Lingua Franca.* Berlin: De Gruyter Mouton; Lopriore L. & Vettorel P.(2015) Promoting awareness of Englishes and ELF in the English Language classroom, in Cogo, A. & Bowles, H. (eds) *International Perspectives on English as a Lingua Franca: Pedagogical Insights* Palgrave/Macmillan.

**Roby Marlina** (PhD, Monash University, Melbourne, Australia) is a Language Specialist at SEAMEO-RELC (Southeast Asian Ministers of Education Organization, Regional Language Centre), Singapore. Prior to joining SEAMEO-RELC, he spent 10 years as a lecturer in the English as an International Language (EIL) program at Monash University. His research interests lie in the curriculum and pedagogy of English as an international language (World Englishes), multicultural education and TESOL. He has published in international journals including *International Journal of Educational Research, Multilingual Education* and *Asian EFL Journal.* He is one of the main editors of the book, *The Pedagogy of English as an International Language: Perspectives from Scholars, Teachers, and Students* (Springer International Publishing).

**Aya Matsuda** (PhD, Purdue University) is Associate Professor of Applied Linguistics in the Department of English at Arizona State University. Her research interests include the use of English as an international language and the pedagogical implications of the global spread of English. Her work focusing on these issues has appeared in various books and journals including *English Today, JALT Journal, TESOL Quarterly* and *World Englishes.* Her edited volume, *Principles and Practices of Teaching English as an International Language* (2012), was published by Multilingual Matters. Matsuda currently services on the board of directors for TESOL International Association and also as a secretary-treasurer of the International Association for World Englishes.

**Raúl Alberto Mora** (PhD, University of Illinois at Urbana-Champaign) is an Associate Professor (with tenure) of English Education and Literacy Studies at the School of Pedagogy Graduate Programs at Universidad Pontificia Boliviariana (UPB-Medellín, Colombia). At UPB, he helped create the MA program in Learning and Teaching Processes in Second Languages and he was the first program coordinator between August 2013 and June 2016. He also serves as a Visiting Professor at several graduate programs in Colombia. His current research explores second language literacies in urban spaces and gaming communities in Medellín, the pedagogical implementation of alternative literacies in second language education and the use of transmedial discourse in sociocultural studies, topics he develops with his research team at the Literacies in Second Languages Project (LSLP).

**Heath Rose** is an Associate Professor of Applied Linguistics in the Department of Education at The University of Oxford. He currently coordinates and teaches the online MSc in Teaching English Language in University Settings. Before moving to the UK, he lectured in Applied Linguistics at Trinity College Dublin. He has published articles in *Applied Linguistics, ELT Journal* and *Modern Language Journal,* and is co-author of the book *Introducing Global Englishes* (2015) and co-editor of *Doing Research in Applied Linguistics* (forthcoming), both published by Routledge.

**Aline M. Sanfelici** is a tenure-track Professor of English at Universidade Tecnológica Federal do Paraná. She holds a PhD and an MA in English from Universidade Federal de Santa Catarina. She has previously served as tenure-track and tenured professor at Universidade Federal do Pará and Universidade Federal do Sul e Sudeste do Pará in Brazil. Her current work addresses issues of literary studies and the teaching of literature.

**Ali Fuad Selvi** is an Assistant Professor of TESOL and Applied Linguistics in the Teaching English as a Foreign Language program at Middle East Technical University, Northern Cyprus Campus. His research interests include the sociolinguistics of English as an international language and its implications for language learning, teaching, teacher education and language policy/planning; and issues related to nonnative English-speaking professionals in TESOL. He is the past Chair of the NNEST Interest Section in TESOL International Association. In addition, he co-authored *Teaching English as an International Language* (2013) published by TESOL Press.

**Nicos C. Sifakis** is an Associate Professor in the School of Humanities of the Hellenic Open University (HOU) and director of the MEd in TESOL program. He holds a PhD in language and linguistics from the University of Essex, UK. He is editor-in-chief of *Research Papers in Language Teaching and*

*Learning* (http://rpltl.eap.gr/). He has published extensively on intercultural communication and pedagogy, teaching and researching English as an international lingua franca, language teaching methodology, distance education, adult education and teacher education.

**Paola Vettorel** is an Assistant Professor at the Department of Foreign Languages and Literatures, University of Verona. Her main research interests include ELF and its implications in ELT practices and materials. Among her recent publications: (2013) 'ELF in international school exchanges: Stepping into the role of ELF users' *JELF* 2/1; (2014) *ELF in Wider Networking: Blogging Practices*, Mouton de Gruyter; (2015) (ed.) *New Frontiers in Teaching and Learning English*, Cambridge Scholars; with Lopriore, L. (2015) Promoting awareness of Englishes and ELF in the English Language Classroom, in A. Cogo and H. Bowles (eds) *International Perspectives on English as a Lingua Franca: Pedagogical Insights*, Palgrave/Macmillan.

**Nugrahenny T. Zacharias** was a teacher educator at the English Teacher Education (ETE) department of Faculty of Language and Literature at Satya Wacana Christian University. Her research interest is in the area of identity issues and the implementation of EIL pedagogy in second language teaching and learning. She has published in various international journals. Her recent coedited book is entitled *Contextualizing English as an International Language: Issues and Challenges* (2013). Currently, she is a Visiting Assistant Professor at Miami University, Oxford, Ohio.

Biographies for the contributors for Chapter 15 are provided after each pedagogical idea in the chapter.

# Introduction

## Aya Matsuda

## Teaching English as an International Language

The unprecedented spread of English and the growing importance of English as an international language (EIL) have complicated the notion of English, English speakers and English-speaking culture, and challenged the taken-for-granted assumptions in the field of English language teaching (ELT). In the past decade or so, scholars (e.g. Alsagoff *et al.*, 2012; Matsuda, 2012a; McKay, 2002) have argued for a paradigm shift in the field of ELT in order to meet the complex and diverse uses and users of English. There is an increasing awareness among English language teachers, too, as demonstrated by the growing number of conference presentations or articles in teacher-oriented journals (Matsuda, 2015), that some of our common pedagogical practices must be re-examined vis-à-vis the current use of EIL. There also seems to be a shared understanding that the current use of EIL is best conceptualized not as one specific variety of international English but rather as a function that English performs in international, multilingual contexts, to which each speaker brings a variety of English that they are most familiar with, along with their own cultural frames of reference, and employs various strategies to communicate effectively.

Although proposed frameworks and approaches may have different names – e.g. English as a lingua franca (ELF)-aware pedagogy (Bayyurt & Sifakis, 2015), global Englishes language teaching (GELT) (Galloway, 2011, 2013; Galloway & Rose, 2015), teaching EIL (Matsuda, 2012a; McKay, 2002) or World Englishes (WE)-informed ELT (Matsuda, forthcoming) – they share much in common in terms of their visions and practical suggestions. For example, they all acknowledge the 'messiness' of English – that there are different varieties of English spoken in different parts of the world for different purposes that are learned in different ways – which clearly contradicts the traditional conceptualization of English in ELT, which tends to ignore such heterogeneity. Furthermore, a common premise of these approaches is that ELT must reflect, and also must prepare students for, this 'messiness' of English, and that the traditional approaches to ELT do not do an adequate job in doing so. While there is nothing wrong with English, cultures or people of the US and the UK, which dominate the English language classrooms globally, there is a concern that addressing only these countries and their Englishes does not sufficiently prepare our students for future use of English, in which they are likely to encounter interlocutors and English varieties from countries other than these two.

More specifically, as Alsagoff (2012: 116) wrote, '[t]he literature on EIL, however diverse in opinion, is united in the desire to move away from teaching for native-speaker competence' and encourages ELT professionals to critically evaluate such fundamental concepts as native speakers, standards and correctness and ownership of English that have influenced every aspect of our profession. Some of the specific pedagogical recommendations that these approaches often share include:

- Increasing exposure to and raising awareness of diverse forms and functions of English.
- Emphasizing communication strategies to negotiate linguistic differences.
- Using cultural materials from diverse sources.
- Facilitating an understanding of and sensitivity toward the politics of EIL (including such issues as multilingualism, linguistic and cultural diversity and identity).

## Importance of Teacher Preparation

The successful implementation of these and other suggested changes in the English language classroom requires and depends on successful innovations in teacher preparation (Dogancay-Aktuna & Hardman, 2008; Matsuda, 2006). Teacher preparation programs in any discipline consistently evolve in order to meet the changing needs of students, teachers and society; the preparation of EIL teachers is no exception. In fact, one may even argue that it is particularly so in the case of EIL teachers because of the magnitude of the transformation that these teachers are expected to go through. As Renandya (2012) wrote:

> To implement an EIL approach, the teachers need to learn and do a lot of things – they need to understand what it means to teach English in the EIL context; they need to know what kinds of roles they should play in promoting EIL pedagogy and what roles they should be critical about if they want to put into practice an approach to teaching English that is compatible with EIL principles; they also need to be willing to learn new knowledge and skills before they can comfortably assume their new roles in teaching EIL. In addition, and perhaps more importantly, they need to develop a favourable attitude towards the teaching of EIL. (Renandya, 2012: 65)

In other words, what is expected of EIL teachers is not merely to acquire new skills and techniques but rather to embrace an entirely new way of thinking about English language teaching and learning based on a newly acquired set of knowledge. And if we expect these teachers to guide their students as they become competent users of EIL, we must also ensure that teacher preparation programs and various professional development opportunities are available to support teachers before and during such a journey.

One reason why teacher preparation programs play a vital role in supporting teachers is that they provide a safe space for transformation that can be slow, which may not be available through a short conference presentation or one-time workshops (although they are indeed important professional development opportunities). A paradigm shift, both in the field and in individuals, is typically a slow process. Kachru (1976) challenged the monolithic view of English from the WE perspective in *TESOL Quarterly* back in the mid-1970s, but such critique did not enter the mainstream teaching English to speakers of other languages (TESOL) discourse until about 30 years later (Matsuda, 2012b). Brown and Peterson (1997: 44) also showed that brief exposure to WE issues is 'unlikely to bring about the kind of paradigm shift called for' and argued that a longer and sustained engagement is essential for deeper and richer understanding of WE issues necessary for EIL teaching. Teacher preparation programs engage student-teachers over time, sometimes for multiple years, and provide them with opportunities to tackle new ideas from multiple perspectives; even if the EIL issues are not explicitly made the central focus on a daily basis, student-teachers may revisit the idea in the context of discussing other ELT issues.

The sustained nature of teacher preparation programs also helps when student-teachers find the transformation challenging and even threatening. These student-teachers who are embarking on the new challenge of teaching EIL, in most cases, are the successful products of English language and language arts curricula that are based on the traditional view of English. Those who learned English as a 'second' or 'foreign' language were taught with an assumption that the Inner Circle varieties, especially US or UK standard English, were the only legitimate instructional model, they were encouraged to aim for the 'native speaker' proficiency and they were probably more successful in doing so than their peers. ELT professionals who are first language (L1) users of English also survived – if not thrived – in language arts curricula that promote standard English prescriptively. English users, whether they have learned it as their L1 or not, often have internalized the monolithic and static view of English of these curricula, and they are now expected to question, challenge and even deconstruct this view. The process of critiquing the fundamentals of the education system which student-teachers have lived through, succeeded in and, in some cases, taught in, can be threatening (although it could also be liberating and empowering for some) because it may feel as though the new perspective dismisses and denies one's past effort and investments in language learning, which is often a significant part of student-teachers' identity. In that sense, teacher preparation programs not only provide the first exposure to the idea of teaching

EIL but also invaluable scaffolding as participating teachers engage with and process the idea to make it their own.

In addition, from a pragmatic point of view, bringing in changes to teacher preparation programs is an efficient way to bring changes into English language classrooms. While a paradigm shift implemented by one language teacher will affect only their students, a shift implemented by one teacher educator will affect multiple teachers, each of whom will have multiple students, and thus the cumulative impact will be greater. Furthermore, teacher educators in many contexts also play influential roles in designing national and regional curricula, which affect teachers with whom they may not have direct contact. The magnitude of influence that teacher educators have is another reason to explore what innovations to bring to the teacher education programs and how to implement them in light of the needs of EIL teachers, students and users today.

## Emerging Changes in TESOL Programs

Changes are slowly but certainly happening in the preparation of English language teachers. Although native speakerism and Inner-Circle bias may still be prevalent in many programs, and even sympathetic teacher educators may think of the EIL perspective as a 'desirable but not necessary' component of teacher preparation (Matsuda, 2009), there are growing interests in incorporating such a perspective into teacher preparation programs. For example, there was a strong presence of sessions related to EIL teacher education at two international conferences I recently attended (The Annual Conference of the International Association for World Englishes in November 2013 and ELF7 in September 2014), which were not only well-attended but also often resulted in active discussions during which some audience members shared their own approaches. The contributors of this volume are examples of scholars and teacher educators who have been actively exploring ways to integrate the EIL perspective into their work with preservice and in-service teachers.

While such attempts are being called by different names, as can be seen in the chapters in this volume, they all work toward the same goal, which is to prepare teachers who are aware of the complexity of the use of English in today's world rather than to perpetuate the view of English with 'native speakers' as the sole target interlocutor and the target proficiency model. More specifically, their teacher education curricula typically emphasize such issues as:

- An informed understanding of today's English, including its forms, uses and users.
- An exploration of the practical implications of the above.
- Critical reflections on key issues as related to the use of EIL today, such as *native speakerism, nonnative English-speaking teachers* and *linguistic imperialism*.

In other words, these approaches to teacher preparation address the theory–practice disconnect in EIL teaching (Matsuda, 2012a; Matsuda & Friedrich, 2011) by creating a space for preservice and in-service teachers to understand the principles of EIL teaching and consider their applications to their local contexts with the ongoing support of teacher educators and peers.

## Overview of This Book

The purpose of this volume, simply put, is to explore ways to prepare teachers of EIL. More specifically, its primary goal is to provide theoretically informed models for EIL-informed teacher education. It identifies the necessary changes in our approaches to prepare English teachers vis-à-vis the use of EIL today, and proposes ways to implement those changes. As in my previous work, the term *EIL* is used to refer to the function that English performs in multilingual, international contexts. *Teaching EIL* is characterized by its commitment to prepare our students to become competent users of English in international contexts (Matsuda, 2012a), and it is used as an umbrella term for several frameworks that I mentioned above, which share a dynamic and diverse view of English, uses and users today (e.g. ELF-aware, GELT, WE-informed). Consequently, I use such phrases as 'preparing teachers to teach EIL', 'EIL teachers' and 'EIL-informed teacher preparation', not as ideas that contrast and distinguish themselves from parallel notions under different names, but rather as an inclusive shorthand.[1]

The chapters in this volume collectively showcase the approaches, program models and pedagogical ideas for teacher preparation that are informed by theories and research in WE, ELF, GE and other relevant areas. Its aim is not to propose a one-size-fits-all curriculum but rather to illustrate diverse approaches to prepare teachers who can meet the diverse needs of English learners in international contexts today.

The volume also attempts to start a conversation on EIL teacher education that cuts across multiple disciplinary communities, particularly WE and ELF. While these communities share many interests, they have developed into independent scholarly communities and the articulation between them tends to be limited. From the pedagogical point of view, however, it would be more constructive to draw from both (and any other relevant) disciplines to make our teacher education practices as EIL-friendly and informed as possible.

With these goals in mind, the volume includes the discussion of theoretical approaches and principles in EIL teacher education as well as a collection of descriptions of existing teacher education programs, courses, units in a course and activities from diverse geographical and institutional contexts. Even though these curricular ideas were originally developed for the specific instructional context that the authors taught in, the detailed description of the rationale behind the pedagogical decisions and the specific discussion of the uniqueness of their pedagogical ideas should allow each reader to revise the ideas in order to make them more appropriate for their own students and contexts.

Part 1 of the volume presents two complementing frameworks for the preparation of EIL teachers. In Chapter 1, after a brief review of the global spread of English and the EIL construct as well as their implications for teaching and teacher education, Bayyurt and Sifakis introduce a three-phased approach to the preparation of ELF-aware teachers. They introduce the ELF TEd projects, which they implemented in Turkey, to illustrate how three stages – exposure, critical awareness and action plan – play out in EIL teacher preparation. Chapter 2 by Dogancay-Aktuna and Hardman presents another approach, namely a situated meta-praxis framework of EIL teacher education, which conceptualizes teacher education as 'an interaction between *place, proficiency, praxis* and a set of *understandings* about language, culture, identity and teaching' (p. 21).

The rest of the book consists of curricular descriptions and pedagogical ideas. Two chapters in Part 2, Teacher Preparation Programs, present examples of ideal scenarios in which the entire program is created based on the EIL perspective. Such a program can consistently and coherently provide opportunities for students to examine all aspects of ELT practices through an EIL-informed lens. Chapter 3 by Mora and Golovátina-Mora presents a two-year, research-oriented master's program for in-service teachers in Colombia that provides 'an epistemological orientation about English that aligns with the current views of English as an international language' (p. 35). In Chapter 4, Kang describes how the US-based TICKET program transformed a traditional in-service teacher training program into 'an innovative teacher education program with a new perspective on EIL in multicultural globalized contexts' (p. 52).

In reality, however, it is rare that we have an opportunity to create or revise the entire curriculum to incorporate the changing needs of our students and of the fields. Implementation at a course level – formally by creating or revising a new course or informally by taking advantage of the flexibility as a course instructor – is often a much more realistic option, as presented in the next two parts of the book.

Four chapters in Part 3 introduce teacher preparation courses that are dedicated specifically to the idea of teaching EIL. Galloway (Chapter 5) describes 'Global Englishes for Language Teaching', which is an 8-week postgraduate course based on the GELT framework (Galloway & Rose, 2015) for in-service and preservice teachers offered at the University of Edinburgh. In Chapter 6, Hino describes a course titled 'Education in Language and Culture'. It is an existing course within a master's program at a national university in Japan, which he offers with his own focus and subtitle 'Principles and practices of EIL education'. 'Practices of Teaching Englishes for

International Communication', described by Marlina (Chapter 7), is another example of a graduate-level course, which is offered within the master's program in Teaching World Englishes for Intercultural Communication in Australia for in-service and preservice teachers. The last chapter (Chapter 8, Selvi) in this section describes an undergraduate 'Global Englishes' course in Northern Cyprus, which presents the overview of English as a global language and its pedagogical implications. The course is strategically positioned as the first of the ELT courses so that it 'has the potential to serve as an intellectual lens which illuminates the process of construction of their professional knowledge base' (p. 117).

Three chapters in Part 4, in contrast, present courses with a focus on another ELT topic, in which the ideas of EIL and Teaching English as an International Language (TEIL) are integrated throughout. Dinh (Chapter 9) demonstrates how the EIL perspectives informed and were integrated into a newly developed course on teaching materials at a Vietnamese university. The focus of Chapter 10 (Diniz de Figueiredo and Sanfelici) is a course on 'Anglophone cultures' from Brazil, which the authors expanded to incorporate the global perspective of English and promoted 'a pluralistic understanding of culture, one that is heterogeneous, continuous and not fixed or essentialized' (p. 149). The final chapter of this section (Chapter 11, Zacharias) features a microteaching course at a university in Indonesia, in which the author introduced the notion of EIL pedagogy and supported student-teachers to create EIL-informed lessons and deliver them.

The next section, Part 5, showcases three self-standing units on EIL pedagogy that have been implemented in different courses. While units are shorter and may appear more limited than a program or a course in terms of the impact that they have on the transformation of student-teachers, they have several advantages, including portability and flexibility. These units can be inserted into a variety of courses, and thus have the potential to reach out to more student-teachers. Also, having a series of such units ready gives teacher educators the flexibility to add as much or little EIL perspective as the context allows. The first example of such units is from Ireland. Rose (Chapter 12) describes a unit called 'A Global Approach to English Language Teaching', which he offered in the middle of the graduate course 'Second Language Teaching'. In Chapter 13, El Kadri, Calvo and Gimenez share an example from a state-funded online teacher education program at a Brazilian university. The unit 'English in the Contemporary World' is offered as part of 'Teacher Education: Linguistic-Communicative Skills and English as a Lingua Franca', which is a one-semester course for the fifth (and final) year of the undergraduate program. The last chapter of this section (Chapter 14 by Vettorel and Lopriore) compares and contrasts two approaches in the new teaching programs implemented relatively recently at Italian universities. The first case offers a discreet unit on WE, ELF and their pedagogical implications as part of the 'English Language' module of the program, while in the second case, such perspectives and issues are embedded and integrated throughout the English language teaching component of the program.

The last section, Part 6, is a collection of pedagogical ideas. The 15 lessons and activities introduced in this chapter were originally developed for a particular group of preservice and in-service teachers, both L1 and second language (L2) users of English, in a particular context, but they are flexible enough to be adopted by or adapted for other audience and contexts. Some of the lessons and activities aim to raise awareness among teachers about the use of EIL, while others help them revise the traditional ELT practices to better meet the needs of EIL users. Some of the tasks can be incorporated into TEIL-focused courses as a key component, while others allow teacher educators who teach traditional ELT courses to bring in a TEIL perspective as a stand-alone activity. The goal of this chapter is to provide some specific and actionable pedagogical ideas as well as to inspire teacher educators by showing the range of activities that can facilitate the preparation of EIL teachers.

## Note

(1) I should note, however, that the use of EIL as an umbrella term is not necessarily universal or the norm. The terms related to the global spread of English and its use and diversity (e.g. EIL, English as a lingua franca [ELF], GELT and WE) are used differently by scholars who investigate these issues, and I do not believe that there is one use that is considered more authoritative than others at this point. In this volume, each author uses these terms in their own way while clarifying their scope and use of these terms vis-à-vis the use described here. In a sense, the varying use of these terms among authors accurately captures the current state of the profession.

## References

Alsagoff, L. (2012) Identity and the EIL learner. In L. Alsagoff, S.L. McKay, G. Hu and W.A. Renandya (eds) *Principles and Practices for Teaching English as an International Language* (pp. 105–122). New York: Routledge.

Alsagoff, L. McKay, S.L., Hu, G. and Renandya, W.A. (eds) (2012) *Principles and Practices for Teaching English as an International Language*. New York: Routledge.

Bayyurt, Y. and Sifakis, N. (2015) Developing an ELF-aware pedagogy: Insights from a self-education programme. In P. Vettorel (ed.) *New Frontiers in Teaching and Learning English* (pp. 55–76). Newcastle upon Tyne: Cambridge Scholars Publishing.

Brown, K. and Peterson, J. (1997) Exploring conceptual frameworks: Framing a world Englishes paradigm. In L.E. Smith and M.L. Forman (eds) *World Englishes 2000* (pp. 32–47). Honolulu, HI: University of Hawai'i Press.

Dogancay-Aktuna, S. and Hardman, J. (eds) (2008) *Global English Teaching and Teacher Education: Praxis and Possibility*. Alexandria, VA: TESOL.

Galloway, N. (2011) An investigation of Japanese students' attitudes towards English. PhD thesis, University of Southampton.

Galloway, N. (2013) Global Englishes and English language teaching (ELT) – Bridging the gap between theory and practice in a Japanese context. *System* 41 (3), 786–803.

Galloway, N. and Rose, H. (2015) *Introducing Global Englishes*. Abingdon: Routledge.

Kachru, B.B. (1976) Models of English for the Third World: White man's linguistic burden or language pragmatics? *TESOL Quarterly* 10 (2), 221–239.

Matsuda, A. (2006) Negotiating ELT assumptions in EIL classrooms. In J. Edge (ed.) *(Re) Locating TESOL in an Age of Empire* (pp. 158–170). Basingstoke: Palgrave MacMillan.

Matsuda, A. (2009) Desirable but not necessary? The place of World Englishes and English as an international language in English teacher preparation programs in Japan. In F. Sharifian (ed.) *English as an International Language: Perspectives and Pedagogical Issues* (pp. 169–189). Bristol: Multilingual Matters.

Matsuda, A. (ed.) (2012a) *Principles and Practices of Teaching English as an International Language*. Bristol: Multilingual Matters.

Matsuda, A. (2012b) World Englishes and TESOL. In C.A. Chapelle (ed.) *The Encyclopedia of Applied Linguistics* (pp. 6240–6246). Oxford: Wiley-Blackwell. See http://onlinelibrary.wiley.com/doi/10.1002/9781405198431.wbeal1293/pdf

Matsuda, A. (October, 2015) World Englishes in TESOL. Focus lecture at the annual meeting of the International Association of World Englishes: Istanbul, Turkey.

Matsuda, A. (forthcoming) World Englishes and English language teaching. In B. Kachru, C. Nelson, Z. Proshina and L. Smith (eds) *The Handbook of World Englishes* (2nd edn). Malden, MA: Wiley-Blackwell.

Matsuda, A. and Friedrich, P. (2011) English as an international language: A curriculum blueprint. *World Englishes* 30 (3), 332–344.

McKay, S.L. (2002) *Teaching English as an International Language*. Oxford: Oxford University Press.

Renandya, W.A. (2012) Teacher roles in EIL. *European Journal of Applied Linguistics and TEFL* 1 (2), 65–80.

# Part 1

# Theoretical Frameworks

# 1 Foundations of an EIL-aware Teacher Education

## Yasemin Bayyurt and Nicos Sifakis

## Introduction: ESL, EFL and the Current Global Reality

The education of teachers of English as a foreign/second language has always been a central concern in teaching English to speakers of other languages (TESOL). In the past, teacher education has focused on academically preparing teachers-to-be or informing in-service English for speakers of other languages (ESOL) teachers about all matters regarding the pedagogy of English as a foreign/second language, taking into consideration the context in which they were to find themselves (Freeman & Johnson, 1998). Context is highlighted as a key aspect of teacher education and one of its essential characteristics is typically linked to the status of English: if English is the dominant language or one of the dominant languages, then ongoing exposure to it outside the classroom is a given; if English is not used extensively, or at all, then exposure to it is limited to the classroom and dependent on the courseware used. In the former case, the context is termed 'English as a second language' (henceforth ESL), the idea being that learners have to ultimately 'add' English to their own first language (L1) because they need it in order to be able to 'survive' in their ESL setting. In the latter case, the context is termed 'English as a foreign language' (henceforth EFL), the idea being that learners need to have adequate knowledge of English which, in most cases, takes the form of a certificate of their proficiency, and may be used either for professional or academic purposes. Although the EFL and the ESL contexts are often conflated, they are very different, and this repeatedly shows in field studies of learners' knowledge and usage of English (e.g. Nayar, 1997; Schauer, 2006).

Despite the differences between EFL and ESL, it would be fair to say that, from the point of view of teaching instruction, these two orientations tend to be treated as not being all that different. The underlying assumption is that, in both contexts, learners have to learn what has come to be termed standard English (henceforth SE), namely, 'the variety whose grammar has been described and given public recognition in grammar books and dictionaries, with its norms being widely considered to be "correct" and constituting "good usage"' (Trudgill & Hannah, 2008: 92). Variations are certainly allowed, but these depend on the context and are not treated as being very extensive. ESL settings are more closely dependent upon the SE variety that is closer to the teaching context (e.g. British English [henceforth BE] in the UK, General America [henceforth GA] in the USA, Australian English in Australia, South African English in South Africa and so on). On the other hand, EFL settings tend to be dominated by one of the two more widely used SE varieties, BE or GA. This picture becomes more complicated as different settings have different types of dependences on different varieties of English (Kirkpatrick, 2007). The very existence of many contexts where English is used successfully and consistently by so-called nonnative speakers has given rise to many new standardized varieties of English, such as Singapore English (Deterding, 2007), Philippine English (Bautista & Bolton, 2008) or Nigerian English (Mesthrie, 2008) and has led many scholars to attack the selection, by policymakers, of GA or BE as the sole varieties that learners should be expected to learn and be examined upon (e.g. Kachru & Nelson, 2006). The spread of English is globally so pervasive that, even in settings with no connection to either a standard or an emerging variety of English, we see successful and at times creative uses of English by so-called nonnative users: this perspective has been termed English as a lingua franca, or ELF (Jenkins *et al.*, 2011, Seidlhofer, 2011).

An important ingredient in English for speakers of other languages (ESOL) teacher education is the reflective component (Kumaravadivelu, 2012). Teachers are not just passive receivers of knowledge and skills, but rather they are expected to be autonomous practitioners who are able to make informed decisions about virtually all aspects of teaching, from researching and responding to their learners' individual needs to selecting and/or adapting courseware to applying appropriate assessment and testing techniques. This reflective component was significantly strengthened in the past two decades by developments such as the so-called social turn in applied linguistics (Block, 2003; Freeman & Johnson, 1998) and postmethod pedagogy (Kumaravadivelu, 1994). These developments showcased the importance of the element of communication, language use, teaching and learning and emphasized the importance of tailoring instruction to the cognitive, affective, cultural and other needs of individual learners.

# The Global Spread of English: Developments and Consequences

While the ESL and EFL constructs have for a long time been acceptable and convenient orientations in the world of TESOL, the rapid and unprecedented spread of English on a global scale in recent years has prompted significant developments in both applied linguistics and TESOL. What follows is a brief understanding of these developments and what has caused them.

English is used very extensively around the world. The term 'World Englishes' (WE) shows the central role and status of English in different domains around the globe. Settings where English was one of the languages enjoying legal recognition (e.g. India, Pakistan, Nigeria or Singapore) are rapidly recognized as 'native speaker' or Inner Circle settings (see above). Similarly, the growing number of competent nonnative users of English around the world has challenged the notion of 'EFL'. The concept of 'foreignness' hints at a distance between the learners and the language they learn (Ehlich, 2009: 27) that is more akin to other major foreign languages, like French, German or Chinese. Yet more and more learners of English in the traditional EFL world feel a sense of ownership toward that language that they do not claim for any other language other than their own L1. Admittedly, this sense of ownership is currently limited to certain domains of usage (for example, face-to-face interaction and online communication involving videogames, chatting, etc.), but it is rapidly expanding to more and more domains (e.g. Grau, 2009) and seems to have an impact on changing users' and learners' attitudes (Kormos *et al.*, 2011; Kubota & McKay, 2009; Ranta, 2010). However, that sense of ownership is not reflected in the classrooms of these EFL settings, where teaching follows the 'traditional' EFL approach, i.e. an approach that prioritizes, almost entirely, learners' exposure to and assessment on the basis of native speaker norms, or SE (Bayyurt, 2012; Sifakis, 2009; Sifakis & Sougari, 2005).

Still, norms of usage are bound to change more rapidly than before and are influenced by successful communicative encounters involving an increasing number of native and competent nonnative users. In fact, the very notion of 'native speaker' is challenged (Graddol, 2006). SE (in any shape or form) is no longer the sole candidate for learning English. Users of English need to be able to adapt to communicative settings that involve other nonnative users. The ability to communicate successfully in new intercultural settings, and to do so using English, is considered a central '21st century' or 'soft' skill by international institutions such as OECD (2015) and UNESCO (Medel-Añonuevo *et al.*, 2001).

The above changes give rise to a number of concerns for teacher education. With the rapid increase in global movement, and as virtual (online) communication becomes more and more established and accepted, the ESL/EFL borders are more blurred than ever before. Curricula and textbooks continue to serve a more traditional perspective of teaching and learning English, in the sense that they typically prioritize learners' exposure to SE (Fay *et al.*, 2010). This is reinforced by the widespread need for the certification of proficiency through high-stakes examinations (Wall, 2005). In certain domains, there is an acceptance of the need for learners to become interculturally competent (for example, the Greek curriculum of 2003 and the Turkish curriculum of 2005, which integrated the Common European Framework's principles of literacy, multilingualism and interculturality).

Teachers have strong convictions about their role in the ESL/EFL classroom that is often in contrast to their perspective about what their learners need in order to be successful communicators. Research shows that, while there is a growing acceptance of the need for learners to use English successfully in communications involving other nonnative users, teachers consider their role in the language classroom to be one of the custodian of SE (Bayyurt, 2006, 2012; Sifakis, 2009; Sifakis & Sougari, 2005). In light of the current situation regarding the widespread use of English globally, these perceptions need to be re-evaluated and perhaps, ultimately transformed (Sifakis, 2007, 2014).

# The EIL Construct and Teacher Education

We see *English as an International Language* (henceforth EIL) as an umbrella term that incorporates orientations about the different roles of English around the world (most notably WE and ELF). As we saw above, the more a setting involves varieties of English that are, or can potentially be, standardized, the more clearly delineated that setting is. This means that WE is more clearly delineated than ELF, which also implies that the concept of EIL is still in the process of development (Matsuda & Friedrich, 2011; McKay, 2002). What is clear in EIL is that it defines a broad spectrum of settings concerning the communication and teaching of English that involve nonnative as well as native speakers. As already mentioned, EIL teacher education is challenging for reasons that are, to a large extent, related both to the fact that it encompasses different perspectives of theorizing and analyzing the spread of English around the world, and to teachers' perceptions about SE and conflicting attitudes toward the role and status of nonnative speaker communication and its intelligibility. In this section, we propose a series of principles to be considered by teacher educators who wish to integrate the EIL construct into teacher preparation seminars.

## The concept of EIL-awareness

One of the shortcomings of EIL, when it comes to teacher education and teaching, is the lack of available curricula. While research in EIL and ELF discourse is widespread, currently there is no commonly accepted perspective with regard to teaching EIL (Matsuda, 2009, 2012) or ELF (Canagarajah, 2007; Park & Wee, 2011). Having said that, there is an increasing number of studies that put forward critiques of and proposals for WE/EIL-informed curricula and materials (e.g. Bayyurt & Altinmakas, 2012; D'Angelo, 2012; Lee, 2012; Matsuda & Duran, 2012; Sharifian & Marlina, 2012), but it is still difficult to find a comprehensive curriculum for EIL teacher education. This is probably due to the fact that, as we have seen, while ESL/EFL is readily specified as a teaching and learning construct, EIL/ELF is still not.

The basic reason for this is that, while ESL/EFL refer to standard varieties of English, EIL/ELF do not. This means that ESL/EFL settings provide extensive courseware that cater to all sorts of learner needs, targeting different proficiency levels, as well as different types of formal and informal assessment of proficiency. On top of that, widespread research over the past 15 years consistently shows that the attitudes of all major stakeholders (teachers, learners, sponsors, parents, etc.) are strongly favorable toward the ESL/EFL/SE orientation (e.g. Bayyurt, 2006; Sifakis & Sougari, 2005; Timmis, 2002), despite the fact that there are, as we have seen, signs of awareness of the shifting role of English in global communication, on the part of both teachers and learners (for a review, see Jenkins, 2007).

At the same time, no one can deny that the world of TESOL undergoes a wave of change that focuses on perceiving communication more in terms of its extensive variability in diverse contexts and less in terms of linguistic form, so that 'language events and experiences are central rather than language as form and meaning' (Blommaert, 2010: 100). Fluidity and dynamism in moving between local and global communities is perceived as more interesting and informative in understanding the development of norms (Canagarajah, 2005; Pennycook, 2007). In this context, the widespread use of English by nonnative speakers around the world cannot but shed light on the skills brought to bear by these speakers (Seidlhofer, 2011), which raises implications for the self-awareness of these users as international users of English (Seidlhofer, 2007) and, by extension, for the ESOL classroom itself (Baker, 2009; Firth, 2009; Maley, 2009; Matsuda & Friedrich, 2011; McKay, 2002; Sifakis, 2004).

It is with the above complications in mind that we suggest that EIL teacher education does not aim at changing teachers' perspectives overnight. Research shows that changing teachers' perspectives is a painstaking process that, even with interested teachers, may require a long period of active engagement with the key issues of EIL (Dewey, 2012; Rajagopalan, 1999; Sifakis, 2009). We consider that it is more effective and practical if the focus is on (a) providing comprehensive information about the current role of English worldwide and (b) incorporating an element of change in teachers' perspectives about that role and the implications it can have for their own teaching context. Essentially, the EIL-aware teacher education model we propose breaks down into three phases (see Figure 1.1):

(a) exposing teachers to the intricacies of the global spread of English and the multiplicities of communicative contexts in today's global reality;
(b) raising their awareness of the challenges those intricacies can have for their own teaching context in a critical and practical way; and
(c) involving them in an action plan that would help them to integrate elements from EIL, ELF and WE research they deem important and relevant for their own teaching context.

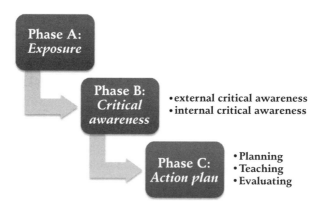

**Figure 1.1** The three phases of EIL-aware teaching education

The three phases blend into each other, with the transitions between them being smooth and gradual. The focus of EIL teacher education, according to our perspective, is not one of indoctrinating teachers into 'buying into' the entire EIL construct (which is, as we have seen, still in the process of developing). The focus is on using existing EIL research as a means of prompting ESOL teachers to grow into more autonomous, independent, critical practitioners, capable of deciding on the extent to which they can integrate EIL issues in their own teaching context. In what follows, we present a more analytical account of the above three phases of what we term EIL-aware teacher education.

### Phase A: Exposure

In this phase, teachers are exposed to the multiplicity and complicatedness of using English today to communicate with other nonnative users. The aims of this phase are twofold. In the first place, teachers are prompted to become aware of the global role of English as a language of convenience in communication. In itself, this can be a journey of discovery for many teachers who may be isolated into believing that only SE 'works'. Their exposure to examples of successful interactions involving nonnative users of English is expected to bring them up to date with the global spread of English. It is advisable that this exposure is done in an experiential way, i.e. with the active involvement of teachers in communications with other nonnative users, who may be fellow teachers, as co-participants in these projects. Trainers can also integrate excerpts from the published literature (e.g. Cogo & Dewey, 2012), from available online corpora (e.g. the VOICE corpus, available at https://www.univie. ac.at/voice; the ELFA corpus, available at http://www.helsinki.fi/englanti/ elfa/elfacorpus; or the ASEAN corpus, available at http://www.ubd.edu. bn/academic/faculty/fass/research/CMACE/home/asean-index.html) and even from YouTube – although, in the latter case, extra care is necessary in selecting appropriate, authentic examples of nonnative discourse in action and avoiding stereotyping.

The second aim of this phase is to prompt teachers to think about the strengths, challenges, shortcomings and also dangers of the global spread of English, as they become aware of the multiplicity of uses of English. For example, among the strengths, it is possible to notice the ease of using a common language in so many communicative settings; among the challenges, the importance of developing accommodation skills that are necessary when interacting with speakers with different proficiency levels; among the shortcomings, the realization that the field of EIL and ELF is under construction and that they themselves can help to contribute to their fuller understanding (Jenkins, 2012); among the dangers, the recognition that EIL/ELF may or may not be relevant to different ways of expression and communication and the awareness that overextending the EIL/ELF constructs to different genres (in spoken and written communications) is neither feasible nor desirable.

### Phase B: Critical awareness

As participants become more aware of the realities of using English internationally, they should be prompted to engage with the challenges that these intricacies can raise for their immediate teaching context. It is important that this is attempted in both a critical and a practical way and that it targets two types of awareness: external and internal.

In the first place, *external critical awareness* refers to teachers' understanding of the ongoing worldwide spread of English. This first stage of critical awareness is closely linked to Phase A (exposure) and asks that teachers move beyond their immediate perspective of reality and begin to think about the status of native speakers, nonnative speakers, the issue of ownership of the English language by native and nonnative users and the key issue of successful communication involving nonnative and native speakers in widely different settings around the globe. The criticality of such awareness lies with the need for teachers to see the inadequacies of SE in meeting the totality of demands of present-day communication (Cogo & Dewey, 2012).

In the second place, *internal critical awareness* refers to teachers' awareness of their own deeper convictions about issues related to communication and teaching. These issues range from the types of English used in different kinds of interactions, the mechanics of accommodation, the beliefs about SE and normativity, to the role of the teacher in the foreign language classroom, including perspectives about what should be considered correct/incorrect, how teacher feedback should work and so on. All of these aspects are important, as research shows that deeper convictions about teaching and learning, together with previous experiences, can significantly impact teachers' instructional decisions (Bayyurt & Sifakis, 2015; James & Pedder,

2006; Kagan, 1992; Sifakis, 2007, 2014; Sifakis & Bayyurt, 2015). At the same time, teachers who have been working in the ESOL environment for a long time are bound to have very specific beliefs about their role as custodians of standard or 'proper' English for their learners and the wider community of their immediate context (Sifakis, 2009) and this has been shown to be in contrast to their growing awareness of the changing role of English as an international lingua franca (Sifakis & Sougari, 2005). It is for this reason that becoming fully conscious of these convictions and taking into consideration the demands of the local context will determine the extent to which these teachers will begin to find ways to adapt or change their teaching practices, making them more EIL-aware. EIL-awareness will also help teachers to feel self-confident as nonnative English language teachers in their pedagogical practice.

### Phase C: Action plan

In this phase, teachers are involved in taking action, experimenting with their understanding of the EIL construct by integrating elements from EIL, ELF and WE research that they deem important and relevant into their teaching practice. The action plan breaks down into three stages. In the first stage, teachers design instructional activities that integrate their awareness of EIL issues and are appropriate for their learners. These activities can vary from minor adaptations of activities or sections of the set textbooks that they use to design entire lessons. It goes without saying that different teaching contexts will raise different demands – for example, teaching young learners is very different from teaching adults and a state school teacher is likely to be allowed more liberties at experimenting with new materials than a private school teacher. The differences will also depend on factors such as the extent to which the setting is examination oriented: the more this is the case, the more pressure the teacher will receive to follow the syllabus of the target examination, which is typically native speaker oriented (Jenkins, 2006; Sifakis, 2009). Planning EIL-aware activities should further take into consideration other stakeholders' perspectives – for example, the parents of younger learners in a private school setting might want their children to be exposed only to native speaker varieties of English, thinking that such exposure will offer them more opportunities for becoming native speakers themselves (see Kordia & Bayyurt-Sarici, 2015).

In the second stage, teachers teach their lessons. It is important for the lesson to be audio- or video-recorded so that it can be viewed or listened to later and analyzed. Finally, in the third stage, teachers evaluate their lessons. This evaluation should be based on two premises: the teacher's own understanding of the EIL construct and the specifications of his/her teaching context. Evaluation can be carried out in various ways:

- Individually/unassisted. If the teacher is on his/her own, it is possible to follow this entire program autonomously, in which case he/she will be unassisted. This may be challenging for the teacher, as it requires a substantial amount of autonomy and maturity, in the sense that the teacher should be able to locate the strengths and inadequacies of the taught lesson and draw his/her own road map of EIL-aware lessons.
- Individually/assisted. In this case, the teacher is assisted by another teacher, perhaps a more experienced tutor with some awareness of EIL, who will act as mentor, pointing out the advantages and problems of the lessons and perhaps helping in designing further EIL-aware activities.
- In teacher groups/unassisted. Teachers can collaborate with fellow teachers in designing and teaching EIL-aware lessons. This is positive because they can learn from one another's experiences, which can be particularly instructive, especially when they all teach in the same context (e.g. primary school). Teacher groups can be very helpful in organizing peer observations and are likely to have a better impact on informing stakeholders (parents, directors of study, etc.) about the advantages of experimenting with EIL-aware lessons.
- In teacher groups/assisted. In more 'organized' teacher education settings, groups of teachers are led by one or more trainers. The role of the trainers should focus on guiding individual teachers through their EIL-aware journey, prompting them to engage with the issues critically and design appropriate EIL-aware lessons for their learners and facilitating dialogue between the group members.

Our experience with the ELF TEd project at Bogazici University (Bayyurt & Sifakis, 2015) has shown that different teachers respond differently to the first two phases of EIL/ELF-awareness.[1] In fact, it is possible to see three types of ELF-aware participants. The first type is *the supporter*, i.e. the teacher who has an overall positive attitude toward EIL/ELF but, for various reasons including his/her immediate teaching environment (e.g. he/she may be working at a private school or with exam prep classes), is not very willing or able to experiment. The second type is *the risk-taker*, i.e. the teacher who is enthusiastic about the new perspectives and willing to experiment with his/her classes. Risk-takers are courageous and do not fear going all the way, applying their own understanding of ELF in their classes and doing their best to make their own learners and other stakeholders EIL/ELF-aware. The third type is *the skeptic*, i.e. the teacher who will come into the program but will resist every question raised in Phase 2 and, at times, might even refuse to enter the EIL/ELF debate, *a priori* rejecting the entire construct as irrelevant and perhaps even inappropriate to his/her context and role as an ESOL teacher.

Bearing the above considerations in mind, the three-phased approach presented here can be tailored to the needs and specifications of each locale. In formal educational contexts, it can extend throughout an entire postgraduate program, with each phase taking up individual modules or courses. It can be tailored to fit an existing program, either at the undergraduate or the postgraduate level, in which case the individual phases would have to be substantially constricted. Depending on the profiling of the participants, one or two of the phases can be focused on more – e.g. teachers with some awareness of EIL could become more involved with the third phase, that of action research. On the other hand, when EIL-awareness becomes established, in the near or more distant future, programs might have to go over Phases 1 and 2 more quickly and focus almost exclusively on the third phase. As regards the project's timeline, again, this would depend on the participants, the scope of the program and the time available. That said, teacher educators should bear in mind that changing teachers' perspectives is time-consuming; ELF-awareness is a demanding and therefore slow process.

## Advantages and Constraints of EIL-aware Teacher Education

As presented above, EIL-aware teacher education can have a series of advantages for everyone involved in it in one way or another – teachers, learners and other stakeholders. Teachers' exposure to and understanding of the realities and challenges of EIL research can prompt them to be creative with their learners and make original decisions about appropriate implementations of EIL-aware pedagogical interventions. This will trigger their development as pedagogues and action researchers. It has been shown that, in certain cases, such an engagement can lead to the transformation of teachers' perspectives about teaching, learning and evaluation (Bayyurt & Sifakis, 2015; Hall et al., 2013). From an instructional perspective, EIL-aware teacher education can help them to appreciate the importance of educational philosophies like differentiated instruction (Tomlinson, 1999), as they are prompted to discover ways to find out about and bring out the best in each individual learner, employing, among other techniques, appropriate group and pair work activities. In many ways, a carefully constructed and implemented EIL-aware program can establish practices that promote effective leadership in teaching and learning, such as 'establishing clear goals, enabling leaders to be role models, providing ESOL professional learning, and empowering teaching and learning for ESOL' (McGee et al., 2015: 92).

As for learners, EIL-aware lessons engage them in communicative activities that let them 'be themselves'. As a result, they have the opportunity to acquire interactional skills that are necessary when engaging with other nonnative users (e.g. using discourse that is relevant to their interlocutors' competency levels, using appropriate accommodation strategies). In this way, they become EIL-aware in their own right, and the same is likely to be the case with learners' parents, who will also become more knowledgeable about the realities of modern-day communication in English.

To maximize the impact of EIL-aware lessons, the following constraints need to be taken into consideration by teacher educators when designing EIL-aware teacher training projects:

(a) *Context.* As mentioned at the outset, where seminars take place is crucial. Different (Inner-, Outer- or Expanding Circle) contexts orientate a particular setting for the use of English and therefore for learners' and other stakeholders' perceptions about the roles of teachers. Where they take place is bound to influence the aim, perspective and focus of the seminar – hence the need for the common theme to be EIL-'awareness'.

(b) *Curricular specifications.* These refer to the target situation, or aims of the lessons. Aims can vary significantly and can influence the extent to which EIL-aware lessons will be accepted by the learners. For example, a high-stakes exam prep class is likely to have a more tightly specified syllabus than a state high school EFL class, rendering the latter more amenable to EIL-aware experimentations.

(c) *Participants' attitudes.* Teacher educators should accept all attitudes, positive or negative, toward EIL. The key is not to force teachers to accept a dogma and radically change the way they think about teaching, learning, assessment and communication, but to get them to think more extensively (as well as intensively, to the extent that they want) about these issues, always with reference to their own specific context and learners' needs. The key in EIL-aware pedagogy is dialogue and creativity on the part of the teachers, not persuasion.

## Glimpses from an ELF-aware Teacher Education Project

In an attempt to understand to what extent the EIL/ELF-aware teacher education model presented above would be applicable, in 2012, we began the implementation of an ELF-aware teacher education project (called ELF-TEd) in Turkey, a traditional EFL context. The participants of the initial phases of the project were 11 in-service English language teachers from private/state primary and secondary schools, and private/state higher education institutions in Turkey. Since then, the project has been extended to involve preservice and in-service teachers from different contexts (Bayyurt & Sifakis, 2015; Sifakis & Bayyurt, 2015).

The project falls under the 'teacher group/assisted' framework delineated above. Teachers are exposed to the ELF/EIL construct by reading selections from the ELF/EIL research literature (book chapters, articles, websites, videos). They are guided in these readings by specially designed reflective questions that guide their thinking and focus their attention on different aspects of the ELF construct. Through these reflective questions, teachers are actively involved in shaping the meaning of ELF-related concepts for themselves, taking into consideration the specifications, realities and needs of their own context. Of key importance in this stage is the sense of community that grows in the participants: teachers exchange perspectives, openly discuss their beliefs about central themes in EIL/ELF and are free to disagree with what they read and with other colleagues. Teacher trainers do not interfere to offer final solutions to these arguments, but simply make sure to keep the dialogue going.

Teachers are prompted to draw specific implications from their readings and responses to the reflective questions that are relevant for their own teaching context. They are prompted to develop applications, or 'instructional interventions', for their own classes, by first adapting existing textbook activities, and then progressively designing their own original activities and full lessons. This is done to the extent that they want/are able to do it. Finally, teachers exchange experiences from the above applications. This is an important learning curve for all participants, as they all become more fully aware of the broad variety of contexts, the different challenges that have to be faced and the different perspectives about the effectiveness of EIL/ELF. They then go on to draw a program for themselves for after the training program and continue to fine-tune EIL-aware applications to the extent that they want/are able to.

Teachers upload their reflections onto the project website (www.teacherdevelopment.boun.edu.tr), whose forum is restricted access only. In addition, fortnightly meetings with the teachers are arranged by the course leaders (the authors), where participants meet and discuss issues related to the readings that are covered up until the time of the meeting. In addition, an online forum was established to give participants the opportunity to discuss the issues related to their readings before the meetings. The course leaders send prompts in relation to the readings that were covered that week to initiate online discussions. These exchanges of ideas create a sense of belonging and solidarity among the participant teachers, enabling them to feel that they belong to a professional community of practice.

## Conclusion

In this chapter, we have presented the foundations of what we term EIL-aware teacher education and a three-stage framework for implementing it in teacher education programs. According to our proposal, the overarching orientation of such a project should be teacher development, not the indoctrination of EIL. In this light, the objectives are:

- to critically engage teachers into forming a comprehensive understanding of the EIL (ELF/WE) construct;
- to prompt teachers to become conscious of their deeper convictions about teaching, learning, assessing, etc., vis-à-vis English, and to help them begin to change these perspectives to the extent that they want/ are able to;
- to prompt teachers to understand the implications of the EIL construct for their own teaching context;
- to assist teachers in applying the EIL construct in their own teaching context, to the extent that they want/are able to.

We see EIL/ELF-aware teacher education as an opportunity for ESOL teachers to develop in two interconnected ways: (a) personally, since engaging with issues that have to do with the deep fundamentals of language use (accommodation needs in communication that involves nonnative speakers of English) and teaching (providing feedback, acting as role model for learners) prompts teachers to become conscious of, challenge and perhaps transform their convictions about communicating in English in today's world; and (b) professionally, since they would be fully informed of new developments in using English in today's world and would have experimented with integrating the EIL/ELF-aware approach (Bayyurt & Sifakis, 2015; Kirkpatrick, 2012; Sifakis, 2014) into their own teaching context. They gain skills that they can market upon besides their competency in teaching according to the EFL/ESL orientation. This will also empower teachers in terms of seeing their value as nonnative English language teachers in the post-EFL world with these newly presented ideas/ideologies based on the EIL/ELF/WE construct.

The EIL-aware teacher education blueprint is applicable to both nonnative and native teachers of English alike. As the number of native speakers of English is almost one-third the number of nonnative speakers of English, the native English teachers need to be trained to gain an EIL-aware perspective toward their English language teaching profession as well. They should be equally informed about the EIL/ELF/WE paradigms and expected to apply these perspectives into their teaching.

Contexts may change and it is expected that different teachers come to these projects with different expectations and convictions about ownership, standardness, correction policies, etc. Therefore, for EIL-aware programs to succeed, their design should take context, existing curricular specifications and participants' attitudes into careful consideration. Where possible, teacher educators play an important role as the 'linchpins' of education (Cochran-Smith, 2003: 5–6) in their function as mentors of EIL-aware teachers.

## Note

(1)   As this project focused on ELF, and as ELF is a subset of EIL, we have decided in this section to use both terms.

## References

Baker, W. (2009) The cultures of English as a lingua franca. *TESOL Quarterly* 43 (4), 567–592.

Bautista, M.L.S. and Bolton, K. (2008) *Philippine English: Linguistic and Literary Perspectives.* Hong Kong: Hong Kong University Press.

Bayyurt, Y. (2006) Non-native English language teachers' perspective on culture in English as a Foreign Language classrooms. *Teacher Development* 10 (2), 233–247.

Bayyurt, Y. (2012) Proposing a model for English language education in the Turkish socio-cultural context. In Y. Bayyurt and Y. Bektaş-Çetinkaya (eds) *Research Perspectives on Teaching and Learning English in Turkey: Policies and Practices* (pp. 301–312). Frankfurt: Peter Lang.

Bayyurt, Y. and Altınmakas, D. (2012) A World Englishes course at a foundation university in Turkey. In A. Matsuda (ed.) *Principles and Practices of Teaching English as an International Language* (pp. 169–182). Bristol: Multilingual Matters.

Bayyurt, Y. and Sifakis, N. (2015) Developing an ELF-aware pedagogy: Insights from a self-education programme. In P. Vettorel (ed.) *New Frontiers in Teaching and Learning English* (pp. 55–76). Newcastle upon Tyne: Cambridge Scholars Publishing.

Block, D. (2003) *The Social Turn in Second Language Acquisition.* Edinburgh: Edinburgh University Press.

Blommaert, J. (2010) *The Sociolinguistics of Globalization.* Cambridge: Cambridge University Press.

Canagarajah, S. (2005) 'Reconstructing local knowledge, reconfiguring language studies.' In S. Canagarajah (ed.) *Reclaiming the Local in Language Policy and Practice* (pp. 3–24). London: Erlbaum.

Canagarajah, S. (2007) Lingua franca English, multilingual communities, and language acquisition. *The Modern Language Journal* 91 (1), 923–939.

Cochran-Smith, M. (2003) Learning and unlearning: The education of teacher educators. *Teaching and Teacher Education* 19 (1), 5–28.

Cogo, A. and Dewey, M. (2012) *Analysing English as a Lingua Franca.* London: Continuum.

D'Angelo, J. (2012) WE-informed EIL curriculum in Chukyo: Towards a functional, educated, multilingual outcome. In A. Matsuda (ed.) *Principles and Practices of Teaching English as an International Language* (pp. 121–139). Bristol: Multilingual Matters.

Deterding, D.H. (2007) *Singapore English.* Edinburgh: Edinburgh University Press.

Dewey, M. (2012) Towards a post-normative approach: Learning the pedagogy of ELF. *Journal of English as a Lingua Franca* 1 (1), 141–170.

Ehlich, K. (2009) What makes a language foreign? In K. Knapp and B. Seidlhofer (eds) *Handbook of Foreign Language Communication and Learning* (pp. 21–44). Berlin: De Gruyter Mouton.

Fay, R., Lytra, V. and Ntavaliagkou, M. (2010) Multicultural awareness through English: A potential contribution of TESOL in Greek schools. *Intercultural Education* 21 (6), 579–593.

Firth, A. (2009) Doing not being a foreign language learner: English as a lingua franca in the workplace and (some) implications for SLA. *International Review of Applied Linguistics* 47, 127–156.

Freeman, D. and Johnson, K.E. (1998) Reconceptualizing the knowledge-base of language teacher education. *TESOL Quarterly* 32 (3), 397–417.

Graddol, D. (2006) *English Next. Why Global English May Mean the End of 'English as a Foreign Language'*. London: British Council. See http://www.britishcouncil.org/learning-research-englishnext.htm.

Grau, M. (2009) Worlds apart? English in German youth cultures and in educational settings. *World Englishes* 28 (2), 160–174.

Hall, C.J., Wicaksono, R., Liu, S., Qian, Y. and Xiaoqing, X. (2013) *English Reconceived: Raising Teachers' Awareness of English as a 'Plurilithic' Resource Through an Online Course*. London: British Council.

James, M. and Pedder, D. (2006) Beyond method: Assessment and learning practices and values. *The Curriculum Journal* 17, 109–138.

Jenkins, J. (2006) The spread of EIL: A testing time for testers. *ELT Journal* 60 (1), 42–50.

Jenkins, J. (2007) *English as a Lingua Franca: Attitude and Identity*. Oxford: Oxford University Press.

Jenkins, J. (2012) English as a lingua franca from the classroom to the classroom. *ELT Journal* 66 (4), 486–494.

Jenkins, J., Cogo, A. and Dewey, M. (2011) State-of-the-art article: Review of developments in research into English as a lingua franca. *Language Teaching* 44 (3), 281–315.

Kachru, Y. and Nelson, C.L. (eds) (2006) *World Englishes in Asian contexts*. Hong Kong: Hong Kong University Press.

Kagan, D.M. (1992) Implications of research on teacher belief. *Educational Psychologist* 27, 65–90.

Kirkpatrick, A. (2007) *World Englishes: Implications for International Communication and English Language Teaching*. Cambridge: Cambridge University Press.

Kirkpatrick, A. (2012) English as an Asian lingua franca: The 'lingua franca approach' and implications for language education policy. *Journal of English as a Lingua Franca* 1 (1), 121–140.

Kordia, S. and Bayyurt-Sarici, J. (2015) Teaching ELF at primary school classrooms: Two small-scale case-studies in Turkey and Greece. Paper presented at the International Conference of Applied Linguistics. Çanakkale Onsekiz Mart University, Çanakkale, Turkey.

Kormos, J., Kiddle, T. and Kata Csizér, K. (2011) Systems of goals, attitudes, and self-related beliefs in second-language-learning motivation. *Applied Linguistics* 32 (5), 495–516.

Kubota, R. and McKay, S.L. (2009) Globalization and language learning in rural Japan: The role of English in the local linguistic ecology. *TESOL Quarterly* 43 (4), 593–619.

Kumaravadivelu, B. (1994) The postmethod condition: (E)merging strategies for second/foreign language teaching. *TESOL Quarterly* 28 (1), 27–48.

Kumaravadivelu, B. (2012) *Language Teacher Education for a Global Society: A Modular Model for Knowing, Analyzing, Recognizing, Doing, and Seeing*. New York: Routledge.

Lee, H. (2012) World Englishes in a high school English class: A case from Japan. In A. Matsuda (ed.) *Principles and Practices of Teaching English as an International Language* (pp. 154–168). Bristol: Multilingual Matters.

Maley, A. (2009) ELF: A teacher's perspective. *Language and Intercultural Communication* 9 (3), 187–200.

Matsuda, A. (2009) Desirable but not necessary? The place of World Englishes and English as an international language in English teacher preparation programs in Japan. In F. Sharifian (ed.) *English as an International Language: Perspectives and Pedagogical Issues* (pp. 169–189). Bristol: Multilingual Matters.

Matsuda, A. and Friedrich, P. (2011) English as an international language: A curriculum blueprint. *World Englishes* 30 (3), 332–344.

Matsuda, A. and Duran, C.S. (2012) EIL activities and tasks for traditional EFL classrooms. In A. Matsuda (ed.) *Principles and Practices of Teaching English as an International Language* (pp. 201–238). Bristol: Multilingual Matters.

McGee, A., Haworth, P. and MacIntyre, L. (2015) Leadership practices to support teaching and learning for English language learners. *TESOL Quarterly* 49 (1), 92–114.

McKay, S.L. (2002) *Teaching English as an International Language: Rethinking Goals and Perspectives*. New York: Oxford University Press.

Medel-Añonuevo, C., Ohsako, T. and Mauch, W. (2001) *Revisiting Lifelong Learning for the 21st Century*. Hamburg: UNESCO Institute for Education.

Mesthrie, J. (ed.) (2008) *Varieties of English 4: Africa, South and Southeast Asia*. Berlin: Mouton de Gruyter.

Nayar, P.B. (1997) ESL/EFL dichotomy today: Language politics or pragmatics? *TESOL Quarterly* 31 (1), 9–37.

OECD (2015) *Skills for Social Progress: The Power of Social and Emotional Skills*. Paris: OECD.

Park, J.S.-Y. and Wee, L. (2011) A practice-based critique of English as a lingua franca. *World Englishes* 30 (3), 360–374.

Pennycook, A. (2007) *Global Englishes and Transcultural Flows*. London: Routledge.

Rajagopalan, K. (1999) Of ELF teachers, conscience and cowardice. *English Language Teaching Journal* 53 (3), 200–260.

Ranta, E. (2010) English in the real world vs. English at school: Finnish English teachers' and students' views. *International Journal of Applied Linguistics* 20 (1), 156–177.

Schauer, G.A. (2006) Pragmatic awareness in ESL and EFL contexts: Contrast and development. *Language Learning* 56 (2), 269–318.

Seidlhofer, B. (2007) English as a lingua franca and communities of practice. In S. Volk-Birke and J. Lippert (eds) *Anglistentag 2006 Halle Proceedings* (pp. 307–318). Trier: Wissenschaftlicher Verlag.

Seidlhofer, B. (2011) *Understanding English as a Lingua Franca*. Oxford: Oxford University Press.

Sharifian, F. and Marlina, R. (2012) English as an international language: An innovative academic program. In A. Matsuda (ed.) *Principles and Practices of Teaching English as an International Language* (pp. 140–153). Bristol: Multilingual Matters.

Sifakis, N.C. (2004) Teaching EIL – Teaching international or intercultural English? What teachers should know. *System* 32 (2), 237–250.

Sifakis, N.C. (2007) The education of the teachers of English as a lingua franca: A transformative perspective. *International Journal of Applied Linguistics* 17 (3), 355–375.

Sifakis, N.C. (2009) Challenges in teaching ELF in the periphery: The Greek context. *ELT Journal* 63 (3), 230–237.

Sifakis, N.C. (2014) ELF awareness as an opportunity for change: A transformative perspective for ESOL teacher education. *Journal of English as a Lingua Franca* 3 (2), 317–335.

Sifakis, N.C. and Sougari, A.-M. (2005) Pronunciation issues and EIL pedagogy in the periphery: A survey of Greek state school teachers' beliefs. *TESOL Quarterly* 39 (4), 467–488.

Sifakis, N.C. and Bayyurt, Y. (2015) Educating the ELF-aware teacher: Insights from ELF and WE in teacher training. *World Englishes*.

Timmis, I. (2002) Native-speaker norms and international English: A classroom view. *English Language Teaching Journal* 56 (3), 240–249.

Tomlinson, C.A. (1999) *The Differentiated Classroom: Responding to the Needs of All Learners*. Alexandria, VA: Association for Supervision and Curriculum Development.

Trudgill, P. and Hannah, J. (2008) *International English: A Guide to Varieties of Standard English* (5th edn). London: Routledge.

Wall, D. (2005) *The Impact of High-Stakes Examinations on Classroom Teaching: A Case Study Using Insights from Testing and Innovation Theory*. Cambridge: Cambridge University Press.

# 2 A Framework for Incorporating an English as an International Language Perspective into TESOL Teacher Education

Seran Dogancay-Aktuna
and Joel Hardman

## Introduction

It is widely accepted today that the global spread of English has led to the emergence of diverse varieties of English that represent different sociocultural norms, political affiliations and bilingual/multilingual identities. Also widely accepted among applied linguists is that English language teachers, both native and nonnative speakers of the language, need to know about varieties of English that they and their students are likely to encounter in and outside of classrooms, and they need to teach their students the sociolinguistic tools to navigate across Englishes. Scholars like Canagarajah (in an interview with Rubdy & Saraceni, 2006; Canagarajah, 2013), Mahboob (2014) and McKay (2002, 2003), among others, argue for a paradigm shift in English language teacher education to recognize English as an international language rather than one linked with particular cultures. Such a paradigm shift would involve giving teachers a comprehensive education that fosters an understanding of language variation and change, the new forms and functions of English, the relationship between language and identity, the negotiated nature of intercultural communication and a more nuanced understanding of bilingual language proficiency. As Renandya (2012) elaborates, the role of the teacher is central to the successful implementation of an English as an international language (EIL) approach:

> Teachers need to understand what it means to teach English in the EIL context; they need to know what kinds of roles they should play in promoting EIL pedagogy and what roles they should be critical about

if they want to put into practice an approach to teaching English that is compatible with EIL principles; they also need to be willing to learn new knowledge and skills before they can comfortably assume their new roles in teaching EIL. In addition, and perhaps more importantly, they need to develop a favorable attitude toward the teaching of EIL. (Renandya, 2012: 65)

The proliferation of scholarly work on World Englishes (WE), in particular books such as Alsagoff *et al.* (2012), Galloway and Rose (2015), Jenkins (2015), Kirkpatrick (2007), Mackenzie (2014), Marlina and Giri (2014), Matsuda (2012), Rubdy and Saraceni (2006), Schneider (2011), Seargeant (2012), Seargeant and Swann (2012) and Zacharias and Manara (2013) as well as a large number of journal articles, provide teacher educators with a range of materials to use in order to implement such a paradigm shift and expand the scope of the education that English language teachers receive. Despite the current abundance of works on global Englishes that can serve as teaching materials, there is, in our view, still not enough guidance for teacher educators who would like to introduce these topics into teacher education curricula (but see 'Part 2: Showcase of EIL Programs, Courses and Pedagogical Ideas' in Matsuda [2012]; McKay and Matsuda's chapters in Alsagoff *et al.* [2012] and Marlina and Giri [2014] Parts 2 and 3 for discussions of EIL-oriented pedagogies). In this chapter, we outline a framework for integrating an EIL perspective into teaching English to speakers of other languages (TESOL) teacher education and then discuss some specific topics, practical activities and resources that can be used by teacher educators. We start by defining what an EIL approach means for us, followed by our model of teacher education in the era of global Englishes and then list our suggestions for teaching.

Our view of EIL parallels that of McKay (2002) and Sharifian (2009) who conceptualize EIL as 'a paradigm for thinking, research and practice' in applied linguistics that emphasizes the international and intercultural value of English against the supremacy of particular users and uses and rejects the idea that there can be any particular variety/model of English that will be the best for diverse contexts of international communication and language teaching (Sharifian, 2009: 2). Furthermore, we see EIL as an overarching construct that encompasses an understanding of WE that includes the relatively stabilized and nativized postcolonial varieties such as Indian English, Nigerian English, etc., as well as an understanding of English as a lingua franca (ELF), defined as the contextually negotiated, fluid and hybrid way of using English as constructed by its nonnative speakers (cf. Marlina, 2014).

# A Situated Meta-Praxis Framework
# of EIL Teacher Education

Our model of EIL teacher education, represented in Figure 2.1, imagines teacher education in terms of an interaction between *place, proficiency, praxis* and a set of *understandings* about language, culture, identity and teaching that are relevant to teaching EIL (this current model is a revised version of one discussed in Dogancay-Aktuna & Hardman [2012]). We believe that an understanding of the international forms and functions of English will give teachers an awareness of the current sociolinguistic profile of the language, expand their views of what it means to be proficient in a global language and help them to decide what is relevant to their contexts of teaching.

By *place*, we refer to both the broad spatial metaphor of Kachru (Inner Circle, Outer Circle and Expanding Circle) and the emergent glocalization of Englishes in a nearly infinite variety of circumstances. Appropriate *proficiency* describes an expert user of both a globally comprehensible English along with locally recognized Englishes (McKay, 2002). *Praxis* is the integration of theory and practice, of thought and desire (Simon, 1992), deployed as pedagogical action.

The *understandings* component of our model refers to concepts, theories and research findings relevant to global English language use and users.

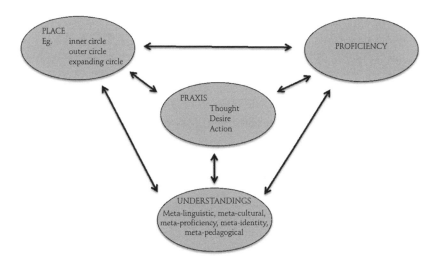

**Figure 2.1** Situated meta-praxis model of EIL teacher education (adapted from Dogancay-Aktuna & Hardman, 2012: 104)

The emergent character of language variation has led to English acquiring various global forms, functions and affiliations (including renationalized/ indigenized varieties). Such variation in language is a natural linguistic development, as is change over time. There is also inherent *hybridity* and *variability* of interactions in Englishes. A 'non-deficit' orientation to such variation in English is needed (Seidlhofer, 2002) to accept and work with the global ownership of English (Galloway, 2013).

There is also a need for understanding the social context in which English is used, and how proficiency and identity relate to that social context. In this volume, Kang discusses the need to develop a proficiency level that builds confidence in one's identity as an English user. There is a need for communication strategies and cross-cultural competence for negotiating meaning across Englishes. EIL/ELF/WE speakers are bi- or multilinguals who express their multiple identities through English. There is need for a situated/contextualized view of English language proficiency for local affiliation (language for identification) and global negotiation (language for communication) (Ushioda, 2013).

The current version of the model (Figure 2.1) attempts to visually emphasize the balance between place, proficiency and understandings to indicate that no one element is inherently more important than any other. We place praxis centrally to communicate its core role in mediating the relationships between the various elements of the model, thus providing a framework for integrating teacher thought (understandings), teacher identity (as an English teacher/user) and classroom action (a situated English language teaching [ELT] pedagogy).

These understandings can be integrated into TESOL curricula as one specialized course or distributed across the main subject areas that form the knowledge base of ELT, namely courses focusing on linguistics/language analysis, second language acquisition (SLA), sociolinguistics and teaching English as a second language (TESL) methodology. Below, we discuss what topics to emphasize and how to do so in each subject area.

## Linguistics and Sociolinguistics Courses

Linguistics courses need to emphasize an understanding of language variation in and across languages as a natural reflection of the speaker's background. Courses focusing on the relationships between language and society need to emphasize the culturally and contextually embedded nature of language in general and of English in particular to show how language use and usage are shaped to reflect the speech communities that use them. They also need to involve discussions about language attitudes and linguistic prejudice. The following themes and activities would reinforce understanding of the situatedness of language:

- Use of dialect variation videos: show students a video that represents different dialects of English (such as *American Tongues*). Have them use a graphic organizer for categorizing features of English dialects (lexical, phonological, syntactic, pragmatic), along with their attitudes toward the feature (positive, negative, neutral). In groups, have students compare and discuss their graphic organizers. Follow up with discussion questions: What is the source of variation in English? Where do your language attitudes come from?
- Engage students in a detailed descriptive linguistic analysis of global varieties of English, including discourse representing WE and ELF interactions, to show them examples of variation and patterns in Englishes, the nativization/appropriation of English across cultures and the linguistic creativity of its newer users. Different groups can be assigned different varieties to analyze, and present their findings to the class.
- Utilize free corpus data, especially including global English varieties (VOICE, ELFA) but also other internet sources (multinational blogs and mass media from Outer and Expanding Circles), to further demonstrate the patterns of variation in academic and business settings in non-English-speaking countries (see Baik & Shim [2002] and Chapters 8–13 in Matsuda (ed.) [2012], for ideas).
- Conduct group or class discussions based on the following as part of knowledge building:

    (1) The history of the English language using the video 'The history of English in 10 minutes' (Open University, https://www.youtube.com/watch?v=H3ZJuCbklqg) to show the hybrid roots of the English language.
    (2) The global uses of English using Kachru's Three Circles Model and McArthur's Circle of World Englishes, widely available in books on global Englishes. In this volume, the contributions by El Kadri and Rose discuss the need to develop teacher understanding of English spread and change (including EIL), and how it affects beliefs toward teaching and learning.
    (3) Alternatives to the native/nonnative dichotomy: (e.g. Cook's [1999] vision of the 'multi-competent' language user; Modiano's [2009] concept of the 'proficient user of English as an International Language/Excellent communicator in EIL'; Rampton's [1990] view of the 'expert user of English').
    (4) Debates on whether or not all native speakers of English are intelligible in the global arena, and whether or not new varieties of English could develop into mutually unintelligible languages the way Latin did.

- Include readings on the cross-cultural pragmatics of global English. Along those lines, in this volume, Hino discusses how to develop an understanding of the 'interactional dynamics' of EIL, and Diniz de Figueiredo and Sanfelici argue for the need to develop an understanding of the relationship between culture, EIL and intercultural communication.
- Assign tasks for teachers to test their own perceptions of various Englishes using Munro *et al.*'s (2006) framework of collecting and evaluating selected samples of accented speech samples (see also Pedrazzini & Nava, 2010, 2011; Song & Drummond, 2009).
- Prepare assignments whereby students trace the spread of English and examine the current sociolinguistic profile of English in a particular country (outside of the 'Inner Circle') of their own choice. The sociolinguistic profile will include an examination of the forms and uses/functions of English in this context and any educational, social and linguistic problems that were triggered or exacerbated by the presence of English. In this volume, Mora and Golovátina-Mora discuss the need for deep reflection on the sociocultural context of English learning, and Selvi argues that teachers need an understanding of English variation around the world and the implications of that variation for teaching and learning.

## Second Language Acquisition and Methodology Courses

Courses in SLA need to put greater emphasis on the sociolinguistic and sociocultural aspects of SLA, including a discussion of the multiple identities of EIL speakers (cf. Alsagoff *et al.*, 2012; Norton, 2000) and identity as 'fluid and amorphous, … constantly and endlessly invented and reinvented' (Kumaravadivelu, 2012: 11). Tasks need to be crafted that encourage discussion of the connections between language, culture and identity, and the role of accents in expressing a speaker's identity (Jenks, 2013). Students need to be introduced to the multiple competencies, diverse motivations and linguistic repertoires of English-speaking multilinguals. Courses on approaches to language teaching need to reinforce an understanding of language learning and teaching that is contextually constrained, and prepare teachers to plan and deliver socioculturally appropriate English language instruction that reflects the complexity of English as a global language with multiple varieties and functions. The following activities attempt to engage students in these discussions.

- Student self-examination: Ask students to recall a language learning experience they have had. In what context did it occur? How do they think that context affected their acquisition? How did/do they 'feel' when speaking a second language? Do they ever feel like someone else? Students can then compare responses to look for shared themes surrounding language and identity. Vittorel, in this volume, argues for the need to prompt teachers to reflect on how WE/EIL/ELF relate to their personal experiences and teaching practices. Such an activity is especially important for native-speaking teachers to engage in as they learn about multi-competence and the value of communication strategies in using a second/foreign language (cf. Ellis, 2009).

- Accent and identity: Provide students with a list of world English accents/varieties (some regional, some nonnative), along with the viewing of one of those YouTube videos of expert accent mimics, and then have students rank-order the list according to perceived prestige/desirability. Have groups compare and discuss their rankings. What are the commonalities in the rankings? Where do those common perceptions come from? How do race, class and ethnicity affect the rankings of accents?
- Introduce ELF as a global code that is dynamic and context-bound hence open to significant negotiation, and talk about the processes of successful ELF interactions as signs of learners' strategic competence and linguistic creativity.
- Distinguish ELF from the nativized varieties of English, English as a Second Language and English as a Foreign Language, and draw attention to motivational differences in their learning and the desired levels of proficiency.
- Problematize the construct of 'proficiency in English' in the era of global Englishes using readings such as Canagarajah (2013) and Mahboob and Dutcher (2014). Discuss the need for a situated/contextualized view of English language proficiency for local affiliation (*language for identification*) and global negotiation (*language for communication*) (Ushioda, 2013).
- Introduce the pedagogies of particularity, possibility and practicality (Kumaravadivelu, 2001) and contrast them with 'best practices'. 'Particularity' refers to the situatedness of teaching in a particular context. 'Practicality' resists the usual theory/practice dichotomy through a theorized and theorizing practice. A pedagogy of 'possibility' acknowledges the sociopolitical reality of education and creates space for the transformation of student identities.
- Engage teachers in critical evaluations of popular approaches, such as communicative language teaching (see Llurda, 2009; McKay, 2002; Sharifian, 2009), that often assume the supremacy of particular cultures of teaching and learning at the expense of local norms and expectations and do not reflect how English is used cross-culturally.
- Reinforce the need and introduce ways for teaching learners pragmatic strategies for intercultural communication (vs. the pragmatics of native

speakers) to negotiate their meaning across Englishes (McKay, 2012; McKay & Bokhorst-Heng, 2008). In this volume, Hino, Dinh and Diniz de Figueiredo and Sanfelici all promote the importance of developing global teachers' competence in intercultural communication.

- Assign critical reflections on various proposals for integrating ELF/WE into TESOL practice using, for instance, Sifakis (2006), Kirkpatrick (2006), McKay (2006), Prodromou (2006), Tomlinson (2006) (all in Rubdy & Saraceni (eds), 2006) as well as chapters in Matsuda's (2012) Part 2 and chapters in Marlina and Giri (2014) where teachers in various parts of Asia critically reflect on their implementation of an EIL approach. Context-dependent pedagogies are discussed by Galloway in this volume, and by El Kadri *et al.* who focus on how differing contexts relate to teacher beliefs toward teaching and learning.

- Assign projects where teachers develop a full/partial course or lesson plans designed to raise learners' awareness of and ability to communicate with global users of EIL. Ask teachers for descriptions of the language model(s) (that is, forms and uses/functions of English) they would select to introduce and their rationalization. Discuss the choices involved in selecting a variety of English for an instructional context (Matsuda & Friedrich, 2012; Pakir, 2009).

- Guide teachers to resources on Englishes to inform the design of their teaching materials and ask for an annotated bibliography, complete with links of free/affordable web-based resources, they could use as teaching resources.

## Conclusion and Praxis

It could be argued that there is a danger in proposing so many necessary 'understandings', as that might imply a theory-heavy transmission model of teacher education. However, many of our 'understandings' are grounded within a framework of variability, context dependence and local emergence. In other words, the focus has been on the *limitations* of any unified set of global understandings. *Praxis* offers a solution to the theory–practice tensions by providing a framework for integrating thought (*understandings*), motivation and action (Simon, 1992).

The integration of these elements does not imply either that practice should simply be the application of theory, or that theory should always bow to the practical constraints of a local context. *Praxis* is an emergent, situated, particularized theorizing. As we have stated before:

Rather than there being an 'essentialized' set of *particular* correct forms of English, or *particular* English-speaking cultures, or *particular* types of proficiency deemed 'target-like,' or *particular* ways of being identified as an EIL speaker, or *particular* 'best practices' in teaching, there are more general, second-order, 'meta' understandings of all these issues that should be the subject of EIL teacher education. (Dogancay-Aktuna & Hardman, 2012: 115)

A variety of instructional activities can help lead students to develop such a *praxis*, some of which were described above. In addition, activities that would fit well in a practicum course include lesson study projects, action research projects or video-stimulated recall. In a lesson study project, students can be asked to collaboratively plan, implement and evaluate a lesson to critically evaluate the outcomes of their pedagogical decisions and actions. The action research cycle (problem identification, investigation, action, reflection, etc.) helps teachers identify relationships between theory, research, knowledge, beliefs and practices. Video-stimulated recall, which asks practicum students to view themselves teaching while being asked to provide explanations for their actions, also prompts engagement with the connections between knowledge, desire and action in the classroom. In this volume, Marlina also pushes for the need to develop teachers' research skills for critically reflecting on classroom action.

In sum, if we are preparing teachers to teach English as a global language to diverse groups of learners, then the principles and practices of TESOL teacher education, that is, the body of knowledge and skills reinforced in TESOL programs, need to be modified to reflect the current sociolinguistic reality of Englishes and reinforce the social situatedness of ELT. This means that pre- and in-service teachers need to gain awareness of the global forms and functions of English and learn how to adapt their teaching to meet the particular demands of specific contexts of learning (see also Selvi and Galloway in this volume). This awareness raising and skill-building should be complemented by reflection activities that challenge teachers to rethink concepts of standard English, accuracy in grammar or usage, definitions of native versus nonnative speakers (Nero, 2012), appropriate methodology and best practices (see also Sifakis' transformative approach to ELF-aware teacher education in Sifakis [2007, 2014] and Bayyurt and Sifakis [2015]). Reflection activities are also needed for teachers to discover their own perceptions of various Englishes to arrive at a 'non-deficit' orientation to variation in English (Seidlhofer, 2002) and to accept its global ownership (Galloway, 2013). Such activities can be built into methodology or practicum courses to help teachers reflect critically on how realistic or effective it is to implement the various ideas on teaching EIL in diverse contexts of teaching, as Wee (2013), Li (2009) and Marlina (2014) also maintain.

As can happen in all cases of introducing change into a situation/ process, there could be challenges for teacher educators to overcome while moving to an EIL paradigm in TESOL teacher education. Some faculty in a department/program, some pre- or in-service teachers, as well as local educational policymakers and parents could maintain the supremacy of a particular variety of English regardless of the context, or hold overt or covert negative attitudes toward specific varieties of English. It is important to recognize their views and concerns and also educate them, as much as possible, when introducing a new paradigm of thinking about and teaching English. It is also important to recognize the role of other languages that serve as lingua francas in particular contexts as discussed by Mufwene (2010), hence our argument for a 'situated' meta-praxis approach to English. As Kubota and McKay (2009) show, for instance, there is a growing presence of non-English-speaking communities in Japan who use Portuguese, Tagalog and Mandarin, just as there is an increasing need for Japanese professionals to learn Mandarin for international communication (Kubota, 2013).

As Modiano (2009: 59) says, 'an understanding of the diversity of English, for production as well as for comprehension, makes one a better communicator'. We argue that this understanding also makes one a better teacher of English, especially when coupled with critical reflections on place, proficiency and meta understandings of language and language learning in our goal to achieve appropriate English language pedagogy.

# Resources on Englishes, including WE, EIL, ELF[1]

American Tongues (1988) by L. Alvarez and A. Kolker. The Center for New American Media.
VOICE https://www.univie.ac.at/voice/page/what_is_voice.
ELFA http://www.helsinki.fi/englanti/elfa/elfacorpus.html.
ACE Asian Corpus of English http://corpus.ied.edu.hk/ace/.
The International Corpus Network of Asian Learners of English http://language.sakura.ne.jp/icnale/.
Center for Global Englishes http://www.southampton.ac.uk/cge/.
International Corpus of English www.ucl.ac.uk/english-usage/ice.
International Dialects of English Archive http://www.dialectsarchive.com.
The Open University: Global English, iTunes University https://itunes.apple.com/gb/course/global-english-language-controversy/id495059946.
The Electronic World Atlas of Varieties of English http://ewave-atlas.org/.
The Bochum Gateway to World Englishes http://www.ruhr-uni-bochum.de/wegate/index.html.
World newspapers www.world-newspapers.com.
New Delhi TV www.ndtv.com.
Radio New Zealand international http://www.rnzi.com/index.php.
Singapore www.channelnewsasia.com.
The History of the English in 10 minutes, by Open University, UK https://www.youtube.com/watch?v=H3ZJuCbklqg.

## Note

(1)   We would like to thank our colleague Dr Gwendolyn Williams (Auburn University, Alabama) for guiding us to some of the above cited resources on global Englishes.

## References

Alsagoff, L., McKay, S., Hu, G. and Renandya, W. (2012) *Principles and Practices for Teaching English as an International Language*. New York: Routledge.

Baik, M.J. and Shim, R.J. (2002) Teaching world Englishes via the internet. *World Englishes* 21 (3), 427–430.

Bayyurt, Y. and Sifakis, N.C. (2015) Developing an ELF-aware pedagogy: Insights from a self-education programme. In P. Vettorel (ed.) *New Frontiers in Teaching and Learning English* (pp. 55–76). Newcastle: Cambridge Scholars Publishing.

Canagarajah, A.S. (2013) Redefining proficiency in global English. In N.T. Zacharias and C. Manara (eds) *Contextualizing the Pedagogy of English as an International language* (pp. 2–11). Newcastle: Cambridge Scholars Publishing.

Cook, V. (1999) Going beyond the native speaker in language teaching. *TESOL Quarterly* 33 (2), 185–209.

Dogancay-Aktuna, S. and Hardman, J. (2012) Teacher education for EIL: Working toward a situated meta-praxis. In A. Matsuda (ed.) *Principles and Practices of Teaching English as an International Language* (pp. 103–118). Bristol: Multilingual Matters.

Ellis, R. (2009) SLA, teacher education and language pedagogy. *Language Teaching* 43 (2), 182–201.

Galloway, N. (2013) Global Englishes and English language teaching: Bridging the gap between theory and practice in a Japanese context. *System* 41, 786–803.

Galloway, N. and Rose, H. (2015) *Introducing Global Englishes*. New York: Routledge.

Jenkins, J. (2015) *Global Englishes: A Resource Book for Students* (3rd edn). Abingdon: Routledge.

Jenks, C. (2013) 'Your pronunciation and your accent is very excellent': Orientations of identity during compliment sequences in English as a lingua franca encounters. *Language and Intercultural Communication* 13 (2), 165–181.

Kirkpatrick, A. (2006) Which model of English: Native-speaker, nativized or lingua franca? In R. Rubdy and M. Saraceni (eds) *English in the World: Global Rules, Global Roles* (pp. 71–83). London: Continuum.

Kirkpatrick, A. (2007) *World Englishes: Implications for International Communication and English Language Teaching*. Cambridge: Cambridge University Press.

Kubota, R. (2013) 'Language is only a tool': Japanese expatriates working in China and implications for language teaching. *Multilingual Education* 3(4). See http://www.multilingual-education.com/content/3/1/4 (accessed 24 August 2016).

Kubota, R. and McKay, S. (2009) Globalization and language learning in rural Japan: The role of English in the local language ecology. *TESOL Quarterly* 43 (4), 593–619.

Kumaravadivelu, B. (2001) Toward a postmethod pedagogy. *TESOL Quarterly* 35 (4), 537–560.

Kumaravadivelu, B. (2012) Individual identity, cultural globalization, and teaching English as an international language. In L. Alsagoff, S.L. McKay, G. Hu and W.A. Renandya (eds) *Principles and Practices for Teaching English as an International Language* (pp. 9–27). New York: Routledge.

Li, D.C.S. (2009) Researching non-native speakers' views toward intelligibility and identity: Bridging the gap between moral high grounds and own-to-earth concerns. In F. Sharifian (ed.) *English as an International Language: Perspectives and Pedagogical Issues* (pp. 81–118). Bristol: Multilingual Matters.

Llurda, E. (2009) Attitudes toward English as an international language: The pervasiveness of native models among L2 users and teachers. In F. Sharifian (ed.) *English as an International Language: Perspectives and Pedagogical Issues* (pp. 119–135). Bristol: Multilingual Matters.

Mackenzie, I. (2014) *English as a Lingua Franca: Theorizing and Teaching English*. Abingdon/ New York: Routledge.

Mahboob, A. (2014) Epilogue: Understanding language variation: Implications for EIL pedagogy. In R. Marlina and R. Giri (eds) *The Pedagogy of English as an International Language: Perspectives from Scholars, Teachers, and Students* (pp. 257–265). Cham: Springer.

Mahboob, A. and Dutcher, L. (2014) Towards a dynamic approach to language proficiency – A model. In A. Mahboob and L. Barratt (eds) *Englishes in Multilingual Contexts* (pp. 117–136). Dordrecht: Springer.

Marlina, R. (2014) The pedagogy of English as an International Language (EIL): More reflections and dialogues. In R. Marlina and R.A. Giri (eds) *The Pedagogy of English as an International Language: Perspectives from Scholars, Teachers and Students* (pp. 1–19). Cham: Springer.

Marlina, R. and Giri, R.A. (eds) (2014) *The Pedagogy of English as an International Language: Perspectives from Scholars, Teachers and Students*. Cham: Springer.

Matsuda, A. (ed.) (2012) *Principles and Practices of Teaching English as an International Language*. Bristol: Multilingual Matters.

Matsuda, A. and Friedrich, P. (2012) Selecting an instructional variety for and EIL curriculum. In A. Matsuda (ed.) *Principles and Practices of Teaching English as an International Language* (pp. 17–27). Bristol: Multilingual Matters.

McKay, S.L. (2002) *Teaching English as an International Language: Rethinking Goals and Approaches*. Oxford: Oxford University Press.

McKay, S.L. (2003) Toward an appropriate EIL pedagogy: Re-examining common ELT assumptions. *International Journal of Applied Linguistics* 13 (1), 1–22.

McKay, S.L. (2006) EIL curriculum development. In R. Rubdy and M. Saraceni (eds) *English in the World: Global Rules, Global Roles* (pp. 114–129). London: Continuum.

McKay, S.L. (2012) Principles of teaching English as an international language. In L. Alsagoff, S.L. McKay, G. Hu and W.A. Renandya (eds) *Principles and Practices for Teaching English as an International Language* (pp. 28–46). New York: Routledge.

McKay, S.L. and Bokhorst-Heng, W. (eds) (2008) *International English in its Sociolinguistic Context: Towards a Socially Sensitive EIL Pedagogy*. New York: Routledge.

Modiano, M. (2009) EIL, native-speakerism and the failure of European ELT. In F. Sharifian (ed.) *English as an International Language: Perspectives and Pedagogical Issues* (pp. 58–77). Bristol: Multilingual Matters.

Mufwene, S.S. (2010) Globalization, global English, and world English(es): Myths and facts. In N. Coupland (ed.) *The Handbook of Language and Globalization* (pp. 31–55). Malden, MA: Wiley.

Munro, M.J., Derwing, T.M. and Sato, K. (2006) Salient accents, covert attitudes: Consciousness-raising for pre-service second language teachers. *Prospect* 21 (1), 67–79.

Nero, S. (2012) Languages without borders: TESOL in a transient world. *TESL Canada Journal* 29 (2), 143–154.

Norton, B. (2000) *Identity and Language Learning: Gender, Ethnicity, and Educational Change*. Harlow: Pearson.

Pakir, A. (2009) English as a lingua franca: Analyzing research frameworks in international English, world Englishes, and ELF. *World Englishes* 28 (2), 224–335.

Pedrazzini, L. and Nava, A. (2010) The ELF of English language teachers. In C. Gagliardi and A. Maley (eds) *EIL, ELF, Global English: Teaching and Learning Issues* (pp. 283–300). Bern: Peter Lang.

Pedrazzini, L. and Nava, A. (2011) Researching ELF identity: A study with non-native English teachers. In A. Archibald, A. Cogo and J. Jenkins (eds) *Latest Trends in ELF Research* (pp. 269–284). Newcastle: Cambridge Scholars Publishing.

Prodromou, L. (2006) Defining the 'successful bilingual speaker' of English. In R. Rubdy and M. Saraceni (eds) *English in the World: Global Rules, Global Roles* (pp. 51–70). London: Continuum.

Rampton, B. (1990) 'Displacing the native speaker': Expertise, affiliation and inheritance. *ELT Journal* 44, 97–101.

Renandya, W.A. (2012) Teacher roles in EIL. *European Journal of Applied Linguistics and TEFL* 1 (2), 65–80.

Rubdy, R. and Saraceni, M. (2006) An interview with Suresh Canagarajah. In R. Rubdy and M. Saraceni (eds) *English in the World: Global Rules, Global Roles* (pp. 200–211). London: Continuum.

Schneider, E.W. (2011) *English Around the World: An Introduction.* Cambridge: Cambridge University Press.

Seargeant, P. (2012) *Exploring World Englishes: Language in a Global Context.* Abingdon: Routledge.

Seargeant, P. and Swann, J. (eds) (2012) *English in the World: History, Diversity, Change.* Abingdon: Routledge.

Seidlhofer, B. (2002) *Habeas corpus* and *divide et impera*: 'Global English' and applied linguistics. In K.S. Miller and P. Thompson (eds) *Unity and Diversity in Language Use* (pp. 198–217). London: Continuum.

Sharifian, F. (2009) English as an International Language: An overview. In F. Sharifian (ed.) *English as an International Language: Perspectives and Pedagogical Issues* (pp. 1–18). Bristol: Multilingual Matters.

Sifakis, N (2006) Teaching EIL - Teaching *International* or *Intercultural* English? In R. Rubdy & M. Saraceni (eds) *English in the World: Global Rules, Global Roles* (pp. 151–168). London: Continuum.

Sifakis, N. (2007) The education of teachers of English as a lingua franca: A transformative approach. *International Journal of Applied Linguistics* 17 (3), 355–375.

Sifakis, N. (2014) ELF awareness as an opportunity for change: A transformative perspective for ESOL teacher education. *Journal of English as a Lingua Franca* 3 (2), 315–333.

Simon, R. (1992) *Teaching Against the Grain: Texts for a Pedagogy of Possibility.* New York: Bergin & Garvey.

Song, K. and Drummond, H. (2009) Helping students recognize and appreciate English language variations. *Foreign Language Research and Education* 12, 201–215.

Tomlinson, B. (2006) A multi-dimensional approach to teaching English for the world. In R. Rubdy and M. Saraceni (eds) *English in the World: Global Rules, Global Roles* (pp. 130–150). London: Continuum.

Ushioda, E. (2013) Motivation and ELT: Global issues and local concerns. In E. Ushioda (ed.) *International Perspectives on Motivation: Language Learning and Professional Challenges* (pp. 1–17). New York: Palgrave Macmillan.

Wee, L. (2013) Book review: Alsagoff *et al.* (eds) (2012) *Principles and Practices for Teaching English as an International Language. TESOL Quarterly* 47 (1), 202–204.

Zacharias, N.T. and Manara, C. (eds) (2013) *Contextualizing the Pedagogy of English as an International Language: Issues and Tensions.* Newcastle: Cambridge Scholars Publishing.

# Part 2

# Teacher Preparation Programs

# 3 A New Model for Reflexivity and Advocacy for Master's-Level EIL In-Service Programs in Colombia: The Notion of 'Learning and Teaching Processes in Second Languages'

Raúl Alberto Mora
and Polina Golovátina-Mora

In *Romeo and Juliet*, William Shakespeare (1597/1900: 1892) wrote, 'What's in a name? That which we call a rose/By any other name would smell as sweet'. Although the Bard's declaration usually holds true, sometimes the answer to the initial question is '*Everything* is in a name'. In the past, graduate programs in English education in Colombia seemed to rely on narrower notions of English didactics and English as a 'foreign language'. Therefore, problematizing certain contemporary issues related to the definitions (Graddol, 2006; Mora, 2015b) and roles for English (Pennycook, 2001) in a globalized world (Blommaert, 2010) are emerging topics in their curricula.

In 2012, when our university commissioned the creation of a new master's (MA) program in language education, we faced the dilemma of naming it. Should we take the traditional route? What kind of alternatives do we want to offer? We knew that we wanted something that would differentiate itself from the other related programs in our city and Colombia. We did not want just a label, but a *blueprint* for our curricular orientation. After conferring with local and international colleagues, we agreed to name this program *MA in Learning and Teaching Processes in Second Languages*[1] (we also use the acronym 'ML2' for unofficial purposes).

Our curriculum proposes an epistemological orientation about English that aligns with the current views of English as an international language, as the umbrella term that encompasses a more global view of English beyond traditional dichotomies such as second/foreign and which embraces the diversity of usage forms for this language worldwide. Informed by research from critical applied linguistics (Pennycook, 2001), literacy (Luke, 2004), bilingual education (Higgins, 2009), linguistic human rights (Skutnabb-Kangas, 2000) and critical pedagogy (Darder, 2003; Kubota, 2004; Pavlenko, 2004), our program intends to engage our graduates in reflexivity (Bourdieu & Wacquant, 1992; Mora, 2011, 2012a, 2014d) about what it means to learn and teach English (in Colombia and worldwide) today. We also expect our students and alumni to participate in moments of *glocalized advocacy* (Joseph & Ramani, 2012; Mora, 2016a; Patel & Lynch, 2013; Roudometof, 2005) about the goals, uses (and misuses) of English today so that we can approach language practices within and beyond the classroom in more critical and equitable frameworks (Mora, 2014e, 2016c).

This chapter provides a glimpse of our program, returning to the initial question about 'What's in a name' to actually explain what *is* in our name, within the aforementioned ideas of reflexivity and glocalized advocacy. We will first provide a historical overview of the beginnings of ML2. Then, we will explain how our program has embraced the idea of 'English as an international language' from a critical standpoint. To do this, we will weave the deconstruction of our name's components (i.e. *Learning and Teaching Processes* and *Second Languages*) with samples from our course syllabi that exemplify how these ideas materialize in our curriculum.

## The Genesis of a Program: Moments of Convergence and Serendipity

Chartering a graduate program, as we have learned, sometimes requires the convergence of different factors. ML2, as it exists today, is an initiative that has evolved since 2009. The first proposal decided to build the program relying on three factors: (a) the academic tradition from the Graduate Specialization[2] in English language teaching (ELT), (b) the critical mass of alumni interested in pursuing their master's degree and (c) a response to the university's advanced education expansion project (Universidad Pontificia Bolivariana, 2005). The initial idea began as a research emphasis in the existing MA in Education called 'Teaching Processes Focused on the Learning of English as a Foreign Language' (Martínez *et al.*, 2011).

This initial proposal began morphing around August 2011. The lead author (Raúl) was hired as a tenure-track assistant professor and was assigned to help revise the initial proposal. However, at the beginning of 2011, our School of Education and Pedagogy was awarded a grant from the Ministry of Education to transform the Graduate Specialization in Literature into a master's program. Winning the grant had a ripple effect across our graduate program, leading our Dean at the time to forego the initial idea (i.e. an emphasis on the MA in Education) and instead develop a stand-alone MA program.

Embracing the new idea, we reorganized the design team, with Raúl as leader of the now called 'ML2 Project'. The design team worked on the ML2 Project proposal, which featured two research emphases on *English* and *Spanish* as second languages[3] (Mora, 2013b; Uribe & Gómez, 2015), between August 2011 and June 2012. The university's academic council approved our proposal in November 2012, the National Ministry of Education followed suit at the end of January 2013 and we welcomed our first cohort on August 2, 2013. As of this writing, we have four cohorts at varying levels of progress. Between July 2015 and March 2016, over a dozen students have successfully defended their theses and graduated between October 2015 and April 2016.

## The Program at Large: A Brief Description

The program is a two-year, research-oriented degree. At present, the program comprises 49 credits (classes count for either two [24 instructional hours] or three [36 instructional hours] credits), divided among 16 courses and four academic areas, as illustrated in Table 3.1.

**Table 3.1** ML2's curricular structure

| Curricular area | Courses by area |
| --- | --- |
| Humanistic Education | • Humanistic Education Seminar<br>• Ethics Seminar |
| Conceptual and Contextual Foundations | • Introduction to English Academic Discourse<br>• Politics, Administration and Management in Education<br>• Reconceptualizing and Recontextualizing Learning and Teaching Processes<br>• Evaluation in Second Language Contexts<br>• Autonomy Education for Critical Thinking |
| Language Emphasis | • English Language I: Issues and Trends in Second Language Acquisition<br>• English Language II: Literacies in Second Languages<br>• English Emphasis I: Interculturality, Multilingualism, Diversity<br>• English Emphasis II: Socio-Critical Approaches in Second Languages<br>• English Emphasis III: Global Issues and Trends in English as a Second Language |
| Research | • Research Seminar I<br>• Research Seminar II<br>• Research Seminar III<br>• Research Seminar IV |

# A Name as a Transition toward English as an International Language: Learning and Teaching Processes in Second Languages

Building the program was an arduous but rather speedy process. *Naming* the program, however, turned out to be slightly more painful. Despite our clear idea for the program's orientation, our choice of a lengthy name raised questions. The name changed from *Teaching Processes Focused on the Learning of English as a Foreign Language* in 2011 to *Learning for Teaching Processes of a Second Language* during the design stage to *Learning and Teaching Processes in Second Languages*. Each version of the name implied revisiting our initial ideas to refine our proposal. As the name changed, so did our epistemological stances. What remained strong, however, was our desire that ML2 would break conventional wisdom about language teachers' professional development. All of our curriculum team had extensive teaching experience and thus we experienced firsthand some of the proposals for professional development in the ELT community. Some of them focused on narrow views of didactics and 'Recipes for Tired Teachers' (Sion, 1985) and were not invested in developing 'organic' (Gramsci, 1971) or 'transformative intellectuals' (Kumaravadivelu, 2003). ML2 has a different agenda in mind. Relying on the idea of reflexivity, or the combination of 'scientific elements and critical consciousness as necessary steps to promote meaningful social change' (Mora, 2014d: What is it?, p. 1), our program confronts our students with this agenda from the first moment they see the name (even going through great lengths so that they all say it properly!), which is reinforced throughout their course of studies.

We will now explain the key components of our name and how they actually constitute the conceptual and epistemological underpinnings of our program. A series of vignettes (Mora, 2016b; Stake, 2010) from the most recent syllabi comprising the five courses in the Language Emphasis Area (Language I and II; Emphasis I, II and III) and two of the Conceptual and Contextual Area (Reconceptualizing and Recontextualizing Learning and Teaching Processes [R&R] and Evaluation in Second Language Contexts) will complement the explanations.

## Learning and Teaching Processes: Challenging the Commutative Property

A very famous arithmetic rule is the commutative property, 'In multiplication, the order of factors being multiplied does not change the product'. For arithmetic, it is true that 3×6 will yield the same result as 6×3. However, in our reflections about *teaching* and *learning* as essential elements of the classroom equation, we realized that the order of factors actually alters the product.

Quite a few graduate programs in Colombia use the names 'Teaching' and 'Teaching and Learning' in their titles. We decided to break that trend, talking about 'learning and teaching processes' instead. We emphasize 'processes' as an awareness that learning is an ongoing event with different stages, both in formal education and more casual training scenarios. As we changed the wording, we also wanted to change teachers' foci. We worried whether talking about 'teaching and learning' might develop a causality relationship that would not assume any learning without teaching. We also wondered if this relationship would force teachers to remain entrenched in instrumental (Mora, 2016c) views of their craft, where they favored hoarding techniques and activities over reflecting on what lies beneath the immediate classroom practice.

Our proposal develops a sense of critical consciousness that although learning and teaching second languages imply instrumental moments of execution, they have epistemological (Mora, 2016c) underpinnings from theories and conceptual trends at the volitive, cognitive and emotional dimensions (Universidad Pontificia Bolivariana, 2012), socially situated under very particular circumstances and features (Gee, 2008; Kumaravadivelu, 1994; Puren, 1998; Street, 2013). Talking about 'learning and teaching processes' then, invites teachers to engage in moments of reflexivity and *conscientização* (Freire, 1979; Mora, 2014a) about their practice as the foundation of a sense of advocacy (Mora, 2014b, 2016c) for their students and peers. Our curriculum has framed those spaces of reflexivity under two questions, as follows.

## What does it mean to *learn* English?

As English teachers, we have all struggled at some point in our careers with losing our sensitivity toward our students' struggles with that second language. Maybe because we are 'native speakers' or we have faced very different learning conditions (such as pursuing a graduate degree abroad), sometimes we forget what being a learner feels like. When we place learning before teaching in our name, we want to trigger a deeper conversation about what it means to learn English today, in light of the new questions (Usma, 2009) and trends (Álvarez, 2014; Lantolf, 2011) related to language acquisition (Atkinson, 2011; Reinhardt, 2012; VanPatten & Benati, 2010).

## What does it mean to learn English *in order to teach it*?

This second question engages our students in a much deeper reflexivity about what we take for granted (or not) when teaching English. This question reminds teachers that, regardless of their level (however they define or measure it), they cannot assume they *know* the language. The question provides a fresh reminder that learning *about* English becomes a necessary precursor to teaching it. It also helps break traditional imaginaries that sometimes default native speakers as better teachers (Mora & Muñoz Luna, 2012), which dovetails with the validation of local teachers that English as an international language (EIL) scholarship has long advocated for.

## Learning and teaching processes: Exploring the English emphasis

Two core issues that link our courses to our transformative view of learning and teaching appeared in our reading of the different syllabi.

### Teachers should confront old and new schools of thought in language education

Involving students in reflexivity and advocacy cannot take place without the confrontation of beliefs and practices as an essential feature of graduate education. Our courses rely on the idea that without these confrontations, real transformation cannot take place. The different courses in English Emphasis invite students to engage in the revision of traditional practices in the English classroom and suggest new approaches to transform the classroom.

For instance, in the course 'English Language I: Issues and Trends in SLA' (Bedoya, 2015), students discuss the need to look at information and communication technologies (ICTs) in our classes through research,

> ICT mediated language learning tasks and environments enjoy nowadays popularity and recognition among L2 researchers, teachers and learners. The extant research shows strong evidence that well planned ICT mediated instruction may be conducive to successful language learning. In our third and fourth sessions we will explore some theoretical and practical aspects concerning the integration of ICT mediated activities into the L2 curriculum. We will also review some successful teaching and learning experiences that will frame our discussion on potential new ICT integration projects. (Bedoya, 2015: 4)

Questioning traditional practices is at the heart of the course 'English Language II: Literacies in Second Languages', as Mora (2015a) explains,

> Literacy and what we mean by it has suffered a number of changes over the years. Whether your definition is simply reading or writing or a more encompassing idea such as 'the process of interpreting and creating text using multiple means and media, including technology, multiple languages, and diverse aesthetic forms of expression, in addition to the written and spoken word', talking about literacy is a contentious issue. (Mora, 2015a: 1)

Martínez (2015), in his course 'Evaluation in Second Language Contexts', argues that 'Chang[ing] the traditional conception and perception of assessment so that it can be differentiated from grading and other practices' is a necessary first step toward 'reveal[ing] the continuities and discontinuities in the evaluation process (as a system) and activate the second language learning processes'. Of course, such transformations are never an easy step to take, as Anderson (2015) in his iteration of 'English Emphasis III', which focused on content and language integrated learning (CLIL), explained,

> You may find that, in many ways, CLIL represents a very different kind of approach to teaching and learning than other approaches with which you are already more familiar. You may wonder whether it is possible to apply CLIL approaches to your current teaching context. Such questions and concerns are normal when we begin [to] learn about what is, in many respects, an often different and still new approach to learning and education. Equally, at the same time, you will find that CLIL draws on many practices and methodologies that are already familiar to you. (Anderson, 2015: 1)

The ML2 curriculum, then, provides a constant space for reflexivity where our students can critically assess their practice as English teachers and infuse them with new models and proposals that align with today's debates in the field of EIL.

### English learning and teaching processes are multidimensional and interdisciplinary

Our curriculum highlights an interdisciplinary perspective for our notions about language learning and teaching. For instance, both iterations of the course 'English Emphasis I: Interculturality, Multilingualism, Inclusion' since 2013 remind us that talking about learning and teaching today should incorporate a sociocultural approach. In the first version of this course titled 'Language, Culture, and Power', Golovátina-Mora (2014) posited,

> The course aims at reflecting over two questions: who is teaching and what do we teach when teaching the languages? The focus will be made on the subject of culture as part of language teaching and the role of language in the social construction of reality. The idea is to propose an interdisciplinary background for understanding the process of the language learning and teaching. (Golovátina-Mora, 2014: 1)

In her version of the course titled, 'Critical Pedagogy and Cultural Politics', Roca-Servat (2015) engages in the discussion of language learning from the vantage point of

> Critical theory and cultural studies. From a critical theory standpoint, the production of knowledge, the means of authority and power relations influence the learning process. A process that should consider

the importance of agency as an act of participating in shaping the world in which we live. (Barroso Tristán, 2013: 1)

Álvarez (2015) also invites students to assume this critical, interdisciplinary view in his proposal for R&R, transcending views of acquisition that only consider the cognitive dimension,

> While it is indeed necessary to acknowledge the relevant role that mental or cognitive process play in language development, we cannot deny the central role of other social and cultural factors in such a process [...] I expect you to look at language teaching and learning as processes that go beyond aspects of linguistic development, communicative competence, skills developments among other concerns that have governed language teaching invisibilizing and that do not allow to see the full picture of what goes on in a language class. While such aspects are relevant, we need to realize that language teaching is informed by factors such as the ones I introduced above. (Álvarez, 2015: 2)

Mora (2015a) acknowledges the interdisciplinary nature of literacy within language learning and teaching,

> Part of developing one's comprehension of these debates and concepts includes the realization, as Lankshear (personal communication, 08/22/13) explained, that 'many of the issues involved in the evolution of thinking about "literacy" seem to grow out of tensions around such paradigms as psycholinguistics, critical theory, sociocultural theory, cultural theory, sociolinguistics, and so on'. (Mora, 2015a: 2)

Finally, Varón Páez (2014), in her version of the course 'English Emphasis III', titled 'Contemporary Trends and Issues in Second Language Teaching and Learning', discussed an interdisciplinary approach to English education,

> The broad aim of the course is to restate the status of the areas surrounding language teaching and learning, which requires the analysis of the most relevant contemporary tendencies in language teaching and learning in addition to the study of a coherent theory of language, whether this comes from linguistics or from some other disciplines. (Varón Páez, 2014: 1)

The field of EIL is highly interdisciplinary, as we explained at the beginning of this chapter. In our curriculum, we have relied both on the interdisciplinary nature of the field and the multiple backgrounds of our faculty to invite spaces for reflexivity about what it means to teach English in Colombia as part of a global call for active scholarship.

# Second Languages: Searching for More Equitable Frameworks

Providing frameworks to understand English within the frameworks of justice (Ladson-Billings, 2015) and equity (Luke, 2004; Mora & Golovátina-Mora, 2011) has been a pressing matter for ML2 since the beginning. Framing English education programs around the notion of 'foreign language(s)' has been the tradition. This notion, we argue, seems to overlook more critical perspectives about English today (Graddol, 2006; Mora, 2013b, 2015b; Pennycook, 2001) and even some of the potential social inequalities germane to the idea of 'foreign' (Mora, 2012b, 2015b). Therefore, we proposed the idea of *second languages* (Mora, 2013b, 2014e, 2015c; Uribe & Gómez, 2015) as our response to the traditional binary opposition of 'second/foreign languages'. Uribe and Gómez (2015) proposed defining second languages as,

> [C]ommunication systems present in a specific context that operate next to (sometimes with) the mother language in that location. In this sense, we recognize that while there may be a predominant language that people use in that particular place, there may be others that people use as a resource for communication. This way, second languages emerge because the context itself and its inhabitants make it happen. (Uribe & Gómez, 2015: Defining the Term, para 1)

Our idea of second languages, we believe, also aligns with ideas such as 'World Englishes' (Smith, 2014), 'English as a Lingua Franca' (Björkmann, 2014) or 'additional language' (Thorne & Black, 2008), as Mora (2013b) explained,

> The idea of second languages is then an approximation to concepts such as additional or new languages, as it acknowledges the diversity in language learning and that speakers may adopt other languages for a myriad or reasons, while advocating that adopting a second language in one specific scenario should never come to the detriment of other languages users already possess, even their mother tongue. (Mora, 2013b: 54)

## Second languages: Exploring the English emphasis

Our curriculum invites students to revisit English today, providing a critical view of the conditions in which it operates within and beyond the classrooms.

A revised view of English questions what new sets of values we must promote and how we must understand the current conditions and frameworks. Our English Emphasis courses provide some interesting examples. In her version of 'English Language I', Golovátina-Mora (2014) prioritized the critical discussion of bilingualism (Mora, 2012b). She invited her students to pay attention to how practitioners make sense of the name (Golovátina-Mora, 2013; Mora, 2012b) and the local and international perspectives and implications around this idea (Baker, 2008; Canagarajah, 2002; Golovátina-Mora, 2012; Stroud, 2007). Varón Páez (2014) focused some of her discussions in 'English Emphasis III' on the context of globalization (Dewey & Jenkins, 2010; Fairclough, 2006; Kramsch & Thorne, 2002; Mackay, 2004), as two of the discussion questions in her course illustrate:

- In what ways have discourses, theories and practices of globalization changed the conditions in which language learning and teaching take place in contemporary language classrooms?
- What are the main challenges imposed by the World Englishes, postmodernism and postcolonialism to the idea of the existence of an English native speaker?

The need for a critical view about postmethod (Kumaravadivelu, 1994, 2001, 2003, 2006) emerged in some courses. In 'English Language I', Bedoya (2015) devoted some sessions to the 'discussion and reflection about the so called postmethod era, to analyze its impact in current language teaching practices, and at the same time, to examine the relevance that L2 teachers still grant to the concept of method'. In the version of 'English Emphasis II: Socio-Critical Approaches in Second Languages', titled 'Critical Pedagogy in Second Language Education', Areiza (2014) situated postmethod within a larger school of thought,

> Language education has increasingly been more sensitive to critical pedagogy or critical pedagogies thanks to Paulo Freire, the Frankfurt School and issues raised by Applied Linguistics (e.g. World Englishes, Colonialism, Culture and Identity, Language policies and planning, feminism, critical literacy, etc.), social constructivism and the postmethod condition. This course will explore how some critical approaches have overtly claimed to shift from a transmissionist pedagogy to a more contextualized, liberating and transformative education. (Areiza, 2014: 1–2)

Finally, there is a sense of awareness that moving toward a more encompassing view of second languages (which, as we have argued, leans very close to ideas regarding EIL), involves a re-examination of our teaching and research methods. In the description of R&R, Álvarez (2015) discusses,

We would examine the factors that have contributed to re-vision the idea of teaching methods, the native speaker as the model for language learning, the role of culture and other constructs. Some of the factors that I will include in this course comprise issues of identity, politics and policy and English language teaching, language teaching pedagogy, World Englishes or English around the globe, interculturality, and Computer Mediated Communication. (Álvarez, 2015: 1)

These re-examinations imply a new view of English teachers, not only as practitioners or researchers, but also as activists, as Mora (2015a) explained in 'English Language II',

Today's language ecologies (Mora, 2014c; 2015b) also require us to reflect on how new technologies and the changes in policy and the world at large are merging within these theoretical conversations. In this sense, it is essential that second language researchers and practitioners be well informed and become active participants in these debates [...] The new views on literacy actually invite us to rethink learning and teaching in new and more meaningful ways. This course is, therefore, an invitation for you to become acquainted with and immersed into these conversations. (Mora, 2015a: 2)

The idea of second languages becomes, then, a space for reflexivity and glocalized advocacy. We invite our teachers to think about the deeper rationales for language learning in Colombia (Mora, 2013a) and to think about the different ideological issues that permeate their classes, from textbook selection (Mora, 2014b) to curricular decisions and translate that into their current teaching and research agendas.

## Discussion: The Road Traveled and the Road Ahead

Three years into chartering our program, we are far from finished. We are assessing our achievements in our curriculum and our ongoing research studies, while raising deeper questions to strengthen our philosophy. The curriculum review that this chapter actually triggered showed us that we have, indeed, surpassed the usual discussions about English as a second language (ESL)/English as a foreign language (EFL) that have long plagued the field of English education. Our proposal of second languages, as an idea of 'international/additional language in disguise', has found a very welcoming audience in our students and our faculty. Opening doors both to non-teaching English to speakers of other languages (TESOL) professionals in our program (such as Polina, who has a background in history and cultural studies) and to scholars who have moved past TESOL into much larger fields (such as Raúl, who now confronts issues in TESOL from his background in literacy research) has become a true asset: The scholarship that these faculty members contribute makes us more interdisciplinary and thus more open to being more critical about English in today's world.

This view of the program is also emerging in our students' MA theses. They are moving from the traditional view of just exploring the improvement of the skills into larger issues. We have studies (both finished and in progress at the time of writing this) looking at children's literacies, language policies in Colombia, social networks, media literacy, conflict resolution, the role of families and ecotourism and English teaching, to name a few. This expanded view of research situates, in fact, our program within a larger international perspective vis-à-vis English.

English education in Colombia keeps evolving (Mora, 2014b). Larger questions and issues appear as our government envisions new and stronger roles for English as a globalizing tool. However, we feel that our program and our philosophy regarding English (and second languages in general) will provide broader spaces to empower our students and engage in the necessary glocalized advocacy that EIL demands of scholars and practitioners. We wish to participate in the worldwide debates about English with a view to devising research that can impact local communities, with the hope that our work can help our practitioners and their students use English, from that view of international language, as a space for equity and for the remainder of this decade and beyond.

## Notes

(1) The original (and official, per Ministry of Education purposes) name of the program is *Maestría en Procesos de Aprendizaje y Enseñanza de Segundas Lenguas.* However, for all related issues to the English Emphasis, we use the name in English.
(2) In Colombia, a specialization degree goes beyond the bachelor's but below the master's, providing deeper professional development via a degree program.
(3) Although this chapter will zero in on the English Emphasis, it is important to point out that all the conceptual and epistemological tenets outlined in the chapter are akin to both emphases.

## References

Álvarez, J.A. (2014) Developing the intercultural perspective in foreign language teaching in Colombia: A review of six journals. *Language and Intercultural Communication* 14 (2), 1–19.

Álvarez, J.A. (2015) *Reconceptualizing and Recontextualizing Learning and Teaching Processes* [Syllabus]. Medellín: MA in Learning and Teaching Processes in Second Languages, Universidad Pontificia Bolivariana.

Anderson, C.E. (2015) *Introduction to Content and Language Integrated Learning* [Syllabus]. Medellín: MA in Learning and Teaching Processes in Second Languages, Universidad Pontificia Bolivariana.

Areiza, H.N. (2014) *Critical Pedagogy in Second Language Education* [Syllabus]. Medellín: MA in Learning and Teaching Processes in Second Languages, Universidad Pontificia Bolivariana.

Atkinson, D. (2011) Introduction: Cognitivism and second language acquisition. In D. Atkinson (ed.) *Alternative Approaches to Second Language Acquisition* (pp. 1–23). London: Routledge Taylor & Francis Group.

Baker, C. (2008) Knowledge about bilingualism vs multilingualism. In J. Cenoz and N.H. Hornberger (eds) *Encyclopedia of Language and Education* (2nd edn; Vol. 6) (pp. 315–327). Dordrecht: Springer.

Barroso Tristán, J. M. (2013) Interview Henry Giroux. *Global Education Magazine, 2*. See http://www.globaleducationmagazine.com/Global-Education-Magazine-School-Day-of-Non-violence-and-Peace.pdf (accessed 15 May 2015).

Bedoya, J.R. (2015) *English Language I: Issues and Trends in Second Language Acquisition* [Syllabus]. Medellín: MA in Learning and Teaching Processes in Second Languages, Universidad Pontificia Bolivariana.

Björkman, B. (2014) English as a lingua franca. *Key Concepts in Intercultural Dialogue* 40. See http://centerforinterculturaldialogue.org/publications (accessed 25 August 2015).

Blommaert, J. (2010) *The Sociolinguistics of Globalization*. Cambridge: Cambridge University Press.

Bourdieu, P. and Wacquant, L. (1992) *An Invitation to Reflexive Sociology*. Chicago, IL: The University of Chicago Press.

Canagarajah, A.S. (2002) Globalization, methods, and practice in periphery classrooms. In D. Block and D. Cameron (eds) *Globalization and Language Teaching* (pp. 134–150). London: Routledge.

Darder, A. (2003) Teaching as an act of love: Reflections on Paulo Freire and his contributions to our lives and our work. In A. Darder, M. Baltodano and R.D. Torres (eds) *The Critical Pedagogy Reader* (pp. 497–510). New York/London: Routledge Falmer.

Dewey, M. and Jenkins, J. (2010) English as a lingua franca in the global context: Interconnectedness, variation and change. In M. Saxena and T. Omoniyi (eds) *Contending with Globalization in World Englishes* (pp. 72–92). Bristol: Multilingual Matters.

Fairclough, N. (2007) *Language and Globalization*. London: Routledge.

Freire, P. (1979) *Conscientização: Teoria e prática da libertação, uma introdução ao pensamento de Paulo Freire*. São Paulo: Cortez & Moraes.

Gee, J.P. (2008) *Social Linguistics and Literacies: Ideology in Discourses* (3rd edn). New York: Routledge.

Golovátina-Mora, P. (2012) On nationalism and bilingualism. Presentation at the Bilingualism Integrative Roundtable, Faculty of Education, Universidad Pontificia Bolivariana, Medellín. See https://vimeo.com/40331366 (accessed 25 August 2015).

Golovátina-Mora, P. (2013) Bilingualism: What's in a name? *Revista Palabra* 3 (1). See http://srvzenu.monteria.upb.edu.co/revistapalabra/?p=186 (accessed 25 August 2015).

Golovátina-Mora, P. (2014) *English Emphasis I: Interculturality, Multilingualism, Diversity* [Syllabus]. Medellín, Colombia: MA in Learning and Teaching Processes in Second Languages, Universidad Pontificia Bolivariana.

Graddol, D. (2006) *English Next: Why Global English may Mean the End of 'English as a Foreign Language'*. London: The British Council.

Gramsci, A. (1971) *Selections from the Prison Notebooks*. London: Lawrence and Wishart.

Higgins, C. (2009) *English as a Local Language: Post-Colonial Identities and Multilingual Practices*. Bristol: Multilingual Matters.

Joseph, M. and Ramani, E. (2012) 'Glocalization': Going beyond the dichotomy of global versus local through additive multilingualism. *International Multilingual Research Journal* 6 (1), 22–34.

Kramsch, C. and Thorne, S.L. (2002) Foreign language learning as global communicative practice. In D. Block and D. Cameron (eds) *Globalization and Language Teaching* (pp. 83–100). London: Routledge.

Kubota, R. (2004) Critical multiculturalism and second language education. In B. Norton and K. Toohey (eds) *Critical Pedagogies and Language Learning* (pp. 30–52). Cambridge: Cambridge University Press.

Kumaravadivelu, B. (1994) The postmethod condition: (E)merging strategies for second/ foreign language teaching. *TESOL Quarterly* 28 (1), 27–48.

Kumaravadivelu, B. (2001) Toward a postmethod pedagogy. *TESOL Quarterly* 35 (4), 537–560.

Kumaravadivelu, B. (2003) *Beyond Methods: Macrostrategies for Language Teaching.* New Haven, CT: Yale University Press.

Kumaravadivelu, B. (2006) *Understanding Language Teaching: From Method to Postmethod.* New York: Routledge.

Ladson-Billings, G. (2015, April) *Justice... just, justice!* Social Justice in Education Award Address at an annual meeting of the American Educational Research Association, Chicago, IL. See https://youtu.be/ofB_t1oTYhI (accessed 25 August 2015).

Lantolf, J. (2011) The sociocultural approach to second language acquisition: Sociocultural theory, second language acquisition, and artificial L2 development. In D. Atkinson (ed.) *Alternative Approaches to Second Language Acquisition* (pp. 24–47). London: Routledge Taylor & Francis Group.

Luke, A. (2004) The trouble with English. *Research in the Teaching of English* 39 (1), 85–95.

Mackay, H. (2004) The globalization of culture? In D. Held (ed.) *A Globalizing World? Culture, Economics, Politics* (pp. 44–80). London: Routledge.

Martínez, J.D. (2015) *Evaluation in Second Language Contexts* [Syllabus]. Medellín: MA in Learning and Teaching Processes in Second Languages, Universidad Pontificia Bolivariana.

Martínez, J.D., Jaramillo, M. and Vallejo, M. (2011) Énfasis: Procesos de enseñanza orientados al aprendizaje de inglés como lengua extranjera. Unpublished manuscript, Universidad Pontificia Bolivariana.

Mora, R.A. (2011) Tres retos para la investigación y formación de docentes en inglés: Reflexividad sobre las creencias y prácticas en literacidad. *Revista Q* 5 (10). See http://revistaq.upb.edu.co/articulos/ver/364 (accessed 25 August 2015).

Mora, R.A. (2012a) Bourdieu y la formación de docentes: Reflexividad sobre los retos y horizontes en el campo de la educación. *Revista Pensamiento Universitari* 23, 55–62.

Mora, R.A. (2012b) What do you mean by <bilingual>?: The multiple dimensions of <bilingualism>. Presentation at the Bilingualism Integrative Roundtable, Faculty of Education, Universidad Pontificia Bolivariana, Medellín. See https://vimeo.com/40725314 (accessed 25 August 2015).

Mora, R.A. (2013a) Have we told our children *why* they should learn another language? A critical discussion on the new roles and questions for language learning in Colombia. Presentation at Seminario Miradas Contemporáneas en Educación, Universidad Distrital 'Francisco José de Caldas', Bogotá, DC. See https://www.youtube.com/watch?v=Yje0AnkuTXo (accessed 25 August 2015).

Mora, R.A. (2013b) The notion of *second languages*: Responding to today's linguistic ecologies. *The Journal for ESL Teachers and Learners* 2, 53–61.

Mora, R.A. (2014a) Conscientização. *Key Concepts in Intercultural Dialogue* 42. See https://centerforinterculturaldialogue.files.wordpress.com/2014/11/key-concepts-conscientizaccca7acc83o.pdf (accessed 25 August 2015).

Mora, R.A. (2014b) Critical literacy as policy and advocacy: Lessons from Colombia. *Journal of Adolescent & Adult Literacy* 58 (1), 16–18.

Mora, R.A. (2014c) Language ecology. *Key Concepts in Intercultural Dialogue* 13. See http://centerforinterculturaldialogue.files.wordpress.com/2014/05/key-concept-language-ecology.pdf (accessed 25 August 2015).

Mora, R.A. (2014d) Reflexivity. *Key Concepts in Intercultural Dialogue* 21. See https://centerforinterculturaldialogue.files.wordpress.com/2014/06/key-concept-reflexivity.pdf (accessed 25 August 2015).

Mora, R.A. (2014e) Rethinking the intersection between technology, digital literacies and language ecologies. *ENLETAWA Journal* 7, 115–128.

Mora, R.A. (2015a) *English Language II: Literacies in Second Languages* [Syllabus]. Medellín: MA in Learning and Teaching Processes in Second Languages, Universidad Pontificia Bolivariana.

Mora, R.A. (2015b) Revisiting today's language ecologies: New questions about language use and literacy practices. [Webinar]. In *Global Conversations in Literacy Research Web Seminar Series*. See http://youtu.be/CMLnXwx3lRY (accessed 25 August 2015).

Mora, R.A. (2016a) Glocalized advocacy. *LSLP Micro-Papers* 37. See http://www.literaciesinl2project.org/uploads/3/8/9/7/38976989/lslp-micro-paper-37-glocalized-advocacy.pdf (accessed 25 August 2015).

Mora, R.A. (2016b) Jaime Garzón's Trickster discourse: His messages, social commentary, and legacy in Colombian comedy. In S. Weaver and R.A. Mora (eds) Special Issue: The Trickster Activist in Global Humour and Comedy. *International Journal of Cultural Studies* 19 (5), 519–534.

Mora, RA. (2016c) Translating literacy as global policy and advocacy. *Journal of Adolescent & Adult Literacy* 59 (6), 647–651.

Mora, R.A. and Golovátina-Mora, P. (2011) Bilingualism – A Bridge to Cosmopolitanism? Keynote presentation at the ELT Conference 2011, Medellín, Colombia.

Mora, R.A. and Muñoz Luna, R. (2012) A critical deconstruction of TV ads for online English courses: Toward a reconstruction of the concept of second language. In L. Gómez Chova, A. López Martínez and I. Candel Torres (eds) *ICERI2012 Proceedings* (pp. 413–421). Madrid: International Association of Technology, Education and Development (IATED).

Patel, F. and Lynch, H. (2013) Glocalization as an alternative to internationalization in higher education: Embedding positive glocal learning perspectives. *International Journal of Teaching and Learning in Higher Education* 25 (2), 223–230.

Pavlenko, A. (2004) Gender and sexuality in foreign and second language education: Critical and feminist approaches. In B. Norton and K. Toohey (eds) *Critical Pedagogies and Language Learning* (pp. 53–71). Cambridge: Cambridge University Press.

Pennycook, A. (2001) *Critical Applied Linguistics: A Critical Introduction.* Mahwah, NJ: Lawrence Erlbaum.

Puren, C. (1998) Del enfoque por tareas a la perspectiva co-accional. See http://www.ugr.es/~portalin/articulos/PL_numero1/puren.pdf.

Reinhardt, J. (2012) Accommodating divergent frameworks in analysis of technology-mediated L2 interaction. In M. Dooly and R. O'Dowd (eds) *Researching Online Interaction and Exchange in Foreign Language Education: Methods and Issues* (pp. 45–77). Bern: Peter Lang.

Roca-Servat, D. (2015) *Critical Pedagogy and Cultural Politics* [Syllabus]. Medellín: MA in Learning and Teaching Processes in Second Languages, Universidad Pontificia Bolivariana.

Roudometof, V. (2005) Transnationalism, cosmopolitanism and glocalization. *Current Sociology* 53 (1), 113–135.

Shakespeare, W. (1579/1900) *The Complete Works of William Shakespeare.* American News Company. See http://www.fulltextarchive.jpegradar.com/pdfs/The-Complete-Works-of-William-Shakespearex8970.pdf (accessed 25 August 2015).

Sion, C. (ed.) (1985) *Recipes for Tired Teachers: Well-Seasoned Activities for the ESOL Classroom.* Reading, MA : Addison-Wesley.

Skutnabb-Kangas, T. (2000) *Linguistic Genocide in Education—or Worldwide Diversity and Human Rights?* Mahwah, NJ: Lawrence Erlbaum.

Smith, L.E. (2014) World Englishes. *Key Concepts in Intercultural Dialogue* 34. See https://centerforinterculturaldialogue.files.wordpress.com/2014/09/key-concept-world-englishes.pdf (accessed 25 August 2015).

Stake, R.E. (2010) *Qualitative Research: Studying How Things Work.* New York: The Guilford Press.

Street, B. (2013) New literacy studies. In M. Grenfell, D. Bloome, C. Hardy, K. Pahl, J. Rowsell and B. Street (eds) *Language, Ethnography, and Education: Bridging New Literacy Studies and Bourdieu* (pp. 27–49). New York: Routledge.

Stroud, C. (2007) Bilingualism: Colonialism and postcolonialism. In M. Heller (ed.) *Bilingualism: A Social Approach* (pp. 25–49). New York: Palgrave Macmillan.

Thorne, S.L. and Black, R. (2008) Language and literacy development in computer-mediated contexts and communities. *Annual Review of Applied Linguistics* 27, 133–160.

Universidad Pontificia Bolivariana (2005) *Plan de investigaciones y de programas de maestrías y doctorados.* Medellín: Author.

Universidad Pontificia Bolivariana (2012) *Maestría en Procesos de Aprendizaje y Enseñanza de Segundas Lenguas: Informe de condiciones de calidad para la obtención del Registro Calificado.* Medellín: Author.

Uribe, S. and Gómez, M.A. (2015) Second languages. *LSLP Micro-Papers* 23. See http://www.literaciesinl2project.org/lslp-micro-papers.html (accessed 25 August 2015).

Usma, J. (2009) Globalization and language and education reform in Colombia: A critical outlook. *Ikala* 14 (22), 19–42.

VanPatten, B and Benati, A.G. (2010) *Key Terms in Second Language Acquisition.* London: Continuum.

Varón Páez, M.E. (2014) *Contemporary Trends and Issues in Second Language Teaching and Learning* [Syllabus]. Medellín: MA in Learning and Teaching Processes in Second Languages, Universidad Pontificia Bolivariana.

# 4 US-based Teacher Education Program for 'Local' EIL Teachers

## Seong-Yoon Kang

## Introduction

Along with the unprecedented empowering status of English as a means of communication in every aspect of global diplomacy, business, education and entertainment, the English language itself, its users and its contexts have inevitably gone through tremendously complicated transitions. Accordingly, it is inevitable that significant changes be made in language policy, teaching materials, attitudes toward varieties of World Englishes (WE) and teacher education programs so that English as an international language (EIL) can maintain its global status as a valid intercultural communication tool used by speakers of different sociocultural backgrounds, keeping its multiple varieties in a global context.

Many linguists, applied linguists and English language teaching (ELT) professionals have tried to theorize on this tremendous shift and present the grounds for the intricateness of English under the umbrella of their own frameworks such as WE (Kachru, 1982, 1985, 1992; Kachru *et al.*, 2009), English as a lingua franca (ELF) (Jenkins, 1996, 2005, 2007) and EIL (Matsuda & Friedrich, 2010; McKay, 2002; Sharifian, 2009).

Despite different perspectives on the continuous changes in diverse users and contexts, they are all based on the continuously changing actualities of the English language in a global context such as the outnumbered English users in the Outer and Expanding Circle countries, the widespread use of English only between nonnative speakers outside the Inner Circle countries and the varieties of WE across the world, to name a few.

These upheavals have questioned the traditional conceptualization of *canon* English – standard or non-standard – in that the English language has been used by diverse users in many different contexts, leading to it being infused with their own societal systems and customs, cultural heritages and local languages (Crystal, 2003; Graddol, 1997, 2006; Kachru *et al.*, 2009; McKay, 2002). In this respect, 'local' EIL teachers, who speak both local language (first language [L1]) and English (second language [L2]) and know local culture and the educational system, are expected to play a prominent role in teaching local EIL students.

Because of numerous contacts with diverse users and contexts, the English language has become heterogeneous, practical and adaptable to specific sociocultural contexts, which has led to a paradigm shift that makes the ownership of English questionable regardless of the supremacy of English. Studies on the linguistic and cultural functions of English have led to reflecting the status quo of English on shaping up a new paradigm that embraces the practicality and appropriateness of English use on an international scale rather than being anachronously fixated on the linguistic chauvinism and ownership of English (Matsuda, 2003; Phillipson, 1992; Phillipson, 2009; Widdowson, 1994). This chapter, thus, introduces the Total Immersion Courses for Chinese and Korean English Teachers (TICKET) at Bloomfield College, New Jersey, which is based on the new paradigm that infuses varieties of English and their diverse users into an ELT classroom setting and that regards English as the *de facto* language for international communication in the multifaceted array of multilingual interactions and plurilingual contexts between English users from diverse linguistic and cultural backgrounds (Kachru, 2011; Kachru & Nelson, 2006; Kachru *et al.*, 2009; Liddicoat, 2005; McKay & Bokhorst-Heng, 2008; McKay & Jenkins, 2009; Murata & Jenkins, 2009; Power, 2005; Svartvik & Leech, 2006). While presenting the theoretical framework and rationale for developing and implementing the US-based teacher education program for English teachers from the Expanding Circle countries, I address how the TICKET program has transformed from a typical traditional teacher training program to an innovative teacher education program with a new perspective on EIL in multicultural globalized contexts and then present the uniqueness (i.e. EIL-ness), challenges and limitations of the program.

## Overview of the Program

The TICKET program is a grant-based teacher education program exclusively for English teachers from the Expanding Circle countries such as the People's Republic of China and the Republic of Korea, funded by their governmental, provincial or municipal education institutes. From its inception until 2011, the TICKET program was merely one of the traditional training programs for English as a second language (ESL)/English as a foreign language (EFL) teachers. The main objective of the program was to learn American English as the *norm-providing* standard and to speak or pronounce with Americans as a role model. English teachers' linguistic proficiency levels were assessed according to their *norm-accepting* linguistic ability to identically or closely imitate American English (i.e. accent) and ways of performing speech acts. They were consciously or subconsciously forced to accept what they practiced throughout the program and to apply what they learned into their own classroom. They were misguidedly trained to reconfirm the superiority of American English, to use American contextual materials and cultural values in the classroom and to keep the homogeneous authenticity of American English (see McArthur, 2001). As a consequence, they felt discouraged, marginalized and inferior as nonnative teachers of English who play only a supplementary role, assisting native English-speaking teachers. They were also apt to lose their confidence and motivation in adopting American cultural norms and values – out of context – into their daily instructional resources. The gaps or tensions between what they construct their roles to be and where they are positioned supplementarily in the classroom may raise 'local' EIL teachers' identity issues (Alsagoff, 2012; Arva & Medgyes, 2000; Llurda & Huguet, 2003; Mahoney, 2004; Tajino & Tajino, 2000; Tang, 1997; Wang & Lin, 2014; Yang, 2000). It was in 2012 when I, as the program director and curriculum specialist, took charge of the TICKET program that indispensably needed a complete overhaul or transformation in order to keep up with the paradigm shift in the global ELT field, considering the emergence of and exposure to multiple varieties of English, an increasing demand for intercultural communicative competence on the world stage, a significant increase in international interactions between nonnative speakers of English and the importance of 'local' EIL teachers and localized teaching and learning materials. The overall frameworks of the program were revised by taking into consideration the theoretical rationales in the ELT field that were different from those of the past program (see Table 4.1).

The learning objectives for EIL teachers, in the past, were mainly to have an opportunity to practice *pure* American English with *educated* Americans, mostly through formal instructions in the school environment, and to learn *pure* American culture for their use in their own classroom. However, the learning objectives of the new TICKET program include the ability to:

- Understand the nature of language and its use in different sociocultural contexts.
- Utilize intercultural communication strategies to compromise sociolinguistic differences and to facilitate exposure and awareness of World Englishes.
- Reflect on their own strengths and weaknesses as EIL teachers to make best use of their competence, performance and professional abilities.
- Have multiple perspectives of the norms and functions of English in the diverse global context.
- Select and develop instructional techniques and strategies using authentic materials and realia from diverse cultural resources.

**Table 4.1** Transition from the old teacher training program to the new teacher education program

| Old TICKET program (2008–2011) | New TICKET program (2012–2016) |
| --- | --- |
| • American English is the standard language in the field of English language teaching (ELT) and should be taught as the norm in the English as a second language (ESL)/English as a foreign language (EFL) classroom. | • American English is merely one of the varieties of English that can be spoken in the use of English as an international language (EIL) in the global context along with other varieties of English. |
| • Only American cultural values and customs should be addressed as the target culture and be used for the pragmatic and contextual clues. | • Learners' and interlocutors' cultural values and customs should be included and utilized as contextual clues and resources along with diverse cultural materials. |
| • Nonnative speakers of English should make an effort to pronounce like native speakers of American English to reach a high level of fluency in English (native-like fluency focused). | • Nonnative speakers of English should learn to effectively communicate in English in the global context (intercultural communicative competence focused). |
| • The program instructors should be US-born native speakers (monolingual preferred). | • The program instructors should be teaching English to speakers of other languages (TESOL)-certified, ESL/EFL teachers (foreign Language (FL) learning experience required and multilingual preferred). |
| • International teachers of English are labelled as 'nonnative English-speaking teachers'. | • International teachers of English are called 'EIL teachers'. |
| • English learners' target interlocutors are Inner Circle native speakers of English. | • English learners' target interlocutors are all English users in the English as a new language (ENL)/ESL/EFL contexts. |

The duration of the program varies from four to eight weeks depending on the requests from dispatching Chinese or Korean institutes. Each program has a cohort of 15 to 20 EIL teachers who are selected out of hundreds of teachers based on their proficiency level and teaching experience.

Almost all of the participating teachers were educated in a monolingual EFL society, in which English is taught at schools as one of the academic subjects for better academic achievement as well as employment opportunities and promotions. Even though they have a significantly limited exposure to English outside the classroom, most of them use English fluently

**Table 4.2** Course schedule (6 weeks)

| Week | Core courses | Elective courses |
|------|--------------|------------------|
| Week 1–4 | TICKET 510 (4 hours/week) | TICKET 500 or TICKET 550 (select one, 4 hours) |
| | TICKET 520 (4 hours/week) | TICKET 560 or TICKET 570 (select one, 4 hours) |
| | TICKET 530 (4 hours/week) | |
| | TICKET 540 (4 hours/week) | |
| Week 5–6 | TICKET 580 (28 hours/week) | TICKET 540 (4 hours/week) |

and accurately in discussing practical, social and professional topics and demonstrate advanced structural accuracy and vocabulary in most formal and informal conversations and writings. Nevertheless, they still feel underprivileged with regard to their authority, credibility and proficiency as EIL teachers in the ELT field (see Selvi, 2014). Therefore, the ultimate goal of the revised TICKET program is to help them to (re)gain confidence in teaching English in English (TEE) and to play a pivotal role in bringing the principles of EIL teaching and learning into English language classrooms. For an example of a six-week course schedule, see Table 4.2.

# Core Courses

## TICKET 500 second language acquisition

This course provides a comprehensive overview of second language acquisition (SLA) theories, methods and hypotheses from the perspectives of behaviorism, innativism, cognitivism and social interactionism. It then examines EIL learners' complex internal and external factors that influence L2 learning processes and outcomes: personality, attitude, learning styles and strategies, language policy and sociocultural factors. This course also addresses current issues and implications in SLA practice/research along with the global status of English, diverse EIL learners, multilingualism and varieties of English.

## TICKET 510 teaching listening and speaking in the EIL classroom

This course provides a basic understanding of the theories and pedagogical techniques that help EIL teachers effectively teach EIL learners the skills of listening and speaking. This course reviews bottom-up (chunking) and top-down (the use of background knowledge) listening processes and discusses/practices effective learning activities and instructional strategies. EIL teachers practice teaching speaking skills with a variety of instructional techniques and learn how to teach the components of the varieties of English as a legitimate instructional model in order to utilize local/diverse authentic materials that express their own identity and cultural values.

## TICKET 520 teaching reading and writing in the EIL classroom

This course helps EIL teachers effectively teach reading and writing skills by overviewing the underlying concepts and practical skills and reviewing teaching methods and strategies for planning, implementing and assessing their instructions. EIL teachers practice instructional strategies for vocabulary/grammar development, reading comprehension and fluency, writing process, critical thinking skills and reading and writing assessment. This course helps EIL teachers refine their competence in selecting socioculturally sensitive reading materials and writing topics from diverse resources.

## TICKET 530 teaching pronunciation in the EIL classroom

This course provides EIL teachers with effective teaching techniques to take better control of their pronunciation (L1 accent) so that both students and teachers themselves can produce effective rhythms and stress in words, phrases and sentences during unrehearsed speech. EIL teachers are provided with ample pronunciation samples from English users of the Inner/Outer/Expanding Circle countries to get used to other varieties of English accents and to improve aural sensitivity to these varieties' rhythm, stress and intonation as well as segmental features both separately and in the context of natural speech. This course further discusses sociocultural identity, intelligibility and comprehensibility among diverse English users.

## TICKET 540 culture and communication: Task-based intercultural activities

This course offers EIL teachers a practical approach to use English as an intercultural communication medium in real-life contexts (New York City) through task-based intercultural activities that hold up as a good example of how to use local cultural values and materials for in-class or outside-the-classroom learning activities. EIL teachers research independently and collaboratively to observe a local story, issue or phenomenon, and present their findings through presentations, reports and personal reflective essays. They learn how to effectively teach their own and diverse cultures in the classroom settings and acknowledge English as a means of intercultural communication.

## TICKET 550 sociolinguistics: English as an international language

This course provides an overview of the political and sociocultural aspects of the global spread of English and reflects on the diverse functions and global status of English in diverse sociolinguistic contexts. EIL teachers critically discuss current issues in the field of ELT in a global context: varieties of World Englishes, diverse sociolinguistic histories, a pluricentric view of English, multilingualism, multiculturalism, native-speakerism, identity issues, language policies and the implications/issues of the use of English in diverse sociocultural contexts.

## TICKET 560 lesson planning and classroom presentation

This course gives EIL teachers an overview of the keys to successful lesson planning and classroom presentation strategies, and introduces a needs-based, learner-centered approach to designing courses, from designing a curriculum and instruction to actual EIL material development. They review widely used, published examples of lesson plans, and practice developing their own lesson plans and teaching materials appropriate for their EIL classroom. EIL teachers also reflect on and analyze their lesson plans with each other and refine them through microteaching sessions and critique sessions.

## TICKET 570 instructional strategies and classroom management

This course reviews various methodologies and techniques for effective instructions and classroom management so that EIL teachers can develop individualized instructional strategies that meet EIL students' needs and interests as well as improve their proficiency levels in all four language skills. EIL teachers discuss their own experiences in designing and using instructional strategies and classroom management skills in their own sociocultural contexts and examine effective strategies and skills. They discuss sociocultural challenges, best practices and current research findings.

## TICKET 580 teaching practicum

This course provides EIL teachers with an opportunity to teach elementary, middle and high school students at local public schools in New Jersey. Visiting EIL teachers observe a variety of school subjects, and collaborate with their host teachers on instructional strategies and learning activities. They also develop lesson plans and teach selected activities under the supervision of the host teacher. Teaching practicum consists of four phases: classroom observation, co-teaching, individual and small-group instruction and whole classroom instruction. They reflect on their teaching experience through poster presentations, video and audio recordings, checklists and coding systems.

# Uniqueness of the Program

The TICKET program puts current major trends in ELT and EIL teacher education into practice, reflecting new perspectives on the multifunctional roles of EIL in multilingual, multicultural contexts. Consequently, it is significantly different from traditional training programs for nonnative English-speaking teachers (NNESTs) of the Expanding Circle countries. It is not uncommon for many teacher training academies and institutes in the Inner Circle countries to exclusively teach their own varieties of English as the only legitimate instructional model. A plethora of one-size-fits-all instructional guidelines, strategies and assessment tools are still deeply rooted in the field of ELT and teaching English to speakers of other languages (TESOL), without acknowledging the diverse English users and sociocultural contexts in the global context (see Farrell & Martin, 2009). In this regard, the TICKET program advocates that 'the effectiveness of English teachers should be determined by their linguistic, instructional, and intercultural competence rather than simply by their linguistic identity' (Sun, 2014). The strengths and advantages of local EIL teachers are emphasized in that they went through the same learning pathway, boulevards or dead ends as their students are going to pass through (Seidlhofer, 1999) and in that they represent themselves as a role model for their students who dream of being a legitimate user of the language (Matsuda, 2012). A series of motivational workshops and pep talks inspire them to feel confident and competent in using and teaching English so that they can make the best use of the high caliber of their 'local' contextually sensitive qualities. They know their students' language, learning process and goals, sociocultural factors and educational systems. They have a significant effect on EIL students' successful learning outcomes in the frontline classroom. Eventually, they are considered highly valued and legitimized as qualified teachers of English since they can teach EIL students in contextually relevant and culturally sensitive ways that satisfy the high demands and requirements of local teachers, language learners and educational stakeholders (see Brown, 2012).

The TICKET program provides EIL teachers with learning materials that dramatically reflect the changing perspectives of English and its use in globalized contexts. In EFL contexts with little exposure to English outside the classroom, they must utilize well-designed textbooks and authentic learning materials with ample sociolinguistic samples so that they can teach their students with competence and confidence, given the fact that 'the quality and quantity of the language input in class is critical in acquiring the language' (Matsuda, 2012: 168). Therefore, instead of using traditional ESL/EFL textbooks that mainly address an artifact of English-speaking countries, the TICKET program uses textbooks and supplemental materials that reflect the effective and appropriate use of English as a communication tool in worldwide real-life environments with English users from diverse sociocultural backgrounds. Furthermore, EIL teachers review a variety of local magazines, newspaper articles, reports, video clips or talks about interesting stories, global issues, inspiring people, science, hidden history, technology and world economy as potential examples of authentic EIL learning materials and classroom application. Through both in-class and outside-the-classroom follow-up activities, they are expected to enhance their global point of view, current international issues, interdisciplinary approach in teaching, critical thinking skills along with four language skills, and improve their core academic language skills. In this regard, a series of workshops and seminars also introduce successful US context-based instructional design models and classroom management techniques (e.g. Lemov, 2014; Wiggins & McTighe, 2005) and take participating teachers to model schools, where these teaching methodologies are being practiced. They see how they apply theoretical concepts to classroom practice so that they can come up with a series of ideas and answers for what/how to teach EIL learners in their sociocultural contexts, how to choose EIL materials and how to create a positive classroom environment that promotes intercultural communication.

The TICKET program also provides task-based 'Lost-in-New York' intercultural activities (e.g. Nunan, 2004) in which EIL teachers visit historic, sociocultural attractions and sites in New York City. Any language reflects its own culture in many ways as culture is related to 'how and why one thinks, learns, worships, fights, and relaxes' (Bedell & Oxford, 1996: 47), and it is mostly expressed by language in the form of 'ideas, customs, skills, arts and tools that characterize a group of people in a given period of time' (Brown, 2000: 177). Therefore, learning another language is inextricably linked with learning its various forms of culture. In this regard, the 'Lost-in-New York' activities are presented as a good exemplary way of applying local historic, sociocultural heritage or resources to actual language classroom activities, leading to utilizing their own historic and cultural resources for their own classroom. The 'Lost-in-New York' activities comprise 10 themes, and each theme has three to four specific tasks or missions from short open-ended questions to personal reflective essays based on their feelings, observations, on-the-spot study, guided tours or information sessions. All of these tasks are completed as small groups or individuals (see Table 4.3).

EIL teachers, before their visits, study historic or cultural events, background information, cultural heritage and interesting anecdotes by utilizing the TICKET activity book that contains all the directions, instructions, history-related background knowledge, research topics and task questions. During their visit to each venue, not only do they actively engage in completing the assigned tasks but they also go beyond their mission to engage in self-directed cultural excursions by searching for any further interesting or significant facts or authentic learning-and-teaching materials for pedagogical purposes. After their visit, they review assigned tasks, reflect on their personal experience, respond to short open-ended questions and reflective essay questions and present their findings and personal reflections along with their own pictures, authentic printed materials or audio and video clips in the classroom. The ultimate purpose of the 'Lost-in-New York' cultural activities is not about going on a sightseeing

**Table 4.3** Ten themes of the 'Lost-in-New York' activities and EIL elements and topics

| Theme | EIL elements and topics |
|---|---|
| Ellis Island and Liberty Island | International and American history, immigration (people, language, culture), pop culture, personal reflection |
| Theater District (Broadway and Times Square) | Multiculturalism, multilingualism, overseas trips, musicals, world economy (signboards) |
| Central Park | City planning and urbanization, vandalism and restoration (community and ethics) |
| Wall Street and 9/11 Memorial | World history and economy, the Great Depression and related pop culture (songs, comic strips, literature), relief programs (Empire State Building), terrorism, world peace |
| United Nations (UN) | International peace and security, human rights (race, sex, language, religion), international relations and cooperation |
| Greenwich Village | Diverse social/cultural/educational/countercultural movements and community, art clubs and galleries |
| American Museum of Natural History | World natural history, environment (climate, water, life), geology, human origins and culture, astrophysics |
| Chelsea and High Line | Diverse cultures, international foods, contemporary art centers and galleries, history/development of High Line (urban park) |
| Metropolitan Museum of Art | European/American/African/Asian/Oceanian/Islamic art collections, diverse costumes/accessories/ancient armor/musical instruments, modern/contemporary art |
| National Museum of the American Indian | Society and culture, religion and philosophy, gender roles, music and art, economy, interracial relations (assimilation) |

trip to downtown New York City, but it is about meaningfully learning every aspect of local culture linked to the learning-and-teaching process and activities and about effectively applying their own or other cultural heritage into their own EIL classroom. In this sense, the 'Lost-in-New York' activities even make it possible for them to first experience and reflect different cultural beliefs and values from their own, and then reflect on *their* cultural aspects at a deeper level than before (McKay, 2012), appreciating and analyzing cultural differences between the two or more cultures. They are expected to establish a mutual understanding without any hindrance in communicating with each other in English, leading to building up 'a sphere of interculturality' (Kramsch, 1993). The 'Lost-in-New York' cultural activities connect linguistic factors and sociocultural structure, appreciate and critically reflect cultural differences and diversities, utilize their own sociocultural resources for communication effectiveness and enhance intercultural communicative competence.

## Challenges and Limitations

The TICKET team strives to furnish quality curricular and extra-curricular courses and activities that prove instructive pedagogically and non-pedagogically from the previous experience, while keeping all the logistics manageable and eliminating potential risk factors. The biggest challenge originates from the gap between what participating teachers expect to do in class and what they are expected to do in class. Considering the fact that they are educated in (or 'they are from') the Confucian societal structure where people tend to have a face-saving (Kim, 1993), self-effacing attitude (Flowerdew, 1998; Gudykunst & Lee, 2003), they sometimes hesitate to take the lead in class activities or discussions, specifically being afraid of making mistakes especially in impromptu tasks or competition-based in-class activities. Some even prefer risk-free, laid-back, lecture-style courses or workshops, which is the way they were taught, mostly concentrating on collecting up-to-date instructional techniques and materials. Almost all of the TICKET courses and workshops are designed to have an interactive, hands-on, learner-centered classroom atmosphere (e.g. Kolb, 1984). Therefore, it is critical for EIL teachers to actively engage in the program at the highest level without feeling overwhelmed or offended. This gap in expectations can be a problem as the success of all the program courses and activities depends on EIL teachers' level of satisfaction and feeling of progress in language use and teaching strategies; it has been a constant challenge to delimit the scale or scope of the program that can maximize the feasibility, effectiveness and accountability of the program while minimizing the negative factors or complaints.

Furthermore, some EIL teachers are reluctant to accept a pluricentric view of English and EIL perspectives. Some of them still believe that their students should learn *standard* Inner Circle Englishes, and they devalue themselves as underqualified or belittle themselves for their L1 accent and limited communication skills. As a matter of fact, it is evidently true that they, as nonnative teachers of English, have often been labeled and marginalized as less idealistic teachers, say, on a lower echelon than

English teachers from English-speaking countries because of the advent and popularity of the communicative language teaching (CLT) method in the global ELT field (Llurda & Huguet 2003; Widdowson, 1994). Throughout the TICKET program, EIL teachers are not stigmatized as 'nonnative teachers of English' or 'trainees' labels that have been prevalently used in the ELT field and ESL/EFL teacher training programs. Rather, they are called 'EIL teachers', 'visiting scholars' or 'bilingual teachers of English' equivalent to the program faculty members and US K-12 teachers. Furthermore, EIL teachers are welcome to criticize all the curriculum and preparatory materials of the program from the perspective of collaboration rather than that of the traditional trainer–trainee or master–apprentice hierarchy, in which trainees are directed to follow, being completely excluded from program development to follow-up management procedures. Nevertheless, some of them do not fully understand the theoretical foundations and framework of the TICKET program and are still hesitant to embrace the new paradigm shift, or the global use of EIL in multicultural settings because EIL perspectives are different from what they were educated in and have learned to teach.

## Conclusion

The demand for teacher education programs for EIL teachers has increased tremendously throughout the world since English is being used as an international communication medium in the era of globalization. Along with the new paradigm shift in ELT and TESOL, the role and need of local EIL teachers who have the same sociolinguistic background as their students are continuously being expanded and emphasized. Accordingly, an increasing number of higher education institutions in the Inner Circle countries are participating in open calls for proposals to attract international teacher education programs, leading to overheated competition among them. Developing and implementing grant-based educational programs for EIL teachers is a challenging task since it requires strong theoretical foundations, good faculty members, detailed action plans, needs assessment, flawless coordination and support, excellent management skills, interesting extracurricular activities, to name a few. However, it is worthwhile for many reasons, including that collaborating with highly motivated EIL teachers provides beneficial professional development opportunities for EIL professionals teaching in the TICKET program as well. The TICKET team and EIL teachers continuously interact with each other even after the completion of the program, leading to a lifelong partnership to find better ways of learning and teaching English in ever-changing sociocultural contexts. Above all, it is rewarding to witness how the TICKET program helps EIL teachers become more competent and confident in teaching EIL in a globalized world.

# References

Alsagoff, L. (2012) Identity and the EIL teacher. In L. Alsagoff, S.L. McKay, G. Hu and W.A. Renandya (eds) *Principles and Practices for Teaching English as an International Language* (pp. 104–122). New York: Routledge.

Arva, V. and Medgyes, P. (2000) Native and non-native teachers in the classroom. *System* 28, 355–372.

Bedell, D.A. and Oxford, R.L. (1996) Cross-cultural comparisons of language learning strategies in the People's Republic of China and other countries. In R.L. Oxford (ed.) *Language Learning Strategies Around the World: Cross-Cultural Perspectives* (pp. 47–60). Honolulu, HI: University of Hawaii Press.

Brown, H.D. (2000) *Principles of Language Learning and Teaching* (4th edn). New York: Longman.

Brown, J.D. (2012) EIL curriculum development. In L. Alsagoff, S.L. McKay, G. Hu and W.A. Renandya (eds) *Principles and Practices for Teaching English as an International Language* (pp. 147–167). New York: Routledge.

Crystal, D. (2003) *English as a Global Language* (2nd edn). London: Cambridge University Press.

Farrell, T.S.C. and Martin, S. (2009) To teach standard English or world Englishes?: A balanced approach to instruction. *English Teaching Forum* 2, 2–7.

Flowerdew, L. (1998) A cultural perspective on group work. *ELT Journal* 52 (4), 323–329.

Graddol, D. (1997) *The Future of English?: A Guide to Forecasting the Popularity of English in the 21st Century*. London: British Council.

Graddol, D. (2006) *English Next: Why Global English May Mean the End of 'English as a Foreign Language'*. London: British Council.

Gudykunst, W.B. and Lee, C.M. (2003) Cross-cultural communication theories. In W.B. Gudykunst (ed.) *Cross-Cultural and Intercultural Communication* (pp. 7–34). Thousand Oaks, CA: Sage.

Jenkins, J. (1996) Native speaker, non-native speaker and English as a foreign language: Time for a change. *IATEFL Newsletter* 131, 10–11.

Jenkins, J. (2005) ELF at the gate: The position of English as a lingua franca. *Humanising Language Teaching* 7 (2). See http://hltmag.co.uk/mar05/idea.htm (accessed 1 February 2016).

Jenkins, J. (2007) *English as a Lingua Franca: Attitude and Identity*. Oxford: Oxford University Press.

Kachru, B.B. (1982) *The Other Tongue: English Across Culture*. Urbana, IL: University of Illinois Press.

Kachru, B.B. (1985) Standards, codification and sociolinguistic realism: The English language in the Outer Circle. In R. Quirk and H.G. Widdowson (eds) *English in the World: Teaching and Learning the Language and Literatures* (pp. 11–30). Cambridge: Cambridge University Press.

Kachru, B.B. (1992) World Englishes: Approaches, issues and resources. *Language Teaching* 25 (1), 1–14.

Kachru, Y. (2011) World Englishes: Contexts and relevance for language education. In E. Hinkel (ed.) *Handbook of Research in Second Language Teaching and Learning* (Vol. 2, pp. 155–172). New York: Routledge.

Kachru, Y. and Nelson, C.L. (2006) *World Englishes in Asian Contexts*. Hong Kong: Hong Kong University Press.

Kachru, B.B., Kachru, Y. and Nelson, C.L. (eds) (2009) *The Handbook of World Englishes*. Oxford: Wiley-Blackwell.

Kim, K.O. (1993) What is behind 'face-saving' in cross-cultural communication. *Intercultural Communication Studies* 3 (1), 39–47.

Kolb, D.A. (1984) *Experiential Learning*. Englewood Cliffs, NJ: Prentice Hall.

Kramsch, C. (1993) *Context and Culture in Language Teaching*. Oxford: Oxford University Press.

Lemov, D. (2014) *Teach Like a Champion 2.0: Techniques that Put Students on the Path to College*. San Francisco, CA: Jossey-Bass.

Liddicoat, A.J. (2005) Teaching languages for intercultural communication. In D. Cunningham and A. Hatoss (eds) *An International Perspective on Language Policies, Practices and Proficiencies* (pp. 201–214). Belgrave: Fédération Internationale des Professeurs de Langues Vivantes.

Llurda, E. and Huguet, A. (2003) Self-awareness in NNS EFL primary and secondary school teachers. *Language Awareness* 12 (3), 220–235.

Mahoney, S. (2004) Role controversy among team teachers in the JET programme. *JALT Journal* 26 (2), 223–243.

Matsuda, A. (2003) Incorporating world Englishes in teaching English as an international language. *TESOL Quarterly* 37 (4), 719–729.

Matsuda, A. (2012) Teaching materials in EIL. In L. Alsagoff, S.L. McKay, G. Hu and W.A. Renandya (eds) *Principles and Practices for Teaching English as an International Language* (pp. 168–185). New York: Routledge.

Matsuda, A. and Friedrich, P. (2010) When five words are not enough: A conceptual and terminological discussion of English as a lingua franca. *International Multilingual Research Journal* 4, 20–30.

McArthur, T. (2001) World English and world Englishes: Trends, tensions, varieties, and standards. *Language Teaching* 34, 1–20.

McKay, S.L. (2002) *Teaching English as an International Language: Rethinking Goals and Approaches*. Oxford: Oxford University Press.

McKay, S.L. (2012) Principles of teaching English as an international language. In L. Alsagoff, S.L. McKay, G. Hu and W.A. Renandya (eds) *Principles and Practices for Teaching English as an International Language* (pp. 28–46). New York: Routledge.

McKay, S. and Bokhorst-Heng, W.D. (2008) International English in its sociolinguistic contexts: Towards a socially sensitive EIL pedagogy. New York: Routledge.

McKay, S.L. and Jenkins, J. (2009) Introduction. In K. Murata and J. Jenkins (eds) *Global Englishes in Asian Contexts: Current and Future Debates* (pp. 1–13). Basingstoke: Palgrave Macmillan.

Murata, K. and Jenkins, J. (eds) (2009) Global Englishes in Asian Contexts: Current and Future Debates. Basingstoke: Palgrave Macmillan.

Nunan, D. (2004) *Task-Based Language Teaching*. Cambridge: Oxford University Press.

Phillipson, R. (1992) *Linguistic Imperialism*. Oxford: Oxford University Press.

Phillipson, R. (2009) *Linguistic Imperialism Continued*. New York: Routledge.

Power, C. (2005) Beyond Babel: Language policies for the 21st century. In D. Cunningham and A. Hatoss (eds) *An International Perspective on Language Policies, Practices and Proficiencies* (pp. 37–49). Belgrave: Fédération Internationale des Professeurs de Langues Vivantes.

Seidlhofer, B. (1999) Double standards: Teacher education in the expanding circle. *World Englishes*, 18 (2), 233–245.

Selvi, A.F. (2014) Myths and misconceptions about nonnative English speakers in the TESOL (NNEST) movement. *TESOL Journal* 5 (3), 573–611.

Sharifian, F. (2009) *English as an International Language: Perspectives and Pedagogical Issues*. Bristol: Multilingual Matters.

Svartvik, J. and Leech, G. (2006) *English: One Tongue, Many Voices*. Basingstoke: Palgrave Macmillan.

Sun, Y. (2014) '8 major trends in the global ELT field'. *TESOL International Association*, blog post, 15 October. See http://blog.tesol.org/8-major-trends-in-the-global-elt-field/ (accessed 10 February 2016).

Tajino, A. and Tajino, Y. (2000) Native and non-native: What can they offer? *ELT Journal* 54 (1), 3–11.

Tang, C. (1997) On the power and status of nonnative ESL teachers. *TESOL Quarterly* 31 (3), 577–580.

Wang, L.Y. and Lin, T.B. (2014) Exploring the identity of pre-service NNESTs in Taiwan: A social relationally approach. *English Teaching: Practice and Critique* 13 (3), 5–29.

Widdowson, H.G. (1994) The ownership of English. *TESOL Quarterly* 28 (2), 377–389.

Wiggins, G. and McTighe, J. (2005) *Understanding by Design* (2nd edn). Alexandria, VA: Association for Supervision and Curriculum Development.

Yang, N.D. (2000) Teachers' beliefs about language learning and teaching: A cross-cultural comparison. *Texas Papers in Foreign Language Education* 5 (1), 39–52.

# Part 3

# Courses Dedicated to Teaching EIL

# 5 Global Englishes for Language Teaching: Preparing MSc TESOL Students to Teach in a Globalized World

## Nicola Galloway

## Introduction

It is important to begin by clarifying the terminology used both in this chapter and on the course itself, given that the multiplicity of terms in use may cause confusion. Here, global Englishes is seen as being an umbrella term which includes World Englishes (WE), English as a lingua franca (ELF) and English as an International Language (EIL) research (Galloway & Rose, 2015: xii). Several definitions of EIL that have been put forward in the literature have been rather exclusionary of ELF research and, therefore, the term global Englishes is the preferred umbrella term. This is by no means an attempt to underestimate the important work of scholars who would position their work within the field of EIL and the course described here exposes students to work in all three fields.

WE, ELF and EIL research has important ramifications for English language teaching (ELT). Despite the fact that the native English-speaker episteme continues to dominate ELT/teaching English to speakers of other languages (TESOL), the pedagogical implications of the global spread of English are receiving considerable attention. There is growing literature on the topic, and in-service and preservice teachers on TESOL programs now have access to a number of global Englishes book sections and chapters devoted to the topic of ELT, entire books on the topic (e.g. Alsagoff, 2012; Matsuda, 2012a) and articles in language teaching journals (e.g. Jenkins, 2012). Several scholars have also suggested ways in which a global Englishes perspective can be incorporated into the ELT classroom, which can be grouped together into a Global Englishes Language Teaching (GELT) framework (Galloway, 2011; Galloway & Rose, 2015). GELT is not a prescriptive model for ELT, but a student-centered framework for curricula that aims to enable TESOL practitioners to critically evaluate their curricula. It emphasizes the need to raise awareness of the issues associated with the spread of English and prepare learners to use ELF in various communities of practice. The goal is still to learn English but this is not necessarily the English spoken by native English speakers. GELT, however, requires a conceptual transition, in terms of both how the language itself is viewed and how it is taught. This may be rather daunting for TESOL practitioners. Galloway and Rose (2015) identify a number of possible barriers to achieving Kumaravadivelu's (2012: 14) 'epistemic break' from native English-speaking norms. One of these is teacher education, although this is an area where change has begun to occur in recent years.

Global Englishes-related subject matter is being increasingly integrated into teacher training programs and postgraduate courses in language education and applied linguistics. This chapter describes a *Global Englishes for Language Teaching* option course on the MSc TESOL program at The University of Edinburgh. It begins with an overview of the program, followed by a detailed description of the course, including the rationale, course content, structure and assessment. It then outlines how it differs from more traditional TESOL practitioner courses and ends with an examination of the challenges of courses such as this.

## Overview of the Program

The MSc TESOL program at The University of Edinburgh is a postgraduate program for in-service and preservice teachers, which allows for one-year full-time contact delivery. It aims to produce graduates who will be able to make a significant contribution to teaching English around the globe. The learning objectives include the ability to:

- understand TESOL-related theories and concepts;
- critically evaluate TESOL and applied linguistics research and literature;
- critically examine TESOL theory and practice in relation to classroom practice;
- consider how to implement change;
- demonstrate the ability to conduct TESOL-related research.

The ethos and goals are essentially international; all courses have an international dimension, the cohort is mostly made up of international students, staff speak an additional language, have international teaching experience and engage in international research. The program is also part of Moray House School of Education's pilot project for the Higher Education Academy, examining internationalizing the curriculum. In 2014–2015, there were 161 students on the program. The program requires an overall International English Language Testing System (IELTS) result of 7 (6.5 minimum in writing) and accepts students without prior teaching experience. Each course has 3 hours a week contact time for 8–10 weeks over 2 semesters (Table 5.1). To progress to dissertation, students must have an average mark of 50%, with 80 credits over 50%. To gain an MSc TESOL, students must pass a combination of *Research Methods 3* and the dissertation with at least 50%.

The program has a focus on TESOL pedagogy and curriculum development and it also has an applied linguistics focus. All members of the teaching staff have doctorates and many have developed optional courses based on their research areas, including:

- *Evaluation and Design of TESOL Materials*
- *Online Language Learning*
- *Theory and Practice of Second Lang Learning*
- *Language Testing*
- *Teaching Text Across Borders*
- *Second Language Teacher Education*
- *Investigating Individual Learner Differences*
- *Language Awareness for Second Language Teachers*
- *Language and Culture Pedagogy*
- *Corpus Linguistics and Language Teaching*
- *Global Englishes for Language Teaching*

The *Global Englishes for Language Teaching* course was introduced in 2014 to reflect the growing use of ELF worldwide, which has numerous pedagogical implications for ELT. Despite the growth in ELF as a global phenomenon,

**Table 5.1** MSc TESOL year structure

**Semester 1**

| Four compulsory courses | |
| --- | --- |
| *TESOL Methodology* | (20 credits) |
| *Second Language Teaching Curriculum* | (20 credits) |
| *Language and the Learner* | (20 credits) |
| *Research Methods 1 Sources of Knowledge* | (10 credits) |

**Semester 2**

| Two compulsory courses | |
| --- | --- |
| *Research Methods 2 Conceptualizing Research* | (10 credits) |
| *Research Methods 3 Planning Research* | (10 credits) |
| Two option courses | (2 × 20 credits) |

**Summer**

| Dissertation | (50 credits) |
| --- | --- |

ELT continues to focus on native English-speaking norms. This course was introduced to address this theory–practice divide. Although many TESOL practitioner programs continue to focus on native English-speaking norms, a growing number of programs are beginning to include global Englishes units, courses and even full programs (Table 5.2). In a survey of 26 UK universities that offer similar postgraduate courses, 10 of these offer courses on global Englishes, one of which is a full program. It should also be pointed out that several other programs offer courses on sociolinguistics in general and intercultural communication. This trend is also evident on a global level, as seen in the job advertisements shown in Table 5.3, which acknowledge the use of English as a global lingua franca.

**Table 5.2** Number of GE courses on masters' programs in TESOL and related fields in the UK

| Institution | Unit/Course/Program | Name |
| --- | --- | --- |
| The University of Edinburgh | Course (MSc TESOL) | Global Englishes for Language Learning |
| University of Durham | Course (MA TESOL) | World Englishes |
| University College London (UCL) | Course (MA TESOL) | Which English? Sociolinguistics and Language Teaching |
| University of Bristol | Course (MA TESOL) | Globalization and the Politics of English |
| University of Bath | Course (MA TESOL) | Teaching and Assessing EIL |
| Birbeck, University of London | Course (MA TESOL) | Language, Culture and Communication |
| Kings College, London | Course (MA Applied Linguistics and ELT) | Sociolinguistics: Language in its Social Context (compulsory) |
| Newcastle University | Course (MA Applied Linguistics and ELT) | English in the World: Global and Cross-Cultural Issues Surrounding ELF |
| UCL Institute of Education | Course (MA TESOL) | English in Diverse World Contexts |
| University of Cambridge | Course (MPhil/MEd in Research in Second Language Education [RSLE]) | Policy Context: International Perspectives on Language Education Policy and Multilingualism |

**Table 5.3** Job advertisements

https://jrecin.jst.go.jp/seek/SeekJorDetail?fn=4&id=D115020145&ln_jor=1&ln=1 (November 2014)

Title: ELF (English as a Lingua Franca) instructor

Department Center for English as a Lingua Franca, Tamagawa University, Japan

https://jobs.soton.ac.uk/Vacancy.aspx?ref=474114F4 (October 2014)

Title: Lecturer in Applied Linguistics (English Language Education, Global Englishes)

Department: Centre for Global Englishes

Requirements: 'The successful candidates will have established research/teaching expertise in ...Global Englishes'.

# Overview of the *Global Englishes for Language Teaching* course

## Rationale

Teacher education and ambivalence to change represent a possible barrier to moving toward GELT in the field of ELT/TESOL (Galloway & Rose, 2015). GELT (Table 5.4) is a very different concept to traditional ELT, and requires TESOL practitioners to reconceptualize both the language and their teaching practice. It is not a one-size-fits-all prescriptive model, but a vision of a curriculum that embodies beliefs about the need to increase choice and emancipate ELF users from adherence to a fixed state of minority native English-speaking norms. Of course, native English may be relevant for some students, but GELT also allows for exposure to the inherent variation in English and aims to raise awareness of the strategies used by multicompetent and multilingual, or translingual, ELF users. Competence is not judged in relation to conformity to native English norms (Widdowson, 2012). Overall, GELT aims to enable TESOL practitioners to critically reflect on their teaching practice through a global Englishes lens and aims to emancipate learners from native English norms.

Practitioners, as important agents of change, are vital in the curriculum evaluation and design process. Teacher education is, therefore, important and TESOL practitioners 'need a meta-understanding about EIL – its forms and histories' (Dogancay-Aktuna & Hardman, 2012: 103). Both Dewey (2012) and Widdowson (2012) note the need for teachers to reconceptualize the notion of language, the very subject they teach. Thus, this course was introduced to provide MSc TESOL students with the opportunity to examine the pedagogical implications of the global spread of English, and enable them to revisit fundamental TESOL theories and

**Table 5.4** GELT

|  | *Traditional ELT* | *GELT* |
|---|---|---|
| Target interlocutor | Native English speakers | Native English speakers and nonnative English speakers |
| Owners | Native English speakers | Native English speakers and nonnative English speakers |
| Target culture | Fixed native English culture | Fluid cultures |
| Teachers | Nonnative English-speaking teachers (same first language) and native English-speaking teachers | Nonnative English-speaking teachers (same and different first language), native English-speaking teachers |
| Norms | Native English and the concept of standard English | Diversity, flexibility and multiple forms of competence |
| Role model | Native English speakers | Successful ELF users |
| Materials | Native English and native English speakers | Native English, nonnative English, ELF and ELF communities and contexts |
| First language and own culture | Seen as a hindrance and source of interference | Seen as a resource |
| Ideology | Underpinned by an exclusive and ethnocentric view of English | Underpinned by an inclusive Global Englishes perspective |

Source: Galloway and Rose (2015: 208).

concepts, introduced in semester one, in light of global Englishes research. Jenkins (2012: 492), however, warns against providing 'specific pedagogic recommendations', noting that,

> ELF researchers have always been careful to point out that we do not believe it is our place to tell teachers what to do, but that it is for ELT practitioners to decide whether/to what extent ELF is relevant to their learners in their context. (Jenkins, 2012: 492)

Thus, just as GELT is not a prescriptive one-size-fits-all model for practitioners, the *Global Englishes for Language Teaching* course was not introduced to tell teachers what to do, or to suggest that the pedagogical practices familiar to them, and those on the program as a whole, are wrong. GELT embraces the diversity of English and the course was introduced to help teachers 'develop a more rationalized, informed perspective on the (de) merits of selecting language norms in the classroom' (Dewey, 2012: 166).

# Description of the Course: Specific Components of the Program/Course

## Aims and objectives

The course examines the theoretical, descriptive and applied aspects of the global spread of English. It aims to address the theory–practice divide and enable in-service and preservice TESOL practitioners to critically reflect on the usefulness of a GELT perspective for their teaching contexts.

## Learning outcomes

The learning outcomes include the ability to:

* demonstrate critical understanding of the theories related to global Englishes;
* critically evaluate approaches to ELT in relation to global Englishes;
* critically analyze global Englishes-related research studies and their implications for pedagogy;
* critically analyze their own teaching context in relation to global Englishes and develop context-specific approaches to incorporate GELT.

## Course content

The course includes eight one-hour pre-lecture workshops, eight one-hour lectures and eight two-hour post-lecture workshops in semester two. It uses a mix of online and face-to-face delivery. Activities include:

* **Introductory activities**
These pre-lecture tasks use the introductory activities in Galloway and Rose (2015) and on the companion website.

* **Reading and discussion**
In addition to core reading, each student in a group of four reads a different article/chapter each week. The reading worksheet (see the companion website to Galloway & Rose, 2015) is used to lead a 10-minute discussion on the reading. Students are given an extensive list of readings appropriate to different teaching contexts.

- **Listening and discussion**
  This task uses audio and visual materials found on Galloway and Rose's (2015) companion website, including interviews, focus groups, observations, video clips, lectures and ELF exchanges.

- **Debating the issues**
  Weekly mini-debate topics take place on an online discussion forum and mini debates are held in the workshop.

- **Materials evaluation and design**
  As Matsuda (2012b) notes, few teachers

  have a rich enough knowledge of and personal experience with all of the varieties and functions of Englishes that exist today, and, thus, they need to rely on teaching materials in order to introduce students to the linguistic and cultural diversity of English. (Matsuda, 2012b: 169)

Workshops provide the opportunity to evaluate and design ELT materials and lesson plans in relation to their teaching contexts, such as those included in Matsuda and Duran (2012). These evaluations form the basis of class presentations and microteaching lessons.

- **Research evaluation and design**
  To support the Research Methods courses (Table 5.1) and encourage critical examination of relevant research, students are given the opportunity to explore research in the field and design their own studies (building on the lesson plans in Matsuda & Duran, 2012).

- **Guest lectures**
  The Edinburgh TESOL and Applied Language (ETAL) seminars, a series of 45-minute seminars held throughout the academic year, provide students with the opportunity to hear from experts on a range of TESOL-related topics. The *Global Englishes Event* included talks from Professor Jennifer Jenkins, Professor Constant Leung, Dr Claire Cowie and Dr Heath Rose. Professor Andy Kirkpatrick also gave a talk at the seminar series. Furthermore, The University of Edinburgh hosted the British Association of Applied Linguistics (BAAL) Language Learning and Teaching Annual Conference and invited Professor Anna Mauranen as a plenary speaker, bringing global Englishes to the forefront of this conference.

- **Course Timetable**
  The course timetable is as follows:

## Pre-course online lecture: The history of English and the global spread of English

As Friedrich (2012) notes,

> If the only constant in lingua franca situations is diversity, then we should anchor our practices in that assumption and educate students to encounter such diversity with respect, curiosity and wisdom. (Friedrich, 2012: 50)

In order to understand the diversity associated with English, the pre-course online lecture begins with a historical overview to highlight that change in English is not new. Examining the global dispersal of English also raises awareness of how English spread to, and is used in, different contexts. Estimating the numbers of English speakers and categorizing them into models (e.g. Kachru, 1992) are also problematized.

## Week one: Language variation and world Englishes research

Week one focuses on language change, language variation and standard language ideology as well as the concepts of ownership and identity in countries where English is spoken as a 'native' and 'nativized' or 'indigenized' language. The WE paradigm is introduced and key terminology in the field of global Englishes is problematized. As noted in the introduction, the global Englishes umbrella term is explained and students are encouraged to critically examine the definitions of WE, EIL and ELF that have been put forward in the literature, debating whether they agree that this umbrella term 'encompasses both centrifugal and centripetal natures of WE, EIL or ELF simultaneously' (Murata & Jenkins, 2009: 5) and whether 'what many EIL scholars have described as EIL fits within the Global Englishes framework' (Galloway & Rose, 2015: x). Pennycook's (2007) theories on global Englishes and Canagarajah's (2013) notion of translingual practice are also briefly introduced. The course aims to show that, while different terms may be employed, these fields are united in a joint desire to move the ELT industry forward. As Alsagoff (2012: 116) notes, 'The literature on EIL, however diverse in opinion, is united in the desire to move away from teaching for native-speaker competence'. This week also introduces standard language ideology, another concept that needs a historical perspective to understand current attitudes.

## Week two: English in global contexts and English as a lingua franca

Week two examines the use of English in the 'rest' of the world, questioning whether it can still be regarded as a 'foreign' language in many parts of the Expanding Circle. There is a movement away from the notion of 'variety' toward a focus on how English operates as a lingua franca, showing how ELF speakers draw on numerous resources and exploit the malleable nature of the language. Students are presented with a theoretical and descriptive overview of ELF research, which aims to help them consider a new perspective on language change and, therefore, help them 'revisit' the language that they are planning to teach. As Dewey (2012) notes,

> It is essential that the knowledge base of language teachers should include an awareness and understanding of the processes of accommodation. For this to happen we must though call into question the suitability of some of the conventional frames of reference in ELT, many of which seem to be characterised by assumptions about language that do not fit well with the sociolinguistics of English in the contemporary world. (Dewey, 2011: 224)

Students reflect on TESOL concepts and theories introduced in semester one in light of ELF research. They also critically examine the criticisms that have been put forward, taking them back to the deep-rooted attachments to 'standard' English presented in week two. Students are encouraged to examine why Seidlhofer's (2001) 'conceptual gap', the problem of engaging with the concept of ELF, something that differs from 'standard' English, is still evident today.

### Week three: Attitudes to English and linguistic imperialism

Week three examines the issues and attitudes surrounding the global spread of English, including the advantages and disadvantages of English's rise as a world lingua franca and the notion of linguistic imperialism. This leads to an examination of language attitudes, and students critically examine various research studies that have been conducted. This examination highlights that positive attitudes toward native English are often related to the dominance of the native English-speaker episteme in TESOL/ELT.

### Week four: English language teaching

As Matsuda and Friedrich (2012: 17) note, the 'linguistic, cultural and functional diversity associated with English today challenges some of the fundamental assumptions of ELT and requires that we revisit our pedagogical practices, especially in classrooms where English is taught as an international language'. Sharifian (2009: 2) also adds that the EIL paradigm, 'calls for a critical revisiting of the notions, analytical tools, approaches and methodologies within the established disciplines such as the sociolinguistics of English and TESOL'. Thus, in addition to encouraging students to reconceptualize the language (week one to three), the course also encourages them to reflect on both their pedagogical practices and fundamental TESOL theories and concepts.

In the core course on Second Language Teaching Curriculum in semester one, students examined the six elements of a curriculum (needs analysis, syllabus, curriculum, evaluation, methodology, and assessment) in a familiar teaching context and suggested some improvements. In this course, we return to this curriculum, critically examining it through a global Englishes lens. For example, students consider whether there is a need to re-examine the concept of qualified teachers (McKay, 2012) and employ multilingual English teachers (METs) (Kirkpatrick, 2009, 2012) and whether teacher training programs sufficiently prepare teachers to expose their students to the diversity of English. We also examine the extent to which current ELT materials prepare students to use ELF and students are encouraged to be critical of communicative language teaching (CLT) textbooks that claim to be 'authentic' and represent 'real-life' English usage based on NES native English speaking (NES) corpora.

Week four also continues the critical examination of relevant research, including studies on attitudes toward:

- English in relation to ELT.
- Native and nonnative English-speaking teachers.
- ELF (teacher and students).
- The ideal English teacher.

There is also an examination of studies on the self-perceptions of nonnative English-speaking teachers. These studies (see Galloway and Rose [2015] for an overview and Jenkins [2007] for an overview of attitudes toward ELF) highlight a strong attachment to native English norms, but students are encouraged to draw on their Research Methods courses (Table 5.1) and be critical of the small sample sizes and use of single methods, as well as a lack of consideration of the many factors that influence these attitudes including the predominance of the native English-speaker model in ELT.

### Weeks five and six: Global Englishes language teaching

Matsuda (2012a: 6) notes that, 'the current state of the discussion of the teaching of EIL poses a great challenge and frustration for teachers'. On the one hand, teachers are being told that their current teaching practices are now inadequate and irrelevant in preparing students to use English globally, yet as the author rightly points out, in many cases, they are not being given any sets of ideas or suggestions to implement change, which unfortunately 'leaves many teachers with no choice but to continue to do what they have been doing, only now feeling less confident about what they deliver to their students' (Matsuda, 2012a: 6). Thus, after a critical evaluation of ELT practice in week four, this course examines what a global Englishes approach may look like in the classroom. The GELT framework (Table 5.4) is introduced alongside six proposals that have been put forward in the literature for change to ELT practice (Galloway & Rose, 2015), which include:

(1)  Increasing WE and ELF exposure in language curricula.
(2)  Emphasizing respect for multilingualism in ELT.

(3)  Raising awareness of global Englishes in ELT.
(4)  Raising awareness of ELF strategies in language curricula.
(5)  Emphasizing respect for diverse culture and identity in ELT.
(6)  Changing English teacher hiring practices in the ELT industry.

Students examine the relevance of these proposals for their teaching contexts, drawing on their knowledge from other courses. Those taking the Online Language Learning course, for example, are encouraged to think of innovative ways to increase ELF exposure via the internet and those taking the Evaluation and Design of TESOL Materials option course are encouraged to examine how to incorporate global Englishes into ELT materials. While the debate surrounding the dominance of NES norms and culture in ELT is not new, and was introduced in semester one with regard to intercultural communication, students are reminded that ELF research throws a new perspective on language change, and to this debate. We return to Kumaravadivelu's (1994) post-methods movement which was introduced in semester one and discuss Dewey's (2012) call for a 'postnormative' condition Dewey (2012). Students are familiar with the quest for new methods in the field of ELT and the more recent calls for context-specific approaches. When considering how to incorporate a GELT perspective in their classrooms, they are encouraged to consider how to adopt context-specific theories of language and communication in accordance with the learners' needs. The importance placed on needs analysis also returns us to the semester one core course on Second Language Teaching Curriculum. In addition to examining the situational and language needs (Brown, 1995) in their respective contexts, the importance is placed on conducting an environment (Nation & Macalister, 2010) or situation (Richards, 2001) analysis is highlighted, which can highlight any possible constraints in their respective contexts. For example, incorporating a GELT perspective into the ELT classroom requires information about the institution (e.g. classroom sizes, materials and internet availability), student body (needs, proficiency level, etc.) and teaching staff (number, skills, workload, etc.). This introduces the possible constraints that those wishing to introduce change may face and they are encouraged to examine the possible barriers to implementing GELT, such as a lack of materials, language assessment, teacher education, attachment to 'standard' English and teacher recruitment practices which favor the native English speaker (Galloway & Rose, 2015). This week ends with an examination of the small number of studies that have investigated the influence of global Englishes instruction on students' attitudes.

## Week seven: The future of English

This final topic examines the current and future trends of the spread (or decline) of English in important domains. Movements to 'internationalize' in higher education are inextricably linked with an increasing role for ELF in the academic domain. On a global level, there has been an increase in programs in English and recruitment of international students, even in countries where English has no official status. Students examine the growth of English medium programs, the increase in Western universities offering programs in places like China and the government policy in places like Japan that aim to attract international students to Japanese universities. There is also a focus on the support offered to international students in universities that focus on 'standard' English academic norms and the increased usage of academic ELF and the associated pedagogical implications.

### Week eight: Presentations

This course is assessed through a group presentation (40%) in week eight and an individual assignment (60%) based on the presentation topic (2500 words). Two options are provided:

(1) Analyze a learning/teaching context in relation to global Englishes, examine relevant research and the pedagogical implications for ELT in your chosen context. Based on this evaluation, recommend changes for ELT practice.
(2) Provide a brief overview of research into one aspect of global Englishes examined on the course. Select two relevant studies and provide a critical examination of them and the implications for ELT practice in a chosen context. Based on this examination, design a 1 hour lesson plan that demonstrates your application of this research.

The group presentation is awarded a mark for group effort and for individual effort. Formative feedback is provided via poster presentations, which are held one week prior to the final presentations.

## Uniqueness of the Course

The *Global Englishes for Language Teaching* course shares many aspects with its more traditional counterparts on teacher education courses in that it focuses on TESOL methodology and curriculum concepts and theories. However, revisiting these concepts, theories and pedagogical practice, in light of global Englishes research puts it at the forefront of current TESOL practitioner programs. An overview of the semester one concepts and theories that are returned to include:

### Curriculum

As Richards (2001: 286) points out, 'once a curriculum is in place, a number of important questions still need to be answered'. Curriculum evaluation is an ongoing process and the GELT framework aims to help

TESOL practitioners evaluate their curricula through a global Englishes lens. Students are encouraged to ask questions, such as

- How are students in my context likely to use English in the future? Is the course addressing these needs?
- Do the national education goals recognize the use of ELF (as in Japan, for example [MEXT, 2003])?
- Are the models of English used in the curriculum relevant?
- Does the curriculum enable students to negotiate with speakers from diverse lingua-cultural backgrounds?
- Do the materials raise awareness of global Englishes?
- Are teachers aware of GELT?
- In what ways would a GELT perspective be suitable for this context?

## Methodology

It is important for TESOL practitioners to understand how the centrality of communication strategies to GELT is not out of sync with current literature in TESOL in which communication is a core focus. For example, strategic competence and communication strategies are central to the concept of CLT, albeit with reference to NES norms. Students are encouraged to examine the different approaches to teaching English that have used over the years. Just as with the move to CLT, practitioners need time and support to implement change. Students are also encouraged to think about the linguistic and cultural diversity in the classrooms they visited on their local school visits, part of the requirement of the core course, and to consider whether global Englishes awareness is necessary for school teachers, and students, in native English-speaking contexts. They are also encouraged to be critical of the applicability of Western-centric TESOL methods to their contexts.

## Intercultural communication and intercultural pragmatics

The Global Englishes for Language Teaching course aims to show that the need for pedagogical change is also being increasingly stressed within the field of intercultural communication (Corbett, 2003). Today, TESOL practitioners need to equip their students with the skills to negotiate with speakers from diverse lingua-cultural backgrounds, which is a central notion to GELT.

## Motivation theory

As with more traditional courses, there is a focus on motivation, which is seen as a key contributor to language learning success. We return to the motivation theories introduced in semester one, but discuss how the global spread of English requires that we re-examine Gardner's (1985) notion of integrative motivation. Students are referred to the study by Kormos *et al.* (2011), which aimed to investigate the motivation of Chilean learners due to the fact that English 'has become an international lingua franca'. Students are encouraged to think about the finding that the most important language learning goal was 'related to the status of English as a lingua franca' (Kormos *et al.*, 2011: 513), considering whether their students' ideal second language (L2) self (Dörnyei, 2009) may be a native English speaker or an expert ELF user, whether the learning environment (e.g. the dominance of the native English-speaker model) and ELF experiences influence students' motivation.

## Second language acquisition (SLA) theories

This course aims to encourage TESOL practitioners to consider the monolingual bias of SLA research that was introduced in semester one, and students are encouraged to examine why there is a 'mismatch between the purpose for which English is most learnt in the world, namely ELF use, and what is focused on in SLA, namely ESL/EFL' (Seidlhofer, 2011: 11–12). We examine the focus on learner activity and involvement in the social-cultural approach, for example, which are also central to GELT, although scaffolding is not necessarily provided by a native English speaker in the latter. Thus, the aim is to improve pedagogical practice by consolidating SLA theories introduced in semester one, and encouraging students to challenge the emphasis on the native English speaker in SLA.

## Corpus linguistics

Unlike more traditional courses, this course questions the use of terms such as 'learner corpus' and also questions whether the various native English corpora, many of which have been used to develop teaching materials, show the real-life use of English today or the well-beaten tracks, which have been taken by 'authorized pathfinders – the educated native speakers who provide the corpus data' (Widdowson, 2012: 16). We return to the native English corpora introduced in semester one, but also introduce those that show the routes taken by nonnative English speakers including the Vienna-Oxford International Corpus of English (VOICE) corpus.

# Challenges and Limitations

Unfortunately, despite the introduction of courses like this, 'the native-speaker episteme has not loosened its grip over theoretical principles, classroom practices, the publication industry, or the job market' (Kumaravadivelu, 2012: 15) and, as noted, there are a number of barriers present to incorporating a GELT perspective. While headway has been made in teacher education, teacher ambivalence to change is still an issue and many TESOL practitioners continue to think that their pedagogical practice should be based on established principles. This ambivalence, however, may also be more related to a sense of 'powerlessness', being at the bottom of the power structure in their institution. There is also a limited amount of materials available and although example activities and lesson plans are provided in Matsuda and Duran (2012) and Alsagoff *et al.* (2012) cover topics such as curriculum, assessment and learning strategies from an EIL perspective, teachers have very few practical suggestions to help them move away from native English norms.

Language testing presents another major barrier. Despite the increasing number of suggestions to move toward tests that focus more on communication accommodation skills (see Galloway & Rose, 2015, for an overview), there continues to be a mismatch between the English used by these test takers and the English they are assessed on. Measuring test takers on their intercultural strategic competence and their ability to use ELF in international situations may also be daunting for TESOL practitioners who are used to testing students on 'errors' or deviations from the 'standard' norm, which needs updating to meet the needs of learners who will use the language as a global lingua franca.

A further 'barrier' relates to attachments to the idea of a 'standard' English and such a deeply ingrained ideology is difficult to challenge. Many TESOL practitioners cling to 'standard' norms and have fixed ideas about how it should be taught. This option course brings into question established modes of thinking about the English language itself, how it should be taught and how TESOL practitioners should be trained. This may not only be daunting for TESOL practitioners, but also for those educating them. However, at The University of Edinburgh, numerous other courses have begun to include a global Englishes perspective since this option course was introduced, making some of them similar to the independent units within courses dedicated to other ELT topics that are outlined in Part 5 of this book.

## Conclusion

To conclude, in order to achieve the macro-level change in ELT called for by Kumaravadivelu (2012), courses such as the one described in this chapter are needed. However, it is also crucial not to alienate experienced teachers by telling them that their current teaching practices are irrelevant and outdated. Many practitioners are ambivalent toward change and questioning familiar pedagogical practice, concepts and theories may create a feeling of unease. Change is challenging and many barriers exist. Action research is also important to ensure that courses such as this are meeting the needs of TESOL practitioners from varied contexts. In 2015, funding was allocated to investigate the attitudes of MSc TESOL students taking this option course toward global Englishes. Their attitudes will be examined before and after taking the course via questionnaires ($n=60$), interviews ($n=5$) and focus groups ($n=10$). A selected number of participants will then also be 'tracked' after graduation in their various teaching contexts to further investigate the possibility of implementing GELT in their respective contexts. This study will provide insights into students taking the course to help inform course evaluation and design. The results will also be useful for those teaching in different contexts, who are interested in ensuring that their TESOL practitioner programs reflect the growth in ELF usage worldwide.

## References

Alsagoff, L. (2012) Identity and the EIL learner. In L. Alsagoff, S.L. McKay, G. Hu and W.A. Renandya (eds) *Principles and Practices for Teaching English as an International Language* (pp. 104–122). New York: Routledge.

Alsagoff, L., McKay, S.L., Hu, G. and Renandya, W.A. (eds) (2012) *Principles and Practices for Teaching English as an International Language*. Abingdon: Routledge.

Brown, J. (1995) *The Elements of Language Curriculum: A Systematic Approach to Program Development*. Boston: Heinle & Heinle Publishers.

Canagarajah, A.S. (2013) *Translingual Practice: Global Englishes and Cosmopolitan Relations*. London: Routledge.

Corbett, J. (2003) *An Intercultural Approach to English Language Teaching*. Clevedon: Multilingual Matters.

Dewey, M. (2011) 'Accommodative ELF talk and teacher knowledge'. In A. Archibald, A. Cogo & J. Jenkins (eds) *Latest Trends in ELF research* (pp. 205–227). Cambridge Scholars Publishing, Newcastle upon Tyne.

Dewey, M. (2012) Towards a post-normative approach: Learning the pedagogy of ELF. *Journal of English as a Lingua Franca* 1 (1), 141–170.

Dogancay-Aktuna, S. and Hardman, J. (2012) Teachers education for EIL: Working toward a situated meta-praxis. In A. Matsuda (ed.) *Principles and Practices of Teaching English as an International Language* (pp. 103–118). Bristol: Multilingual Matters.

Dörnyei, Z. (2009) Motivation, language identity and the L2 self. In Z. Dörnyei and E. Ushioda (eds) *Motivation, Language Identity and The L2 Self* (pp. 9–42). Bristol: Multilingual Matters.

Friedrich, P. (2012) ELF, intercultural communication and the strategic aspect of communicative competence. In A. Matsuda (ed.) *Principles and Practices of Teaching English as an International Language* (pp. 44–54). Bristol: Multilingual Matters.

Galloway, N. (2011) *An investigation of Japanese students' attitudes towards English*. PhD thesis, University of Southampton.

Galloway, N. and Rose, H. (2015) *Introducing Global Englishes*. Abingdon: Routledge.

Gardner, R.C. (1985) *Social Psychology and Second Language Learning: The Role of Attitudes and Motivation*. London: Arnold.

Jenkins, J. (2007) *English as a Lingua Franca: Attitude and Identity*. Oxford: Oxford University Press.

Kachru, B.B. (1992) *The Other Tongue: English Across Cultures* (2nd edn). Urbana, IL: University of Illinois Press.

Kirkpatrick, A. (2009) *Teaching English as a Lingua Franca*. Hong Kong: The Hong Kong Institute of Education.

Kirkpatrick, A. (2012) English as an Asian lingua franca: The 'Lingua Franca Approach' and implications for language education policy. *Journal of English as a Lingua Franca* 1 (1), 121–139.

Kormos, J., Kiddle, T. and Csizer, K. (2011) Systems of goals, attitudes, and self-related beliefs in second-language-learning motivation. *Applied Linguistics* 32 (5), 495–516.

Kumaravadivelu, B. (1994) The postmethod condition: (E)merging strategies for second/foreign language teaching. *TESOL Quarterly* 28 (1), 27–48.

Kumaravadivelu, B. (2012) Individual identity, cultural globalization and teaching English as an international language: The case for an epistemic break. In L. Alsagoff, S.L. McKay, G. Hu and W.A. Renandya (eds) *Principles and Practices for Teaching English as an International Language* (pp. 9–27). New York: Routledge.

Matsuda, A. (ed.) (2012a) *Principles and Practices of Teaching English as an International Language*. Bristol: Multilingual Matters.

Matsuda, A. (2012b) Teaching materials in EIL. In L. Alsagoff, S.L. McKay, G. Hu and W.A. Renandya (eds) *Principles and Practices for Teaching English as an International Language* (pp. 168–185). New York: Routledge.

Matsuda, A. and Duran, C.S. (2012) EIL activities and tasks for traditional English classrooms. In A. Matsuda (ed.) *Principles and Practices of Teaching English as an International Language* (pp. 201–238). Bristol: Multilingual Matters.

Matsuda, A. and Friedrich, P. (2012) Selecting an instructional variety for an EIL curriculum. In A. Matsuda (ed.) *Principles and Practices of Teaching English as an International Language* (pp. 17–27). Bristol: Multilingual Matters.

McKay, S.L. (2012) Teaching materials for English as an international language. In A. Matsuda (ed.) *Principles and Practices of Teaching English as an International Language* (pp. 70–83). Bristol: Multilingual Matters.

Mickan, P. (2013) *Language Curriculum Design and Socialisation*. Bristol: Multilingual Matters.

Murata, K. and Jenkins, J. (2009) *Global Englishes in Asian Contexts Current and Future Debates*. Basingstoke: Palgrave MacMillan.

Nation, I. and Macalister, J. (2010) *Language Curriculum Design*. New York/Abingdon: Routledge.

Pennycook, A. (2007) *Global Englishes and Transcultural Flows*. Abingdon/New York: Routledge.

Richards, J. (2001) *Curriculum Development in Language Teaching*. Cambridge: Cambridge University Press.

Seidlhofer, B. (2001) Closing A Conceptual Gap: The Case For A Description Of English As A Lingua Franca. International Journal of Applied Linguistics, 11: 133–158. doi:10.1111/1473-4192.00011.

Seidlhofer, B. (2011) *Understanding English as a Lingua Franca*. Oxford: Oxford University Press.

Sharifian, F. (2009) English as an international language: An overview. In F. Sharifian (ed.) *English as an International Language: Perspectives and Pedagogical Issues* (pp. 1–18). Bristol: Multilingual Matters.

Widdowson, H.G. (2012) ELF and the inconvenience of established concepts. *Journal of English as a Lingua Franca* 1 (1), 5–26.

# 6 Training Graduate Students in Japan to be EIL Teachers

## Nobuyuki Hino

## Introduction

The present chapter mainly describes and discusses the author's classroom practice in English as an International Language (EIL) teacher education. This course, entitled 'Education in Language and Culture' with my own subtitle 'Principles and Practices of EIL Education', is offered in the master's (MA) program in the Graduate School of Language and Culture at Osaka University, a major national university in Japan.

The official overall aim of the course 'Education in Language and Culture' is to discuss foreign language teaching from lingua-cultural perspectives. All classes at the Graduate School of Language and Culture are electives, and the specific content of each class is largely left to the instructor's discretion as long as it complies with the basic goal of the course. Thus, it is my own decision to dedicate the class to issues of EIL pedagogy, with the belief that this topic will best help the students, many of whom are prospective teachers of English, to deepen their understanding of foreign language education from intercultural viewpoints.

After completion of the MA program, many Japanese students will teach English at junior or senior high schools in Japan. Some go on to a PhD program, usually the one offered at this graduate school, many of whom will eventually obtain university positions. Junior or senior high school English teachers who are on leave also sometimes enrol in this class as recurrent education. On the other hand, the careers chosen by international students (approximately half of the enrollees out of the total class size of 7–17 in recent examples) are various.

It should be noted at the outset that the term 'EIL' is employed in this chapter with three different connotations. Depending on the context, it is used either as an umbrella term in accordance with Matsuda's definition (in this volume), or to refer to a school of thought founded by Larry E. Smith (e.g. 1983) or to an integrated paradigm proposed by the author (e.g. Hino, 2001).

# Background and Context for the Course

This section briefly discusses some of the historical background of EIL teacher training, leading to the author's classroom practice.

## Impact of Smith's concept of EIL on teacher trainers in Japan

As in many other parts of the world, native-speakerism (Holliday, 2006; Houghton & Rivers, 2013) is prevalent in English language teaching (ELT) in Japan. This fact is symbolically evident in the Japanese expression *neitibu chekku* (native check), or check by native speakers. This term, routinely employed among users of English in this country, signifies a belief that no English written by a Japanese person can be made public before it is proofread by a native speaker of the language. On the other hand, historically speaking, starting with Hidezaburo Saito's classic proposal as far back as 1928, '(T)he English of the Japanese must, in a certain sense, be Japanized' (Saito, 1928: Preface), some influential Japanese thinkers have argued for years in favor of nonnative Englishes as a means of representing indigenous values in international communication.

Most notably, Masao Kunihiro, a cultural anthropologist and a pioneer simultaneous interpreter, discussed the significance of the de-Anglo-Americanization of English in Kunihiro (1970), a volume to which the origin of the Japanese term *kokusai eigo* (English as an International Language) can be attributed. Takao Suzuki also pointed out in Suzuki (1975) the importance of distinguishing EIL from Anglophone English, naming the former *Englic* to highlight the difference. Both of these books became bestsellers in Japan, making their philosophies known not only to linguists but also to the general public. Indeed, while scholars working under the paradigm of World Englishes (WE) (Kachru, 1985, 1997) tend to assume that the motives for the original models of English are restricted to the Outer Circle (e.g. Andreasson, 1994; Bamgbose, 1998), those calls for endonormative models of English have proven fairly popular in Japan as an exceptional case in the Expanding Circle.

It was in the context of this sociolinguistic background of Japan that Larry E. Smith's (1976, 1978, 1981a) concept of EIL had a major impact, especially in the late 1970s, on a number of Japanese university professors of ELT, many of whom were involved in teacher training. Those leading ELT scholars from Japan had opportunities to attend seminars and workshops by Smith at various events held at the East-West Center in Honolulu, Hawaii. With their previous exposure to indigenous Japanese philosophy on the de-Anglo-Americanization of English since the early 1970s, the ELT researchers and teacher trainers from Japan were ready to accept the new paradigm of ELT proposed by Smith, who himself was also a professional teacher trainer.

Thus, EIL teacher training in Japan was chiefly initiated by the Japanese professors directly influenced by Larry E. Smith. My classroom practice in EIL teacher training described in the present chapter has also evolved from this stream of thought.

## Smith's graduate class in EIL in 1981 as the starting point

The author had a chance to take a course taught by Larry E. Smith, offered as a part of the MA program in English as a second language (ESL) at the University of Hawaii at Manoa in the spring semester of 1981, which was entitled 'English as an International Language'. This course by Smith, which might historically be the first regular graduate class with the formal aim of EIL teacher education, laid the foundation for my current pedagogical practice.

As the teaching materials for his class, Smith distributed copies of a collection of papers on EIL, when EIL studies were in their infancy. Among them were proofs of Smith (1981b), that is, Smith's edited volume published later the same year. Also, some of the journal papers in this collection were eventually included in Smith (1983), another edited volume now regarded as a classic in the field.

Though this class was a relatively small-sized seminar with nine students, its population still represented some diversity – one each from Japan (myself), Mainland China and Fiji, along with American students including one from the Mariana Islands. The diverse student demographics provided an authentic EIL environment in the classroom. While students were expected to express their own values and identities, their Englishes were required to be intelligible to one another as well. In other words, the students, who were either preservice or in-service ELT teachers, experienced in this classroom the very situation that they were talking about, that is, EIL interaction. Class discussions also centered around cross-cultural issues in EIL, to which international students were able to make meaningful contributions by offering their non-American perspectives. These experiences gave me the initial motivation for creating a similar environment years later at Osaka University, by remodeling my graduate class as English-medium instruction (EMI) (Doiz et al., 2013; Jenkins, 2014) despite the overwhelming dominance of Japanese as the medium of instruction in the socio-educational tradition of Japan.

The graduate class taught by Smith not only introduced the students to sociolinguistic theories of EIL but also discussed their pedagogical implications. For example, concerning the issue of materials for teaching EIL, one of the questions posed by Smith to the students was 'We should go beyond the superficiality of things like merely changing the Anglophone names into local names, but how?', which remains a fundamental problem in the cultural content of EIL textbooks even today.

A few possible techniques for teaching EIL were also demonstrated in Smith's class. On one particularly noteworthy occasion, Richard A. Via, Smith's colleague at the East-West Center and a well-known Broadway-actor-turned-educator, gave a mini workshop as a guest lecturer for the class on the use of a role-play technique called 'Talk-and-Listen', which he had developed for EIL education in collaboration with Smith (Smith & Via, 1983; Via & Smith, 1983). Via's core philosophy was to remain oneself even in acting, which was in line with the basic idea of EIL. In his workshop held in Smith's class, Via let the students act out the 'Talk-and-Listen' skit, with his follow-up comments. This experience made me realize the importance of demonstrating in class how EIL theories could be put into actual pedagogical practice.

In a word, Smith's graduate class 'English as an International Language' in 1981 was the genesis of EIL teacher education, from which we can learn a great deal for our current efforts.

## A survey on EIL perspectives in ELT teacher training in the early 1980s

A questionnaire survey on ELT teacher training conducted by Jack C. Richards and myself, published as Richards and Hino (1983), contained a rare inquiry into the perception of the diversity of English in the context of ELT teacher training in the early 1980s. The survey results show what it was like around the dawn of EIL teacher education.

The participants were 116 ELT teachers in Japan, mostly foreign, who taught at various institutions such as universities, private language schools and senior high schools, the majority of whom ($n=95$) were from the US. For this survey, the respondents were divided into two groups, that is, those who had not studied in a graduate ELT program before and those who had already done so. A key question asked of the former was 'If you were to study in an MA program in TESL/TEFL, which areas would you like to study?', while the parallel question addressed to the latter was 'Indicate which of the following areas you studied in your courses and their usefulness in your present job(s)'. All the items in the questionnaire were to be answered with a three-rank scale, as those were the days before the five-point scale became a standard in ELT research.

Among the items for both groups was 'varieties of English', which I had inserted into the questionnaire from an EIL perspective, with Richards' permission. For the benefit of those who had not enrolled in a graduate ELT program before, this concept was explained on the question sheet as the 'study of American English, British English, and other native and nonnative varieties of English'. From an EIL standpoint, I would have wanted to place more emphasis on the 'nonnative' element in this notation, but it did not seem to be realistic in 1982.

As to what areas the respondents without previous ELT training at the graduate level would like to study, 'varieties of English' ranked only 24th out of 29 options, whereas 'teaching of listening', 'teaching of speaking' and 'second language acquisition' turned out to be the first, second and third choice, respectively. Regarding what classes had actually been taken by those who had enrolled in a graduate ELT program, 'varieties of English' was again rated 24th among 33 options topped by 'phonology/phonetics' with 'transformational grammar' as a close second. Likewise, in the ranking of subjects found to be useful by the latter group of respondents, 'varieties of English' was 24th out of 33 content areas, far behind such items as 'practice teaching' (first), 'classroom management' (second) and 'second language acquisition' (third).

In sum, it was shown in this survey that the diversity of English was generally underrepresented in graduate ELT programs in those days, and that ELT teachers also did not feel very strongly about the need to study such an area. These research results made me realize, in 1982, the need to raise awareness about EIL among the stakeholders of ELT teacher training programs – administrators, teacher trainers and trainees alike.

## Overview and Key Features of the Course 'Principles and Practices of EIL Education'

Emerging out of the background described above, how does the author train graduate students in Japan to be EIL teachers?

Being part of an academically oriented graduate curriculum with a PhD program rather than that of a teachers' college, the immediate objective of the course is not necessarily to provide teacher training per se but to discuss the theories and practices of EIL education. However, the fact that the majority of the students plan to be ELT teachers is always taken into consideration in the planning and implementation of the class.

The basic framework of my MA class at Osaka University is as described earlier in the introduction section. This is a year-long course, though technically divided into two semesters with separate grades. The class meets once a week for 90 minutes, with a total of 15 sessions for each semester.

Though the yearly syllabus of this class varies every time, it typically starts with a series of my introductory lectures on EIL, followed by short presentations on reading assignments and/or demonstrations of EIL pedagogy by each student, combined with whole-class discussions and small-group discussions. We discuss a wide range of issues in EIL, from its theoretical aspects such as the concept of indigenization contrasted with the Sapir–Whorf hypothesis, to practical and pedagogical topics including materials, methodologies, models, testing and teacher training for EIL.

With regard to the fact that some of the students are those who did not study ELT as undergraduates, basic linguistic and pedagogical concepts are explained in class when necessary, such as the difference between the phonemic level and the phonetic level in phonology, the notions of validity and reliability in testing and the communicative approach vs. the audio-lingual approach in the history of language teaching.

In the following, three major features of this class are briefly discussed: (1) an EIL paradigm appropriate for local contexts; (2) bridging theory and practice in EIL; and (3) experiencing authentic EIL communication in class.

## EIL paradigm appropriate for local contexts

While teacher training is essentially of a practical nature, a certain theoretical framework should still be provided to the students as a systematic basis for their educational practice. For my graduate class, it is a paradigm of EIL tailored to the needs of the Expanding Circle including Japan.

The Kachruvian WE paradigm that has dominated the discourses on EIL for the past several decades is a theory that grew out of research in the intra-national use of postcolonial or Outer Circle Englishes. As such, it is often inappropriate to directly apply the WE paradigm to issues of EIL in the Expanding Circle, though there is still a lot to learn from WE studies.

As a basic theoretical framework, this class adopts the author's version of EIL, proposed in works such as Hino (2001, 2009, 2012a, 2012c) for ELT in the Expanding Circle. This paradigm builds on Larry E. Smith's (1976, 1978, 1981a) classic concept of EIL, while also incorporating other relevant theories, including WE (Kachru, 1976, 1985, 1986, 1997), English as a Lingua Franca (ELF) (Jenkins, 2000, 2007; Seidlhofer, 2011) and nonsectarian studies such as Kirkpatrick (2007), as well as indigenous schools of thought in Japan on de-Anglo-Americanized Japanese English (Kunihiro, 1970; Saito, 1928; Suzuki, 1975) mentioned earlier.

Thus, the concept of EIL employed for this course is both eclectic and original. For example, partly under the influence of Smith's philosophy, the teaching of EIL is defined here as a form of diversity education aimed at cross-cultural tolerance. Also, while WE and ELF are founded upon the notions of 'variety' and 'variation', respectively (Widdowson, 2015), EIL is conceptualized in my paradigm as 'variations of varieties', integrating both positions. Furthermore, drawing on the traditional Japanese view of international English, the feasibility of endonormative models for Englishes in the Expanding Circle (including Japanese English) is explored, irrespective of the fact that such an idea is largely limited to the Outer Circle in the WE school and is also considerably de-emphasized in the ELF paradigm due to its focus on the fluid and dynamic nature of the language.

## Bridging theory and practice in EIL

A problem in many fields of academic discipline is the gap between theory and practice, and EIL studies is by no means an exception. My policy for graduate classes is to present concrete examples first, followed by an explanation of the relevant theories.

After a general orientation in the first meeting, I usually start the course by showing authentic examples of EIL communication to illustrate what EIL actually means. For this purpose, I make use of various recordings, including those of a weekly radio ELT program in Japan for which I served as a lecturer from 1989 to 1990. The recordings of this radio course *English for Millions* present my talks with speakers of nonnative varieties of English from Hong Kong, Malaysia, Bangladesh, Sri Lanka, the Philippines and France. With the excerpts of this EIL talk show, I expose the students to the linguistic and cultural diversity of EIL at the beginning of the first semester.

Likewise, various examples of actual practice in teaching EIL are shown to the students, including my undergraduate ELT classes, before going into theoretical discussions. For example, I teach my first- and second-year undergraduate ELT classes at Osaka University with a method now known as IPTEIL (Integrated Practice in Teaching EIL) (Hino, 2012b; Hino & Oda, 2015), in which students watch, read and discuss real-time news that is broadcast or written in varieties of English representing linguistic as well as cultural diversity, provided by various English-language media across the world such as *ADTV* (India), *ABS-CBN* (Philippines) and *Al Jazeera* (Qatar), to name just a few.

Many of the graduate students come to observe my undergraduate ELT classes, though I have never required them to do so. After the class observation, some of the graduate students continue to participate in the undergraduate class every week for their learning of EIL even with no credits.

One of the tasks for students in my graduate class is to come up with their own ways of teaching EIL and to demonstrate them in class. For their reference, I introduce the students to the five approaches in classroom EIL pedagogy analyzed in Hino (2010, 2013), which are 'providing knowledge of EIL', 'exposure to varieties of EIL', 'simulated role-play in EIL', 'content-based approach to EIL' and 'participation in the community of EIL users', though not to the exclusion of other possible approaches.

I also tried this teaching demonstration task in my MA class in the Graduate School of World Englishes at Chukyo University, who did quite well on this assignment. One student brought McDonald's menus from several parts of the world as teaching materials, citing the examples of local adaptation as a metaphor for the indigenization of English, thereby teaching the language while introducing a central idea of EIL at the same time. Another Chukyo student used some scenes from a Bollywood movie that came with Indian English as well as Indian values as an expression of non-Anglophone linguaculture. For the same task recently given at Osaka University, a few students made use of YouTube videos that represented nonnative varieties of English, which are certainly useful resources for EIL education these days.

## Engaging students in authentic EIL interaction in class

One of the most important aspects of my graduate course at Osaka University is authentic EIL interaction in class. This has been made possible by teaching the course as EMI, though English-medium content classes are still more of an exception rather than a norm for traditional higher education in Japan even in language-related fields.

I have been teaching my graduate class at Osaka University as a self-initiated EMI course for nine years, after teaching it basically in Japanese for 11 years. In line with governmental initiatives toward the globalization of higher education in Japan, Osaka University now has official EMI programs in various departments both at the graduate and the undergraduate level, yet the Graduate School of Language and Culture has not adopted such a system. While it probably makes sense to respect the traditional belief among human scientists of this country in the value of scholarship pursued through the medium of Japanese, teaching an academic subject in English attracts many international students whose linguistic barriers are lowered by EMI, and also invites other students, both local and international, who are interested in the concurrent learning of content and English.

For example, in the fall semester of 2013, this class had four students from Japan, and one each from Thailand, Laos and Mainland China, with a teaching assistant (TA) from the United States. In fall 2014, it had seven students from Japan, joined by five from Mainland China, three from Germany and one each from Iran and Papua New Guinea, along with the American TA. Some of these international students belonged to departments other than the Graduate School of Language and Culture, which suggests that EMI may be in greater demand than supply.

Given the diverse international student population mostly comprising speakers of nonnative varieties of English, it is my intention to design this course as a new type of Content and Language Integrated Learning (CLIL) (Coyle *et al.*, 2010) class, where the language of instruction is redefined as EIL rather than Anglo-American English. I call this approach Content and ELF Integrated Learning (CELFIL) (Hino, 2015) by adopting the concept of ELF with its emphasis on interactional dynamism. The fact that the subject of this class is EIL education makes CELFIL particularly productive here, as the students are provided with opportunities to personally engage in authentic EIL communication in the same classroom.

This course is indeed where small-group discussions have proven to be highly useful, as they allow the students to experience the interactive and dynamic nature of EIL, regardless of the issue of potential cultural incompatibility (Hino, 1992; Matsuda, 2012; McKay, 2003) between such Western pedagogy and traditional East Asian values. I make sure that each group has some international diversity, and that all group members are shuffled every time so that the students may have chances to interact with many different types of interlocutors. For instance, in one session, a group comprised students from Japan, China, Germany and Iran, while another group comprised those from Japan, China, Germany and Papua New Guinea. In these small-group discussions, students practice conversational rules such as turn-taking as well as communication strategies including accommodation and negotiation of meaning.

## Outcome of the Course

As briefly mentioned above, many of the Japanese students in my graduate classes at Osaka University become junior or senior high school ELT teachers after completion of the MA program. Others advance to our PhD program, some of whom I supervise in their dissertation projects, and many of them eventually assume university positions.

From 2008 to 2009, I observed classes taught by two Japanese alumni, and interviewed them about the impact of my graduate course on their classroom practice. One was a public senior high school ELT teacher who had completed the MA program. The other, an alumnus both from the MA and PhD program, was an assistant professor in the department of education at a national university, teaching an ELT methodology course for prospective junior and senior high school teachers. The results of this small research have revealed that taking my graduate class helped them, among other things, to be aware of the legitimacy of showing the teacher's own nonnative English to the students as one possible model. In view of the fact that only Inner Circle and Outer Circle Englishes have been fully accepted as legitimate models in the WE paradigm (Kachru, 1976, 1997), this finding in the Expanding Circle is particularly significant in terms of the issue of language attitudes. As mentioned earlier, the EIL paradigm for my graduate class is based upon the premise that original models should be allowed not only for the Inner and Outer Circle but also for the Expanding Circle (Hino, 1987).

The senior high school teacher took my graduate class while she was on leave for recurrent education. For the purpose of investigating 'before and after', I asked her, 'How does your graduate study in the concept of EIL influence your teaching in senior high school now?' She answered that the biggest influence was that she did not hesitate to present her own English in front of her students any more. She also added that she was now convinced that the students could learn a lot in class from her conversation with the Assistant Language Teacher (ALT) from abroad.

To the university professor, another former student of my graduate class, I addressed this question – 'What do you keep in mind when you teach your ELT methodology course?' He answered that he had been telling prospective teachers that they should not depend on CDs too much in demonstrating spoken English. He said that he always made it clear to the future ELT teachers that the primary model of English in class should be their own English. This philosophy is in exact agreement with the one expressed by the high school teacher above, and may be regarded as one of the salient outcomes of taking my graduate class in EIL education.

## Challenges and Limitations

A major challenge and a limitation for this graduate class in EIL education is the gap between the ideals of EIL and the present realities of ELT, especially with respect to the 'examination culture' of Japan. That is, when the students actually start to teach English in school or university, many of them face the demand for preparing their students for examinations – university entrance exams for high school students and standardized tests such as TOEFL (Test of English as a Foreign Language), TOEIC (Test of English for International Communication) or IELTS (International English Language Testing System) for university students. The fact that all these examinations are based on native-speaker norms often puts substantial restrictions on the teachers' efforts in the form of washback effects when they try to incorporate the concept of EIL into their teaching practice.

On the other hand, a change toward EIL is in sight for ELT in Japan. For example, the cultural content of ELT textbooks in Japanese public junior high schools (Hino, 1988; Matsuda, 2002) nowadays represents a diversity of cultures including that of nonnative speakers of English such as the students' own (Hino, 2009). The current course of study for senior high school English, issued by the Ministry of Education in 2009, even explicitly states that in choosing teaching materials 'consideration must be given to the fact that varieties of English are used across the world as a global means of communication' (translation mine). Also, English as a global language beyond the Anglo-American frame of reference has become a popular theme at annual conferences of the Japan Association of College English Teachers, a leading ELT organization in Japan. There are many more tangible instances showing that the teaching of English in Japan is moving in the direction of EIL, though slowly, which suggests that EIL teacher training is worthy of serious undertakings in Japan today.

## Conclusion

This chapter has discussed several aspects of the author's practice in training graduate students in Japan to be teachers of EIL, after presenting its historical background including Larry E. Smith's pioneering efforts in this area. It is hoped that these experiences will serve as a useful reference for EIL teacher educators today.

Teacher training in EIL, which leads prospective ELT teachers to an innovative educational practice, is a scheme for social reform. In the author's view, its ultimate goal is to contribute to the construction of a symbiotic society where people with various different values can live in peaceful harmony with one another. Many of the alumni from the author's graduate class are already active as ELT researchers, administrators and teachers in universities, boards of education and senior and junior high schools in Japan and abroad. I look forward to seeing them help make this world a better place to live for the small and the weak.

# Acknowledgments

This research is partly supported by the Japan Society for the Promotion of Science, Grants-in-Aid for Scientific Research (C) 15K02678, 2015-2017. I am grateful to Mr Simon Yu for helping me with proofreading.

## References

Andreasson, A. (1994) Norm as a pedagogical paradigm. *World Englishes* 13 (3), 395–409.

Bamgbose, A. (1998) Torn between the norms: Innovations in world Englishes. *World Englishes* 17 (1), 1–14.

Coyle, D., Hood, P. and Marsh, D. (2010) *CLIL: Content and Language Integrated Learning*. Cambridge: Cambridge University Press.

Doiz, A., Lasagabaster, D. and Sierra, J.M. (2013) Future challenges for English-medium instruction at the tertiary level. In A. Doiz, D. Lasagabaster and J.M. Sierra (eds) *English-Medium Instruction at Universities: Global Challenges* (pp. 213–221). Bristol: Multilingual Matters.

Hino, N. (1987) *TOEFL de 650-ten: Watashi no eigoshugyo* [*650 on the TOEFL: My Experiences in Learning English*]. Tokyo: Nan'undo.

Hino, N. (1988) Nationalism and English as an international language: The history of English textbooks in Japan. *World Englishes* 7 (3), 309–314.

Hino, N. (1992) The yakudoku tradition of foreign language literacy in Japan. In F. Dubin and N.A. Kuhlman (eds) *Cross-Cultural Literacy: Global Perspectives on Reading and Writing* (pp. 99–111). Englewood Cliffs, NJ: Regents/Prentice Hall.

Hino, N. (2001) Organizing EIL studies: Toward a paradigm. *Asian Englishes* 4 (1), 34–65.

Hino, N. (2009) The teaching of English as an international language in Japan: An answer to the dilemma of indigenous values and global needs in the Expanding Circle. *AILA Review* 22, 103–119.

Hino, N. (2010) EIL in teaching practice: A pedagogical analysis of EIL classrooms in action. In N. Hino (ed.) *Gengobunka-kyoiku no aratanaru riron to jissen* [*New Theories and Practice in Education in Language and Culture*] (pp. 1–10). Osaka: Graduate School of Language and Culture, Osaka University.

Hino, N. (2012a) Endonormative models of EIL for the Expanding Circle. In A. Matsuda (ed.) *Principles and Practices of Teaching English as an International Language* (pp. 28–43). Bristol: Multilingual Matters.

Hino, N. (2012b) Participating in the community of EIL users through real-time news: Integrated Practice in Teaching English as an International Language (IPTEIL). In A. Matsuda (ed.) *Principles and Practices of Teaching English as an International Language* (pp. 183–200). Bristol: Multilingual Matters.

Hino, N. (2012c) Negotiating indigenous values with Anglo-American cultures in ELT in Japan: A case of EIL philosophy in the Expanding Circle. In A. Kirkpatrick and R. Sussex (eds) *English as an International Language in Asia: Implications for Language Education* (pp. 157–173). Dordrecht: Springer.

Hino, N. (2013) Kokusaieigo ni okeru komyunikeshon-noryoku no yosei [Teaching communicative competence in English as an international language]. In K. Kataoka and K. Ikeda (eds) *Komyunikeshon-noryoku no shoso* [*Aspects of Communicative Competence*] (pp. 429–455). Tokyo: Hituzi Syobo.

Hino, N. (2015) Toward the development of CELFIL (Content and ELF Integrated Learning) for EMI classes in higher education in Japan. *Waseda Working Papers in ELF* 4, 187–198.

Hino, N. and Oda, S. (2015) Integrated Practice in Teaching English as an International Language (IPTEIL): A classroom ELF pedagogy in Japan. In Y. Bayyurt and S. Akcan (eds) *Current Perspectives on Pedagogy for English as a Lingua Franca* (pp. 35–50). Berlin: De Gruyter Mouton.

Holliday, A. (2006) Native-speakerism. *ELT Journal* 60 (4), 385–387.

Houghton, S.A. and Rivers, D.J. (eds) (2013) *Native-Speakerism in Japan: Intergroup Dynamics in Foreign Language Education*. Bristol: Multilingual Matters.

Jenkins, J. (2000) *The Phonology of English as an International Language*. Oxford: Oxford University Press.

Jenkins, J. (2007) *English as a Lingua Franca: Attitude and Identity*. Oxford: Oxford University Press.

Jenkins, J. (2014) *English as a Lingua Franca in the International University: The Politics of Academic English Language Policy*. Abingdon: Routledge.

Kachru, B.B. (1976) Models of English for the Third World: White man's linguistic burden or language pragmatics. *TESOL Quarterly* 10 (2), 221–239.

Kachru, B.B. (1985) Standards, codification and sociolinguistic realism: The English language in the Outer Circle. In R. Quirk and H.G. Widdowson (eds) *English in the World: Teaching and Learning the Language and Literatures* (pp. 11–30). Cambridge: Cambridge University Press.

Kachru, B.B. (1986) *The Alchemy of English: The Spread, Functions and Models of Non-native Englishes*. Oxford: Pergamon Press.

Kachru, B.B. (1997) World Englishes 2000: Resources for research and teaching. In L.E. Smith and M.L. Forman (eds) *World Englishes 2000* (pp. 209–251). Honolulu, HI: University of Hawaii Press.

Kirkpatrick, A. (2007) *World Englishes: Implications for International Communication and English Language Teaching*. Cambridge: Cambridge University Press.

Kunihiro, M. (1970) *Eigo no hanashikata* [*English Works for You*]. Tokyo: Simul Press.

Matsuda, A. (2002) Representation of users and uses of English in beginning Japanese EFL textbooks. *JALT Journal* 24 (2), 182–200.

Matsuda, A. (2012) Teaching materials in EIL. In L. Alsagoff, S.L. McKay, G. Hu and W.A. Renandya (eds) *Principles and Practices for Teaching English as an International Language* (pp. 168–185). New York: Routledge.

McKay, S. (2003) Teaching English as an international language: The Chilean context. *ELT Journal* 57 (2), 139–148.

Richards, J.C. and Hino, N. (1983) Training ESOL teachers: The need for needs assessment. In J. Alatis, H.H. Stern and P. Strevens (eds) *Georgetown University Round Table on Languages and Linguistics 1983* (pp. 312–326). Washington, DC: Georgetown University Press.

Saito, H. (1928) *Saito's Japanese-English Dictionary*. Tokyo: Nichieisha. (Reprinted in 2002, Tokyo: Nichigai Associates.)

Seidlhofer, B. (2011) *Understanding English as a Lingua Franca*. Oxford: Oxford University Press.

Smith, L.E. (1976) English as an international auxiliary language. *RELC Journal* 7 (2), 38–53. Also in Smith, L.E. (ed.) (1983) *Readings in English as an International Language* (pp. 1–5). Oxford: Pergamon Press.

Smith, L.E. (1978) Some distinctive features of EIIL vs. ESOL in English language education. *The Culture Learning Institute Report*, 5–7 and 10–11 June. Also in L.E. Smith (ed.) (1983) *Readings in English as an International Language* (pp. 13–20). Oxford: Pergamon Press.

Smith, L.E. (1981a) English as an international language: No room for linguistic chauvinism. *Nagoya Gakuin Daigaku Gaikokugo Kyoiku Kiyo* 3, 27–32. Also in L.E. Smith (ed.) (1983) *Readings in English as an International Language* (pp. 7–11). Oxford: Pergamon Press.

Smith, L.E. (ed.) (1981b) *English for Cross-Cultural Communication*. London: Macmillan.

Smith, L.E. (ed.) (1983) *Readings in English as an International Language*. Oxford: Pergamon Press.

Smith, L.E. and Via, R.A. (1983) English as an international language via drama techniques. In L.E. Smith (ed.) *Readings in English as an International Language* (pp. 111–116). Oxford: Pergamon Press.

Suzuki, T. (1975) *Tozasareta gengo, nihongo no sekai* [*A Closed Language: The World of Japanese*]. Tokyo: Shinchosha.

Via, R.A. and Smith, L.E. (1983) *Talk and Listen: English as an International Language via Drama Techniques*. Oxford: Pergamon Press.

Widdowson, H. (2015) ELF and the pragmatics of language variation. *Journal of English as a Lingua Franca* 4 (2), 359–372.

# 7 Practices of Teaching Englishes for International Communication

## Roby Marlina

## Introduction

Teaching English as an International Language (EIL) does not seem to be an unfamiliar perspective, concept or movement in the teaching English to speakers of other languages (TESOL) discipline. For the last three decades, EIL and World Englishes (WE) scholars have called for the need to base the teaching of the English language or an English language teacher-education program on the EIL paradigm that advocates the following views of English: (1) English is a heterogeneous language; (2) English is spoken/used predominantly by plurilingual users of English; (3) English, as a heterogeneous language, reflects diverse cultural values, beliefs, systems and practices; and (4) English is not exclusively owned by the so-called 'native-speakers' (Matsuda, 2012a; McKay, 2002, 2012; Smith, 1983). However, both Matsuda (2012a) and Marlina (2014a) have observed that the teaching of EIL still remains at a theoretical level. In a review of the latest literature on teaching EIL, Wee (2013) emphasizes the need for future works to address how realistic it is to teach EIL. Thus, this chapter (and other chapters in this edited volume) aim to address this gap by illustrating how teaching EIL can be 'practicalized' especially in a teacher education program. Specifically, I discuss how a course ('Practices of Teaching Englishes for International Communication' – POTEIC) can be an example of a way to equip teachers with knowledge, attitudes and skills to teach EIL. Reflecting critically on my experiences as the lecturer of this course, this chapter also presents challenges that I have encountered when teaching this course.

## Master of Applied Linguistics (Teaching World Englishes for Intercultural Communication)

POTEIC is one of the courses taught within the Master of Applied Linguistics (Teaching World Englishes for Intercultural Communication) program – formerly known as the Master of Arts in English as an

International Language program (see Sharifian & Marlina, 2012) – at Monash University, Australia. This 1.5-year long program (or three semesters) is designed for both pre-service and in-service English teachers who aim to gain and expand their knowledge of the recent development of English in the context of globalization; and to learn how to operationalize this knowledge in their current and/or prospective professional workplace settings including classrooms. In addition to gaining theoretical and practical knowledge and skills, this program has also been designed to allow students to develop research skills, and thus, to conduct research projects in areas such as teaching EIL, WE, English as a lingua franca and intercultural communication. To help students achieve these aims, the program offers the choice between Pathway 1 (coursework only) and Pathway 2 (coursework plus a 16,000-word research dissertation) (Table 7.1).

The Master of Applied Linguistics (Teaching World Englishes for Intercultural Communication) program has attracted both domestic and international students from diverse linguistic and cultural backgrounds. Most students are pre-service and in-service secondary English language teachers with zero or some teaching experience. There are also a large number of international students who are English language university lecturers in their home country, and are interested in advancing their

**Table 7.1** Study pathways for the Master of Applied Linguistics (Teaching World Englishes for International Communication)

| Pathway 1 (coursework only) | Pathway 2 (coursework+dissertation) |
| --- | --- |
| Semester 1: | Semester 1: |
| • APG5347: Research Methods in Applied Linguistics | • APG5347: Research Methods in Applied Linguistics |
| *Either one of the following courses:* | *Either one of the following courses:* |
| • APG5349: World Englishes<br>• APG5652: Language and Intercultural Communication | • APG5349: World Englishes<br>• APG5652: Language and Intercultural Communication |
| Semester 2: | Semester 2: |
| • APG5047: Issues in teaching EIL<br>• APG5042: POTEIC | • APG5047: Issues in teaching EIL<br>• APG5042: POTEIC |
| Semester 3:<br>*Any two of the following courses:* | Semester 3: |
| • APG5044: Professional internship<br>• APG5348: Second language acquisition<br>• APG5702: Bilingualism<br>• APG5856: Research project | • APG5848: Research thesis |

professional knowledge in English language teaching. This program has also attracted experienced teachers of languages other than English (such as Japanese and Chinese), as well as those from different fields of study (such as history and economics) who are interested in becoming English language teachers. There are also a few translators/interpreters, as well as office workers who anticipate that their future responsibilities are likely to involve English language teaching.

## POTEIC

POTEIC is a course that was developed in response to one of the main limitations of the EIL program discussed in Sharifian and Marlina (2012), i.e. the practicality of teaching EIL. As Sharifian and Marlina (2012: 150–151) state, 'our EIL students who are currently teachers or pre-service English teachers are still entirely uncertain about how to implement the imparted theoretical knowledge of teaching EIL in an actual classroom setting'. A program that engages students in learning about teaching EIL is still inadequate if 'no opportunities are given to practice "teaching" EIL' (Sharifian & Marlina, 2012: 150–151). Thus, POTEIC was developed in late 2012, and officially offered in 2013 with an aim to introduce students to the practical aspects of teaching WE in a variety of multilingual, and intra/international contexts. Upon completion of this 12-week course, students are expected to have developed the following learning outcomes:

- Demonstrate advanced understanding of the practical aspects of teaching WE in a variety of international contexts.
- Exhibit the skills to teach WE in a variety of international contexts.
- Develop a learning curriculum for teaching Englishes for international communication.
- Critically engage in evaluating practices of teaching WE.
- Profile pedagogical ideas that are informed by the latest literature on teaching Englishes for international communication.

In order to achieve the above learning outcomes, students are engaged in discussing the topics, and in working on the pedagogical activities outlined in Table 7.2.

The prescribed readings for this course are the edited books by Alsagoff *et al.* (2012), *Principles and Practices for Teaching English as an International Language,* and Matsuda (2012a), *Principles and Practices of Teaching English as an International Language.* However, as postgraduate students, they are required to read widely especially empirical works and/or practice-oriented papers published in journals that are relevant to the course such as, to name a few, *TESOL Quarterly, English Today, World Englishes, Asian Englishes* and *ELT Journal.*

**Table 7.2** Topics and a brief description of POTEIC weekly lesson

| Week | Topic | Description |
|---|---|---|
| 1 | Introduction to teaching EIL | In this week, students are engaged in critically discussing and reviewing the traditional assumptions of ELT, and are introduced to the basic principles of teaching EIL. |
| 2 | EIL teaching materials | Based on the principles of teaching EIL in Week 1, students are engaged in reviewing the existing ELT textbooks. They learn how to develop teaching materials that are 'glocally' relevant. |
| 3 | EIL pedagogical practices | In this week's seminar, students learn to develop and implement pedagogical practices/activities that engage English language learners in learning how to communicate effectively across cultures and Englishes. |
| 4 | Testing in EIL | This lesson provides students with an opportunity to review and redesign the existing local and international English language tests based on the current international use of English, and the notion of 'critical language testing' (CLT). |
| 5 | Observation practicum | In these weeks, students observe a first-year undergraduate EIL course on 'International Communication' taught by experienced EIL instructors. They can observe as many two-hour seminars as they wish. Furthermore, students are required to develop a lesson plan and to discuss their lesson plan with the lecturer in charge. |
| 6 | Observation practicum+EIL lesson preparation | |
| 7 | Teaching practicum | Students deliver a 60-minute lesson to the first-year undergraduate EIL students whom they observed in previous weeks. A debriefing session with the lecturer in charge on their teaching performance is carried out at the end of their lesson. |
| 8 | Teaching practicum | |
| 9 | Teaching grammar of Englishes | In this week, students learn about the notion of 'standard English' as a polycentric dialect, and learn to develop pedagogical activities based on this notion. |

*(Continued)*

**Table 7.2** Continued

| Week | Topic | Description |
|------|-------|-------------|
| 10 | Teaching reading across cultures | Students in this week are engaged in a discussion on a social/discourse perspective of reading; and how this can be implemented in a classroom setting. |
| 11 | Teaching writing across cultures | Students are engaged in critiquing the monolithic view of writing. Learning how to teach English language learners to take ownership of their writing practices is a focus of this week's lesson. |
| 12 | Teaching speaking/listening across cultures | This week focuses on finding, developing and teaching listening materials which expose English language learners to world Englishes. Students are also engaged in developing pedagogical activities based on an interactional approach to teaching speaking across cultures and Englishes. |

As POTEIC is a practice-oriented course, students are required to complete the following assessment tasks which mainly engage them in learning and experiencing the practical aspects of teaching EIL.

## Assessment Task 1: Classroom observation report

In the observation practicum weeks (Weeks 5 and 6), students observe a first-year undergraduate EIL course on 'International Communication' (a synopsis of this course can be found in Sharifian and Marlina [2012]), and most importantly, observe how experienced EIL lecturers engage their students in learning about English language variation and its implications for communication. Though POTEIC students can observe as many seminars as they wish, they are required to choose only two seminars on which their reflective observational report is to be based. In this report, they are expected to address the following guiding questions:

- What have you learned from the EIL-oriented lesson(s) you have observed?
- How does the teacher implement the principles of teaching EIL?
- Do you believe that his or her teaching materials and pedagogical approaches have raised his or her students' awareness of linguistic and cultural diversity, and have inspired them to appreciate this diversity? Explain.
- Is there anything you would have done differently? If yes, what are they and why?

- In light of your observation of the EIL-oriented lesson, do you believe that the guiding theoretical principles of teaching EIL need to be revised or extended?

## Assessment Task 2: Teaching practicum portfolio and report

The teaching practicum portfolio and report is the major practice-oriented assessment task for POTEIC as it involves and assesses: (1) the teaching of a 60-minute EIL-oriented lesson; (2) the development of a lesson plan; (3) the design of EIL-oriented teaching materials and activities; and (4) the writing of a critical reflective report on Teaching English as an International Language (TEIL) based on the students' teaching practices.

Prior to the practicum weeks, students are asked to select the week in which they prefer to teach. Students have a choice to teach either a lesson on 'politeness in international communication' (Week 7) or 'writing in an intercultural context' (Week 8).

Before their lesson, POTEIC students are required to

- Develop a 60-minute EIL-oriented lesson plan in which the chosen topic, teaching objectives, materials and resources and sequences of the lesson are clearly written.
- Develop at least two learning activities on the chosen topic, and of which the ideological assumptions behind the activities are informed by the principles of teaching EIL.
- Arrange a time with the lecturer in charge to discuss their lesson plan and teaching materials.

During their lesson, POTEIC students are encouraged to

- Constantly monitor and observe their students' responses to the learning materials, their students' discourses of or attitudes toward linguistic and cultural diversity and their students' attitudes toward their classmates from different lingua-cultural backgrounds.
- Monitor their pedagogical strategies.

After the lesson, POTEIC students are required to

- Discuss their teaching performance with the lecturer in charge, involving a critical conversation on the strengths and limitations of the lesson based on the criteria sheet (see Appendix) that the lecturer uses to assess their teaching practice.
- Document what they have monitored during their lessons, as well as the discussions they have had with the lecturer.

- Write a report that addresses the following questions in light of the principles of teaching EIL, the students' observations of their classroom during the lesson, the students' reflections on their own teaching practices and the lecturer's comments and assessment:

    (1) Do you believe that your pedagogical approaches have raised students' awareness of linguistic and cultural diversity, and have inspired them to appreciate this diversity? If so, what did you do?
    (2) Do you experience any challenges in conducting an EIL-oriented lesson? If so, what are the challenges? Why?
    (3) To what extent do you believe that there is (or are) something (or things) 'missing' in the principles of teaching EIL? Do you believe that the principles have equipped you for teaching in a 'real' or 'authentic' EIL classroom? Justify.
    (4) To what extent do you believe that your lesson can be implemented in your teaching context? Justify.

## Assessment Task 3: Mini EIL lesson

From Weeks 9 to 12, students are engaged in learning how to teach linguistic macro-skills and micro-skills. Therefore, this assessment task requires them to develop and implement one pedagogical activity during the seminar that teaches their chosen skill based on the principles of teaching EIL discussed in the selected week or previous weeks. Specifically, students must:

- Choose one macro-/micro-skill that they are interested in teaching, and a focus for the lesson (e.g. a lesson on the present progressive tense or on writing an argumentative piece).
- Choose their own teaching context and participants (e.g. upper-intermediate, young adult university students of English in South Korea).
- Develop a 20–25 minute lesson in which the learning activities are based on the principles of teaching EIL, and should engage language learners in developing the chosen skill.
- Implement their activity during the seminar in which their classmates are asked to take on the role of the chosen participants.
- (After the implementation) Discuss the extent to which their lesson is informed by the principles of teaching EIL, and why the lesson suits their chosen teaching context.
- (After the implementation) Discuss with their classmates the strengths and limitations of their lesson in general and/or the learning activities in particular.

# The EIL-ness of POTEIC

An ideal EIL teacher education program, as Bayyurt and Sifakis (2015) assert, should have two integral components: (a) comprehensive information about the current role of English worldwide, and (b) an element of change in both the teachers' perspectives about that role and the implications that such a program can have for their own teaching context. As observed in the structure of the Master of Applied Linguistics (Teaching World Englishes for International Communication) program in Table 7.1, prior to undertaking POTEIC, students develop familiarity with and advanced theoretical knowledge of Englishes in the world and its implications by undertaking the 'theory-oriented' courses in which the changing sociolinguistic reality of English and its pedagogical implications, as well as intercultural communication are the core foci: World Englishes (a 12-week course on the global spread of English and Englishes in various Kachruvian circles), Language and Intercultural Communication (a 12-week course on communication across Englishes and cultures) and Issues in Teaching English as an International Language (a 12-week course on the theoretical perspectives of and issues in teaching English as a pluricentric language). Driven by an aim to engage students in critically reconsidering any preconceived views on the role of English and the teaching/learning of English, these theory-oriented courses constantly encourage students to reflect on and critically evaluate their own experiences of teaching, learning and using English in light of various theoretical perspectives that challenge communicative and pedagogical practices that explicitly or implicitly glorify certain use/users of English and marginalize others.

However, in order to prompt students to see how knowledge they have gained from an EIL-aware teacher education program is applicable or relevant to their teaching context, a 'practical' component needs to be integrated into the program. In addition to Bayyurt and Sifakis's (2015) components, an ideal EIL teacher education program should go beyond simply 'talking about' the current sociolinguistic reality of English or how to teach EIL. It needs to offer an opportunity to *experience* and *apply* theoretical knowledge (i.e. teaching EIL) in a real classroom setting, and to *evaluate* how such knowledge can be implemented in students' own teaching context and/or classroom. This has, to a large extent, guided the design and the delivery of the curriculum of POTEIC.

In addition to discussing the theoretical principles of teaching EIL in a seminar, POTEIC allows students to see how these principles can be practicalized in a real authentic classroom setting. Table 7.2 shows that every weekly seminar of POTEIC (except the practicum weeks) is guided by a particular theoretical framework(s) or pedagogical principle(s). As a practice-oriented course, students are mostly engaged in either developing EIL-oriented learning activities (including tests) or reviewing and redesigning existing learning activities based on these theoretical frameworks/principles. The (re)design of these activities is often also based on the students' choices of settings and participants. For example, in Week 3's seminar on EIL teaching materials, students are introduced to Matsuda's (2012b) framework for EIL materials development, selection and evaluation. They are provided with existing language teaching materials such as from *Headway* or *Interchange*, and are then asked to review its local and international relevance and appropriateness based on Matsuda's framework. Thereafter, students are assigned the role of language teaching materials writers which requires them to redesign those teaching materials based on the framework as well as the guiding principles of teaching EIL discussed in Week 2's seminar. This 'theory-review-redesign' approach is often the routine or pattern of POTEIC seminars.

The opportunities to experience and apply the principles of teaching EIL can also be seen in both teaching and observation practicum, as well as the mini EIL lesson. Students are required to observe real/authentic EIL-oriented lessons taught by experienced EIL educators, and to practice teaching EIL. Specifically, during the observation practicum, they are encouraged to observe and discuss what they have learned from observing the teaching materials, the pedagogical practices, the assessment tasks, the classroom grouping, teacher–student interactions, student–student interactions and teachers' feedback. The teaching practicum also allows students to experience and apply frameworks and/or principles that they have learned in the seminar through developing their own EIL-oriented lesson plans and teaching materials, and delivering an EIL-oriented lesson. Since students may not necessarily be familiar with the context of the teaching practicum, the mini lesson provides students with an opportunity to develop an EIL-oriented lesson plan and EIL-oriented teaching materials based on the context (settings and students) of their choice. According to POTEIC students, both the teaching practicum and the mini lesson have enriched their knowledge of teaching EIL and, to a large extent, prepared them for teaching EIL in both familiar and unfamiliar contexts. This, shared by one of the students, is crucial as English language teachers' mobility across the globe tends to characterize today's English language teaching employment landscape.

Furthermore, as EIL curriculum and pedagogy research, especially the practicality of implementing an EIL-oriented curriculum and pedagogy as well as its efficacy, is still in its infancy stage (Brown, 2012; Marlina, 2014b; Matsuda, 2009), POTEIC also engages students in critically reviewing and evaluating the theoretical frameworks and guiding principles based on their experiences of observing and teaching an EIL-oriented lesson. For example, the teaching practicum assessment task requires students to use their experiences of teaching the first-year undergraduate EIL course to critically review the principles and to evaluate its suitability to their own teaching contexts. Also, students are encouraged to discuss and justify the extent to which their mini EIL lesson suits their chosen teaching context. My observations of their critical reflections have revealed that not only do students discuss the EIL-ness of their activities, but also how the linguistic, cultural, educational, economic and political landscape of their context allows and/or may challenge its implementation.

In addition, students are also encouraged to discuss the extent to which those frameworks or principles can be extended. For example, in writing up their observational reports, not only do students explain how the pedagogical principles or frameworks are applied by the experienced EIL educators, but also discuss if there is anything else that they have learned from the observation that can be added to the existing pedagogical principles or frameworks. Based on my research, analysis of POTEIC students' writings and conversations with students during the debriefing sessions, the incorporation and discussion of sociopolitical questions or issues (Pennycook, 2000) in an EIL-oriented lesson need to be added into the guiding principles or frameworks for teaching EIL or preparing teachers to teach EIL (Marlina, 2014b).

## Challenges

As mentioned before, POTEIC is a recently established course. The evaluation of this course's performance from the students' perspectives has generally been relatively positive. The practical nature of the course and the knowledge/experiences of teaching EIL gained from both observation and teaching practicum are what students have highlighted as the strengths of the course. However, as this is a new course, both my students and I feel that some areas need further improvement. Specifically, students claim that observing how experienced EIL lecturers teach EIL for a period of two weeks is largely inadequate to prepare them for the teaching practicum as they are still relatively new to the EIL paradigm, its pedagogical implications and therefore practical applications. Although they have already completed courses that engage them in learning about various perspectives that advocate the pluricentricity of English prior to POTEIC, some students have still not developed enough confidence to stand in front of a class and teach EIL, English with an EIL perspective or intercultural communication. During the teaching practicum, this group of students often struggle to either respond adequately to questions from the undergraduate students or provide in-depth explanations to guide them in developing an understanding and/or appreciation of linguistic and cultural diversity. There are several occasions where lessons are finished earlier than the required duration, and classroom discussions are short and occasionally irrelevant. When analyzing the underlying discourses of the lessons, linguistic and cultural diversity tend to be approached from a 'sympathetic' point of view, which is not in line with the paradigm of EIL. For example, one lesson on writing in an intercultural context is concluded with: *'we should learn to feel sorry for those who can't write in an American style. So, we need to learn to be more understanding'*. When discussed at the debriefing session, some of the POTEIC students claim that EIL, WE or English as a lingua franca are 'calls' made by nonnative speakers to ask for a sympathetic recognition of their inability to use English like so-called 'native speakers', and their difficulties in adapting to or internalizing native-speakers' 'cultures'. This has also led me to wonder (1) if there is a need for EIL, WE or English as a lingua franca to be discussed as one of the weekly seminar topics perhaps at the beginning of the course and (2) if the teaching practicum should only be an alternative task for students who are still not familiar with the paradigm and have not yet developed enough confidence to teach EIL.

Having students who share similar views and are passionate in advocating the paradigm certainly indicates one's successful attempts in inspiring others to be EIL-aware or EIL-informed teachers. However, as strong proponents of the EIL paradigm, the teaching approach of some of my overly passionate POTEIC students tends to be slightly 'authoritative'. Comments from the undergraduate students that may challenge the EIL paradigm are often responded to in the following way: *'No, you can't say that!'*, *'you shouldn't be thinking in that way'*, *'you must know that we are different'*. These comments have prevented learning from taking place as the undergraduate students refuse to engage in classroom discussions, and resist offering further opinions when prompted to answer discussion questions. When discussing their seemingly confrontational feedback strategies and their undergraduate students' reactions at the debriefing session, these students do not seem to view these as problematic. In fact, some of the POTEIC students strongly believe that an EIL teacher should be assertive and strong, and must show an authoritative personality in order to 'make' students change their attitudes, and 'make' them aware that their views are 'wrong'. The resistance of the undergraduate students to engage in classroom discussions is interpreted by some of the POTEIC students as an acceptance of their 'mistakes' for offering 'wrong and inappropriate' views. What my POTEIC students may not have realized is that the teaching of EIL should aim toward 'inspiring' – as opposed to 'making' – students learn to understand and appreciate linguistic/cultural diversity (Marlina, 2014b). As an 'anti-normative' paradigm (Kubota, 2012), the EIL paradigm and the teaching of EIL challenge deeply ingrained assumptions, beliefs or preconceived views of language use, language teaching and language learning that are often regarded as 'normal'. Pedagogically, an EIL lesson that challenges those 'normative' ideologies cannot simply be a matter of persuading, 'making' or 'telling' students to think otherwise. All of this has, therefore, prompted me to consider incorporating a topic on classroom feedback strategies that motivate and inspire EIL students to develop an understanding and appreciation of linguistic and cultural diversity in the POTEIC course curriculum.

# Conclusion

In response to the global expansion of English and its outcomes of being an international language, EIL scholars have emphasized the need to professionally guide English language teachers to learn to be teachers of Englishes. Though principles of or frameworks for teaching EIL have been proposed by several key EIL scholars, they still remain at a theoretical level, leading Wee (2013) to question the extent to which the implementation of this principle or framework is realistic. To address this gap, this chapter has shown that, through the descriptions of the POTEIC curriculum, the implementation of the guiding principle or framework for teaching EIL seems to be more realistic than idealistic. In order to prepare teachers to teach EIL, a comprehensive knowledge of the outcomes of English being an international language and an awareness/knowledge of the pedagogical principles of teaching EIL are essential. However, this knowledge alone is still insufficient. Teachers also need to be given opportunities to experience and apply this theoretical knowledge through observing experienced EIL teachers, developing an EIL-oriented lesson and teaching an EIL-oriented class. Since teachers know more about their contexts, they need to be provided with a space to evaluate and review the extent to which the teaching of EIL can be applied to their teaching contexts. Although this course seems to have established a way to inspire teachers to teach EIL, there are still several challenges which are mainly related to students' unfamiliarity with the epistemological lens of the EIL paradigm, the pedagogical principles and its practical applications. Thus, more opportunities for students to discuss this lens and to practice teaching EIL are needed. It is hoped that this chapter has provided English language teacher educators with an example of a way to prepare future teachers to teach English as a pluricentric language.

# References

Alsagoff, L., McKay, S.L., Hu, G. and Renandya, W.A. (eds) (2012) *Principles and Practices for Teaching English as an International Language*. New York: Routledge.

Bayyurt, Y. and Sifakis, N. (2015) Foundation of an EIL-Aware Teacher Education. A paper presented at the 21st Annual Meeting of the International Association of World Englishes (IAWE), Istanbul, Turkey.

Brown, J.D. (2012) EIL curriculum development. In L. Alsagoff, S.L. McKay, G. Hu and W.A. Renandya (eds) *Principles and Practices for Teaching English as an International Language* (pp. 147–167). New York: Routledge.

Kubota, R. (2012) The politics of EIL: Toward border-crossing communication in and beyond English. In A. Matsuda (ed.) *Principles and Practices of Teaching English as an International Language* (pp. 55–69). Bristol: Multilingual Matters.

Marlina, R. (2014a) The pedagogy of English as an International Language: More reflections and dialogues. In R. Marlina and R. Giri (eds) *The Pedagogy of English as an International Language: Perspectives from Scholars, Teachers, and Students* (pp. 1–19). Switzerland: Springer International Publishing.

Marlina, R. (2014b) Teaching English as an International Language in Australia: Voices from the Australian university classroom. Unpublished PhD thesis, Monash University.

Matsuda, A. (2009) Desirable but not necessary? The place of World Englishes and English as an international language in English teacher preparation program in Japan. In F. Sharifian (ed.) *English as an International Language: Perspectives and Pedagogical Issues* (pp. 169–189). Bristol: Multilingual Matters.

Matsuda, A. (2012a) *Principles and Practices of Teaching English as an International Language*. Bristol: Multilingual Matters.

Matsuda, A. (2012b) Teaching materials in EIL. In L. Alsagoff, S.L. McKay, G. Hu and W.A. Renandya (eds) *Principles and Practices for Teaching English as an International Language* (pp. 168–185). New York: Routledge.

McKay, S.L. (2002) *Teaching English as an International Language*. Oxford: Oxford University Press.

McKay, S.L. (2012) Principles of teaching English as an international language. In L. Alsagoff, S.L. McKay, G.W. Hu and W.A. Renandya (eds) *Principles and Practices for Teaching English as an International Language* (pp. 28–46). New York: Routledge.

Pennycook, A. (2000) The social politics and the cultural politics of language classrooms. In J.K. Hall and W.G. Eggington (eds) *The Sociopolitics of English Language Teaching* (pp. 89–103). Clevedon: Multilingual Matters.

Sharifian, F. and Marlina, R. (2012) English as an International Language: An innovative program. In A. Matsuda (ed.) *Principles and Practices of Teaching English as an International Language* (pp. 140–153). Bristol: Multilingual Matters.

Smith, L.E. (1983) *Readings in English as an International Language*. Oxford: Pergamon Press.

Wee, L. (2013) Book review: L. Alsagoff, S.L. McKay, G. Hu and W.A. Renandya (eds) (2012) *Principles and Practices for Teaching English as an International Language*. *TESOL Quarterly* 47 (1), 202–204.

# Appendix

APG4020: Practices of Teaching Englishes for International Communication
Teaching Practicum Criteria Sheet

| Criteria | E | G | NI |
|---|---|---|---|
| Knowledge of the field (overall) | | | |
| Understanding of English as an International Language (EIL) | | | |
| Understanding of teaching EIL | | | |
| Lesson plan (overall) | | | |
| Structure of the lesson plan | | | |
| Clarity/relevance of the goals/objectives of the lesson | | | |
| Sequence of the lesson | | | |
| Teaching materials and pedagogical practices (overall) | | | |
| Engage students in understanding and learning about world Englishes | | | |
| Inspire students to learn to respect and appreciate diverse Englishes and cultures | | | |
| Engage students in learning to work across Englishes and cultures | | | |
| Encourage students to learn to take 'ownership' of their use of English | | | |
| Evidence of 'intercultural-grouping' | | | |
| Clarity of classroom instructions and feedback | | | |
| Comment: | | | |

E=excellent; G=good; NI=need improvement.

# 8 Preparing Teachers to Teach English as an International Language: Reflections from Northern Cyprus

## Ali Fuad Selvi

## Introduction

The unprecedented global demand, use and appropriation of English as an International Language (EIL) necessitate immediate and sustainable responses in various domains of the English language teaching (ELT) enterprise (Alsagoff *et al.*, 2012; Marlina & Giri, 2014; Matsuda, 2012; McKay, 2002; McKay & Bokhorst-Heng, 2008; Selvi & Yazan, 2013; Sharifian, 2009). Over the past couple of decades, the paradigm shift operationalized along the dimensions of the 'critically oriented scholarship', encompassing World Englishes (WE), English as a lingua franca (ELF), Global Englishes Language Teaching (GELT) and EIL perspectives, has served as a prime impetus for the re-examination and reconceptualization of the deeply inherent values and practices in ELT in light of the present-day sociolinguistic realities of English. More specifically, we have been witnessing a significant shift in our understanding of the 'native speaker' (NS) as a goal and benchmark for learning and a model of competence (Cook, 2002), teacher quality (Braine, 2010; Selvi, 2011, 2014) and the monolingual and monocultural approach to language teaching (Zacharias, 2003). Recently, these efforts called for moving beyond the conceptual dichotomies of uniform experience to construct learner, user and teacher identity as well as manifestations of linguistic, cultural, ethnic, national, professional and gender-oriented marginalization and privilege (Park, 2012; Rudolph *et al.*, 2015).

Scholarship drawing upon critically oriented frameworks has created a compelling case for the transformation of teacher education practices (Doğançay-Aktuna, 2006; Doğançay-Aktuna & Hardman, 2008; Matsuda, 2006). That is, scholars have called for teaching and teacher education practices conducive to the contextualized lived experiences of individuals negotiating identity within and across borders (e.g. Motha *et al.*, 2012), and affording teacher candidates the contextually sensitive knowledge, skills and dispositions to deconstruct and challenge dominant and often essentialized approaches to education, within societies and ELT located therein (Selvi & Rudolph, forthcoming). However, as Matsuda (2009: 171–172) rightfully acknowledges, 'in spite of the increasing attention given to the teaching of EIL,... we know much less when it comes to the question of how such ideas as World Englishes and EIL are dealt with in teacher preparation programs'.

In order to address the dearth of and the need for more sustainable teacher education practices within the growing EIL and second language teacher education (SLTE) literature, the present chapter offers a comprehensive account of an undergraduate-level course entitled 'Global English', which aims to examine the linguistic, social and political impact of the spread of English around the world with specific emphasis on the set of implications for English language teachers. In particular, it begins by providing an overview of the specifics of this course (e.g. context, participant profile, scope, objectives, tasks and assignments), and then identifies the tensions and challenges embedded in the local teaching–learning context vis-à-vis the principles of ELT and EIL. Finally, it underscores the critical roles and responsibilities to be shared by teacher educators and teacher learners throughout the course and beyond. Ultimately, it is hoped that this chapter (and the volume in which it appears) accentuates the vitality of the link between EIL pedagogy and EIL teacher education, and contributes to the emerging discussions of teacher preparation through constant negotiation with glocal needs, realities and challenges at multiple levels (Tudor, 2003).

In the midst of the plethora of perspectives and acronyms calling for a reconceptualization of the traditional professional and intellectual knowledge base of ELT (e.g. ELF, WE, GELT and EIL), it is an undoubtedly useful and stimulating practice for the ELT profession(als) to operationalize the terms underpinning their views and practices. Departing from this realization, I contend that the operational formulation of 'EIL' in this chapter is aligned with Matsuda's view (this volume: p. xiii), which conceptualized EIL as 'a function that English performs in international, multilingual contexts, to which each speaker brings a variety of English that they are most familiar with, along with their own cultural frames of reference, and employ various strategies to communicate effectively'. For this reason, it needs to be treated as a more encompassing view that subsumes other dynamic and critically oriented paradigms and approaches to English uses, users and functions today (e.g. ELF, GELT and WE). Following Matsuda's lead, the motivation behind using terms such as 'preparing teachers to teach EIL', 'EIL teacher education' and 'EIL-aware teacher education' throughout this chapter was not to treat them as mutually exclusive conceptualizations juxtaposed with similar notions but rather adopt them as a pragmatic and more-encompassing choice in a diversity of orientations.

# Description of the Course

In order to provide a comprehensive account of the course under scrutiny, it is essential to depict a larger picture delineating the program and the institution in which it is offered as well as a broad overview of the learners in this course. This will be followed by a discussion describing the specific parameters of the course comprising curricular components, instructional goals and intellectual dimensions.

## The big(ger) picture: Institution, program and the course

The Global English course is usually offered in fall semesters in 'departmental elective' status in the undergraduate program in teaching English as a foreign language (TEFL) at Middle East Technical University, Northern Cyprus Campus (METU NCC).[1] The program has an institutional aim of preparing preservice teachers to work as ELT professionals in the contexts of Turkey, Northern Cyprus and beyond. As stated in the mission statement showcased on the program's website, the program 'aims to instruct and train qualified teachers with a superior knowledge of English, critical teaching and thinking skills, and broad intellectual curiosity of languages and cultures' (METU NCC TEFL, 2015). A great majority of the TEFL program participants are of Turkish and Turkish Cypriot origin, representing a wide variety of socioeconomic backgrounds. Graduates of the TEFL program begin their professional careers as certified English teachers in Turkey and Northern Cyprus at various educational settings ranging from pre-K to post-secondary levels. They often assume positions as English teachers, curriculum designers and material developers at public and private institutions of primary, secondary and tertiary education, as well as in other professional areas (e.g. translation/interpretation, tourism, international business) requiring advanced English language skills.

Being one of the most popular elective courses of the TEFL program, the Global English course is listed as a 200-level course, and therefore mostly welcomes students in the second year of their studies. This is particularly significant since second-year students in this program take the Global English course at the beginning of a sequence of ELT (English Language Teaching Methodology I & II, Teaching Language Skills, Teaching English to Young Learners, Material Design and Adaptation, Language Testing and Assessment) and educational sciences (Introduction to Education, Educational Psychology, Classroom Management, Turkish Education System and School Management) courses. To be more specific, due to its strategic location within the TEFL program curriculum, the Global English course has the potential to serve as an intellectual lens that illuminates the process of construction of their professional knowledge base. Oftentimes, most of the elective courses offered by the TEFL program, including Global English, are also open to interested students from various programs across the campus. The popularity of the course among students within and beyond the TEFL program as well as its intriguing intellectual scope for users of English from diverse ethnolinguistic and cultural backgrounds makes it an interesting choice for students from other programs and disciplines as well. This situation gives (non-TEFL major) students 'the opportunity to engage directly with the humanities and reach across disciplinary boundaries in developing skills of critical intellectual engagement' and directly supports the overall mission of the institution in helping students develop 'humane and moral values and an open-mindedness for contributing to a global community' (METU NCC TEFL, 2015).

## Curricular components, instructional goals and intellectual dimensions

This part of the chapter adopts a more focused approach, and delineates a comprehensive account of the Global English course with specific emphases on its curricular components, instructional goals and intellectual dimensions. To begin with, the course aims to familiarize students with the global spread of EIL, emerging uses, users and contexts of English around the world and the implications of these ideas for English language teaching and learning. The course places specific emphasis on the set of implications for English teachers and learners. More specifically, participants successfully completing this course will be able to:

- define the global language (and what makes English language a global language);
- use key sociolinguistic concepts and terms related to language study;
- identify various models of WE and the roles played by different varieties of English;
- discuss the future of English as an international language;
- perhaps most importantly, make explicit connections to contextually sensitive pedagogy to serve English language learners in their future teaching contexts.

In order to meet these instructional goals and objectives, the course employs a wide variety of instructional materials. These include (1) textbooks (Jenkins, 2014; Kirkpatrick, 2007); (2) reference books (Block & Cameron, 2002; Crystal, 2003; Graddol, 1997, 2006); (3) EIL pedagogy-oriented books (Alsagoff et al., 2012; Marlina & Giri, 2014; Matsuda, 2012; McKay, 2002; McKay & Bokhorst-Heng, 2008; Selvi & Yazan, 2013; Sharifian, 2009);

(4) online resources such as websites/webpages like the Universal Declaration of Human Rights, and archives like The Speech Accent Archive, IDEA (International Dialects of English Archive); and (5) other resources in the form of articles from scholarly journals, book chapters, news pieces, commentaries and other relevant materials.

Building upon constructivist approaches to learning and teaching, the course places considerable emphasis on attendance and participation as a manifestation of mutual responsibility toward the members of the learning community. Therefore, students enrolled in this course are reminded that regular attendance and participation in in- and out-of-class (online) discussions are essential in order to benefit from the instructional and interactional nature of this course. They earn a grade for participation and attendance that takes into account the quality and substance of their contribution to the collaborative learning of the class community. In light of the controversial scope and nature of the course content, they are expected to listen and respond to their classmates, always be open to different perspectives, provide thoughtful contributions to class discussions and most importantly be respectful to other members of the learning community. In order to strengthen and evaluate students' understanding of the course content, the course employs a range of formal (e.g. midterm and final examinations, quizzes, projects, dictionary entries, essays, teaching tips/lesson plans) and informal (e.g. observations, checklists and discussions) forms of assessment. A list including the various course assignments used in this course together with their descriptions and categories in light of the framework by Bayyurt and Sifakis (2015) is showcased in Appendix A.

## Uniqueness of the Course

The Global English course differs significantly from its older and more traditional counterparts that do not incorporate ideas from the critically oriented scholarship (e.g. EIL, ELF and WE). More specifically, it introduces the students to varieties of English and the implications of these varieties for English language teaching and learning in specific contexts. The course also examines the linguistic, social and political reasons and consequences of the spread of English around the world – where, when, why and how new forms of English have emerged. It also places specific emphasis on the set of implications for English teachers and learners. From the standpoint of the principles of EIL pedagogy, this course:

- presents a comprehensive account of diverse uses, users and functions of English;
- places emphasis on ELF, WE and EIL paradigms;
- challenges the NS-oriented worldview in ELT;
- problematizes the ownership of English;

- aims to broaden the traditional basis of culture;
- promotes mutual intelligibility/comprehensibility as the defining goal in interaction;
- connects teacher education practices to the EIL principles;
- redefines teacher skills and competencies through the EIL lens.

In their recent work, Bayyurt and Sifakis (2015) delineate three specific phases in critically oriented (ELF/EIL/WE-aware) teacher education programs and courses. These are (1) *theory* – which involves being 'informed' about and 'aware' of the information pertinent to EIL principles and pedagogy and making sense of these notions for their own context; (2) *application* – which entails developing lesson plans situated on the principles of ELF/EIL/WE for the participants' local context so that their learners become aware of the parameters of and issues related to the unique status of EIL; and (3) *evaluation* – which encompasses 'self' and 'peer' evaluation with the overarching aim of critical reflection through forum discussions on various aspects of the lesson being taught or watched. Built upon the principles of transformative learning theory (Mezirow, 1991; Sifakis, 2007), this framework of ELF/EIL teacher education and training utilizes teacher education activity to (a) offer opportunities for teacher candidates to realize, embrace and challenge the widely held and deeply inherent NS-dominated values in ELT; (b) help them be informed about ELF/EIL and what it represents for the diverse uses, users and contexts of the English language; and (c) transform teacher candidates into ELF/EIL 'pedagogues', who are charged with spearheading ELF/EIL-related activities in their local teaching contexts and encouraging their learners to become ELF/EIL users. Thus, the Global English course makes a deliberate attempt to include a wide variety of pedagogical tasks, assignments, activities and experiences that are aligned with the 'theory', 'application' and 'evaluation' levels of this framework (see Appendix A). In other words, the uniqueness of the course lies in its innovative approach of combining the theoretical bases of SLTE with the practical implications of EIL pedagogy at multiple levels.

## Challenges and Limitations

While EIL pedagogy and EIL-informed teacher education practices offer many potential tangible benefits for the present and future of ELT, the critical question is whether these practices (units, courses or programs) would offer a sustainable alternative to the existing structures and practices. Obviously, there have been a number of challenges and key limitations to the implementation process of the Global English course.

First of all, the perennial challenge of situating the course and framing the EIL-aware/informed knowledge base within the larger curriculum of TEFL programs has always been there and will never go away. In other words, while some programs may adopt EIL principles as a common thread running through the entire curriculum and (in)forming the knowledge base construction of teacher candidates in the program, others may choose to follow an 'infusion' approach and thus confine EIL principles (and related experiences) to one course or even one unit within a course. Although there are potential pros and cons to each approach and having at least some discussion of the EIL principles is regarded as more desirable than not having any discussion of the critically oriented scholarship, the way EIL principles are framed, dealt with and utilized within teacher education programs always remains a pedagogically sensitive matter for teacher educators. In its current stance within the overall curriculum, the Global English course may inadvertently give the false impression that EIL principles and issues are not needed in other courses since anything and everything related to EIL is covered in this course. However, it is more desirable to have both stand-alone courses dedicated to the present-day sociolinguistic realities of EIL and to support the infusion of EIL-informed ideas, experiences and approaches throughout the teacher education curriculum, and even beyond.

Situating the Global English course and framing the EIL-aware knowledge base within the larger curriculum of the TEFL program is also a delicate task from the perspective of educators who are primarily charged with the implementation of the teacher education program. More specifically, the epistemological and ontological commitments surrounding the EIL course content and the related pedagogical idea(l)s may stand out as ideological fault lines among the faculty members. In other words, as primary stakeholders responsible for the organization, implementation and assessment of any given teacher education program, teacher educators may exhibit varying degrees and forms of interest in, investment with and commitment to EIL principles and EIL-aware teacher education. To be more specific, while some teacher educators recognize this as a central driving force and guiding framework that (in)forms their practices, others may only be conceptually aligned with these principles and not necessarily take the initiative to (in)form their work through the lens of EIL principles. In such cases, teacher learners' engagement with EIL principles is left at the level of abstraction. That is, they learn 'about' it without really establishing strong, sustainable and praxis-driven ties to their practice. Finally, on the other end of the spectrum is the complete absence of EIL principles from the picture of teacher education practices and experiences. This situation may be attributed to three different scenarios: (1) teacher educators may either not be informed about EIL principles (i.e. unawareness), (2) they may be in epistemological and conceptual disagreement with EIL principles (i.e. disagreement, rejection and resistance) and (3) they may acknowledge EIL principles but see no value in them within the scope of teacher education (i.e. reluctance).

This relative position along the EIL teacher education continuum by colleagues comprising the same teacher education program may manifest itself in volatile, loosely connected and sometimes even contradictory practices and experiences. While hearing comments of rejection, resistance and reluctance regarding the EIL principles is certainly discouraging given that teacher education is a collaborative activity, it actually should urge EIL-minded teacher educators to think about two important issues: First, construing the internal dynamics of the program (e.g. trying to understand the sources of rejection, resistance and reluctance) and forging practical and pragmatic pathways in the given situation to ensure a continued professional growth (e.g. maintaining a reliable communication channel with teacher candidates and infusing EIL principles into the other courses in the teacher education program); and second, seeking opportunities for dialogue to reach out to their colleagues in the program with the ultimate aim of understanding, uncovering and rectifying any misconceptions they might have regarding the EIL issues.

Another major challenge stems from one of the strengths of the course – the 'elective' status. The Global English course is offered in 'departmental elective' status for the TEFL program participants. However, it is also open to students from across the METU NCC community in 'non-departmental elective' status. Therefore, it is quite common to have a group of TEFL students with some additions of students from other disciplines. It is both a blessing and a curse to have a group of students from diverse ethnolinguistic, racial and academic backgrounds. While it certainly pushes the intellectual scope and rigor of the course, it brings a new set of challenges in terms of classroom dynamics, course aims, expectations and assignments. The overall roles and responsibilities of the teacher educator increase exponentially, and encompass maintaining different 'voices' and 'perspectives' in the classroom, redefining more individualized course expectations from the various groups of students (e.g. TEFL vs. non-TEFL), accommodating diversity in the course assignment options and providing a much more individualized instruction in and beyond the classroom.

Finally, another significant challenge is due to the specific positioning of the course within the TEFL program. More specifically, since a considerable number of ELT methodology courses (e.g. ELT Methodology I and II, Teaching Language Skills I and II, Teaching English to Young Learners) are spread over the second and third years of the curriculum, program participants, who are mostly at the beginning of their second year, do not bring an extensive disciplinary knowledge which may be remolded with the EIL pedagogy and principles. Through the lens of Bayyurt and Sifakis (2015), this situation means not being able to address all three phases and thus inescapably limiting the course content largely to the 'theory' phase with relatively little or no emphasis on 'application' and 'evaluation'.

Collectively, the points detailed in this section may seem to be impediments or points of challenge to the implementation of the Global

English course. While some of these issues may be context specific (e.g. the positioning of the course in the curriculum), others (e.g. the diversity of course participants; the rejection, resistance and reluctance of other faculty members; the infusion model to integrate EIL principles into the teacher education curriculum) may be found in various programs where a similar course is offered. Teacher educators teaching EIL courses (or wishing to integrate EIL courses into their local teacher education programs) may be informed about these potential issues and devise (in)formal, systematic, creative and collaborative solutions to ensure the sustainable integration of EIL issues into the knowledge base of teacher candidates in their program.

## Conclusion

The ever-diversifying global sociolinguistic landscape of the uses, users and contexts of EIL, and the necessity to better meet the increasingly complex needs of EIL users stand out as pressing priorities in the agenda of ELT, as a profession, as an activity and as a field of scholarly inquiry. These glocal winds of change also permeate into the area of teacher education, and more specifically SLTE. Although traditional university-based teacher education programs tend to mostly be confined to the walls of the classroom, they both inform and are informed by the broader sociocultural, political and economic contexts in which they occur and for which they prepare the teacher workforce. Therefore, the idea of infusing EIL principles into teacher education practices is more relevant than ever. In order to shed some light on this matter, the current chapter provided a description of an undergraduate elective course on Global English in a teacher education program. More specifically, it described the curricular parameters, pedagogical dimensions and instructional challenges associated with the course, as situated in the broader programmatic and institutional context.

In closing, I would like to leave the readers with the notion of 'shared accountability' for the future of preparing teachers to teach EIL. That is, the transformation of EIL principles into teaching and teacher education practices sensitive to the dynamics of the local teaching context as well as to teachers' socio-historically situated negotiations of identities and diverse lived experiences and potential future professional trajectories, contexts and learners necessitate a distinct set of roles and responsibilities for the stakeholders of the ELT activity (e.g. research, teacher education programs, curricula, teacher educators and teacher candidates). Therefore, more research is needed to forge new intellectual pathways to acknowledge and expand the diverse needs of EIL users today, and generate more concerted efforts to carefully mediate the professional growth of the teachers within the framework of EIL principles.

## Note

(1)  Established as a major higher education project in 2005, Middle East Technical University, Northern Cyprus Campus is a branch campus of the main campus located in Ankara, Turkey. The campus is physically situated in Güzelyurt (Morphou) region of Cyprus, a bitterly divided island in the eastern Mediterranean with a rich and turbulent past, a dynamic present and an imagined more peaceful future.

## References

Alsagoff, L., McKay, S.L., Hu, G. and Renandya, W.A. (2012) *Principles and Practices for Teaching English as an International Language*. London: Routledge.

Bayyurt, Y. and Sifakis, N. (2015) Developing an ELF-Aware Pedagogy: Insights from a Self-Education Programme. In P. Vettorel (ed.) *New Frontiers in Teaching and Learning English* (pp. 55–76). Newcastle upon Tyne: Cambridge Scholars Publishing.

Block, D. and Cameron, D. (2002) *Globalization and Language Teaching*. London: Routledge.

Braine, G. (2010) *Nonnative Speaker English Teachers: Research, Pedagogy and Professional Growth*. New York: Routledge.

Cook, V.J. (2002) *Portraits of the L2 User*. Clevedon: Multilingual Matters.

Crystal. D. (2003) *The Cambridge Encyclopedia of the English language* (2nd edn). Cambridge: Cambridge University Press.

Doğançay-Aktuna, S. (2006) Expanding the socio-cultural knowledge base of TESOL teacher education. *Language, Culture and Curriculum* 19 (3), 278–295.

Doğançay-Aktuna, S. and Hardman, J. (2008) *Global English Teaching and Teacher Education: Praxis and Possibility*. Alexandria, VA: TESOL Publications.

Graddol, D. (1997) *The Future of English*. London: British Council.

Graddol, D. (2006) *English Next*. London: British Council.

Jenkins, J. (2014) *Global Englishes: A Resource Book for Students* (3rd edn). London: Routledge.

Kirkpatrick, A. (2007) *World Englishes: Implications for International Communication and English Language Teaching*. Cambridge: Cambridge University Press.

Marlina, R. and Giri, R. (2014) *The Pedagogy of English as an International Language: Perspectives from Scholars, Teachers, and Students*. Dordrecht: Springer.

Matsuda, A. (2006) Negotiating ELT assumptions in EIL classrooms. In J. Edge (ed.) *(Re-) locating TESOL in an Age of Empire* (pp. 158–170). Basingstoke: Palgrave-MacMillan.

Matsuda, A. (2009) Desirable but not necessary? The place of World Englishes and English as an international language in English teacher preparation programs in Japan. In F. Sharifian (ed.) *English as an International Language: Perspectives and Pedagogical Issues* (pp. 169–189). Bristol: Multilingual Matters.

Matsuda, A. (ed.) (2012) *Principles and Practices of Teaching English as an International Language*. Bristol: Multilingual Matters.

McKay, S.L. (2002) *Teaching English as an International Language*. Oxford: Oxford University Press.

McKay, S.L. and Bokhorst-Heng, W.D. (2008) *International English in its Sociolinguistic Contexts: Towards a Socially Sensitive EIL Pedagogy*. New York: Routledge.

Mezirow, J. (1991) *Transformative Dimensions of Adult Learning*. San Francisco, CA: Jossey-Bass.

Middle East Technical University Northern Cyprus Campus, Teaching English as a Foreign Language Program (METU NCC TEFL) (2015) Mission. See http://efl.ncc.metu.edu.tr/mission/ (accessed 1 July 2015).

Motha, S., Jain, R. and Tecle, T. (2012) Translinguistic identity-as-pedagogy: Implications for language teacher education. *International Journal of Innovation in English Language Teaching* 1 (1), 13–27.

Park, G. (2012) 'I am never afraid of being recognized as an NNES': One teacher's journey in claiming and embracing her nonnative-speaker identity. *TESOL Quarterly* 46 (1), 127–151.

Rudolph, N., Selvi, A.F. and Yazan, B. (2015) Constructing and confronting native speakerism within and beyond the NNEST movement. *Critical Inquiry in Language Studies* 12 (1), 27–50.

Selvi, A.F. (2011) The non-native speaker teacher. *ELT Journal* 65 (2), 187–189.

Selvi, A.F. (2014) Myths and misconceptions about the non-native English speakers in TESOL (NNEST) Movement. *TESOL Journal* 5 (3), 573–611. See http://dx.doi.org/10.1002/tesj.158 (accessed 23 August 2016).

Selvi, A.F. and Yazan, B. (2013) *Teaching English as an International Language*. Alexandria, VA: TESOL Press.

Selvi, A.F. and Rudolph, N. (forthcoming) Teachers and the negotiation of identity: Implications and challenges for second language teacher education. In J. de Dios Martínez Agudo (ed.) *Native and Non-native Teachers in English Language Teaching*.

Sharifian, F. (2009) *English as an International Language: Perspectives and Pedagogical Issues*. Bristol: Multilingual Matters.

Sifakis, N.C. (2007) The education of the teachers of English as a lingua franca: A transformative perspective. *International Journal of Applied Linguistics* 17 (3), 355–375.

Tudor, I. (2003) Learning to live with complexity: Towards an ecological perspective on language teaching. *System* 31 (1), 1–12.

Zacharias, N.T. (2003) A survey of tertiary teachers' beliefs about English language teaching in Indonesia with regard to the role of English as a global language. MA thesis, Assumption University of Thailand.

# Appendix A

Course assignments, descriptions and categories

| Course assignment pool | Assignment descriptions | Category* |
|---|---|---|
| The Online Dictionary of Global English | This dictionary will serve as a go-to source for students, teachers and researchers who are interested in various aspects of the Global English phenomenon. The online dictionary project consists of two major sections:<br><br>(1) Concept Keywords – these are keywords which provide interested readers with some basic, accessible and brief information regarding the theoretical and practical issues on various concepts in Global English. A typical concept keyword entry includes a discussion which frames the issue and investigates the topic under examination with succinct definitions and explanations, followed by a list of some important quotations about the topic. The authors are also expected to include a list of references used in their entries, other valuable readings on the issue and online resources (e.g. webpages, news articles and YouTube videos) that they would recommend to someone who wants to learn more about this topic. Some of these keywords include code-mixing, English on the internet, Indian English, intelligibility, language death, linguistic imperialism and nonnative speaker.<br><br>(2) Who's Who in Global English? – this section aims to introduce key scholars who work in the area of Global English. A typical scholar entry includes brief biographical information about the scholar (e.g. name, current affiliation, email address/website) followed by a brief biography and scholarship (list of books, articles and other works by this person, specifically on Global English) and any online resources (e.g. webpages and YouTube videos) that they would recommend to someone who wants to learn more about this topic. Some of these scholars include but are not limited to Aya Matsuda, Ahmar Mahboob, Braj Kachru, David Crystal, Sandra Lee McKay and Suresh Canagarajah. Students are expected to contribute to this project by adding at least three concept keyword entries and one scholar entry. | Theory |

| Essay on Global English | This is an interdisciplinary essay that examines a particular topic related to English as a global language in more depth than we have addressed in class. Some of the topics for the essay may include nonnative English-speaking teachers, the ownership of English and its implications for users and learners/teachers of English, the medium of instruction debate in the local context, linguistic landscaping, the global spread of English and language death. A typical essay includes a clear discussion of the problem/phenomenon, a literature review and the discussion of implications for the future of English and English language teaching. | Theory |
|---|---|---|
| Online discussions (Learning Management System of Facebook group page) | Throughout the semester, students in this course are invited to share their reflections on weekly topics and guiding questions on the class discussion board/Facebook page and have the opportunity to engage in meaningful conversation with other members of the learning community. These discussions are informal but intelligent, critical and reflective responses to weekly readings, class discussions and activities. Primarily, they are intended to help the members of our learning community to demonstrate their synthesis of the course content and to encourage them to think about their own learning processes. They are always encouraged to use this as an opportunity to think about how to apply this in their teaching contexts. Students can respond to guiding questions, elaborate on areas of interest, agreement/disagreement with readings or discussion leader, ask extension questions, analyze readings/issues from multiple perspectives, make connections between course readings/topics and their own experience, continue an unfinished discussion or respond to interesting issues that came up during our in-class discussions. | Theory |

| Adapting, evaluating and designing instructional materials | Since instructional materials constitute an integral part of English language teaching practices, teachers spend a considerable amount of time finding, selecting, evaluating, adapting and designing instructional materials on a daily basis in order to support their teaching and their students' learning. For this reason, this assignment gives course participants an opportunity to examine factors and guidelines that they need to take into account when evaluating the readily available materials and designing effective instructional materials. The assignment consists of two major sections:<br><br>(1) Evaluating a textbook through EIL lens: The course participants choose one of the commercially available textbooks used in their local teaching settings. They evaluate the entire book by using a checklist informed by various principles of EIL pedagogy. The final report should contain the checklist developed for this assignment as well as a comprehensive analysis, comments and conclusions about the book. Students are also recommended to point out some directions for possible adaptations for classroom use. If possible, a brief oral presentation of the report is shared in a large group discussion.<br><br>(2) Adapting and developing instructional materials through EIL lens: The course participants choose one section (unit, lesson or activity) from a commercially available textbook used in their local teaching settings. They are asked to adapt this section using the EIL principles to better suit the characteristics of their potential future students. They design and/or create additional instructional materials to complement the existing section and develop a lesson plan utilizing the materials they created. In their large-group oral presentation, they discuss (or demonstrate) the new activity and present their rationale for the adaptation with some concrete reference to the principles of EIL pedagogy. | Application and evaluation |

| | | |
|---|---|---|
| EIL lesson plan | This assignment aims to promote students' understanding of the critical importance of the EIL pedagogy and gives them a chance to establish a connection between theoretical discussions and pedagogical practices. The assignment consists of two major portions: (1) a 50-minute lesson plan that integrates, promotes and raises awareness with respect to intercultural communication; and (2) a one-page description of the connection between the lesson taught and the EIL pedagogy. In this project, students are free to create a hypothetical (e.g. learner characteristics [e.g. age, gender, or proficiency levels], institutional setting, level, grade) or use an actual teaching context (e.g. local intensive English program). | Application and evaluation |
| Teaching tip | Teaching tip presentation will give course participants an opportunity to employ the specific techniques introduced, get used to classroom management procedures and gain the teaching experience necessary for their actual teaching practices. For this assignment, they are expected to create a lesson plan for 50 minutes and teach a portion of the lesson (max. 10 minutes) to our class participants who will act as their hypothetical 'students'. In addition, presenters are required to submit a written lesson plan on the day of their presentation and a one-page reflection on the entire process. The brief reflection may include the course participants' responses to such questions as 'How did it go?', 'What went (not so) well?' and 'If you had the opportunity to teach this lesson again, would you do anything differently? What? Why?' among others. | Application and evaluation |

*Based on the three-layered (theory–application–evaluation) framework by Bayyurt and Sifakis (2015).

# Part 4

# EIL-informed Courses on Another ELT Topic

# 9 Preparing Preservice Teachers with EIL/WE-oriented Materials Development

## Thuy Ngoc Dinh

## Introduction

This chapter reports on the Materials Development course at a university of education in Vietnam. It is one of the electives within the four-year teaching English to speakers of other languages (TESOL) program, offering a bachelor's (BA) TESOL degree that educates students to become teachers of English in different educational sectors, particularly in high school. The course was designed by the author, in consultation with other staff members, approved by the department and implemented for the first time in the first semester of 2014 for third-year students.

The prescribed reading for the course is a combination of theoretical discussions and research from English language teaching (ELT) textbooks, English as an International Language (EIL)/World Englishes (WE) and relevant disciplines. The course addresses the selection, revision, development and use of materials in light of the current function of EIL.

The university is among many universities in Vietnam that offers the language teacher education program. Upon graduation, students can use their degrees to enter the ELT profession. This TESOL program is divided into five streams of education: language skills, linguistics, ELT, literature/culture and practicum. Together with these streams, students also learn other courses with a focus on Vietnamese Studies, such as Vietnamese cultural studies, politics and philosophy. Table 9.1 provides a snapshot of the TESOL courses in the program.

During the four-year TESOL program, the students spend the first two years building their fundamental skills and knowledge of English, and spend the third and fourth years on ELT-specific issues. For graduation, students can choose to either take a research project or complete three core courses: computer-assisted language learning, assessment in ELT and learners' autonomy. Upon completion, students are expected to have mastered English language study skills and teaching skills, using different methodologies and multiple learning resources.

**Table 9.1** A snapshot of the TESOL program curriculum at the university in 2014

| Streams | Courses | Core | Elective | Credits | Total periods (1 period=45 min) |
|---|---|---|---|---|---|
| | | Status | | | |
| Language skills (20 core and 3 elective courses) | Listening 1, 2, 3, 4 | × | | 2 each | 30 each |
| | Listening 5, 6 | | × | 2 each | 30 each |
| | Reading 1, 2, 3, 4, 5 | × | | 2 each | 30 each |
| | Reading 6 | | × | 2 | 30 |
| | Writing 1, 2, 3, 4 | × | | 2 each | 30 each |
| | Research writing | × | | 2 | 30 |
| | Speaking 1, 2, 3, 4, 5 | × | | 2 each | 30 each |
| | Grammar | × | | 2 | 30 |
| Linguistics (5 core and 2 elective units) | Phonology | × | | 2 | 30 |
| | Morphology | × | | 2 | 30 |
| | Syntax | × | | 2 | 30 |
| | Semantics | × | | 2 | 30 |
| | Discourse analysis | × | | 2 | 30 |
| | Sociolinguistics | | × | 2 | 30 |
| | Contrastive linguistics | | × | 2 | 30 |
| Language teaching (4 core and 2 elective units) | ELT Methodology 1 | × | | 2 | 30 |
| | ELT Methodology 2 | × | | 4 | 60 |
| | ELT Methodology 3 | × | | 4 | 60 |
| | Study skills | × | | 2 | 30 |
| | Information Communication Technology in ELT | | × | 2 | 30 |
| | Materials development | | × | 3 | 45 |
| Literatures and cultures (3 core and 4 elective units) | English Literature 1 | × | | 2 | 30 |
| | English Literature 2 | | × | 2 | 30 |
| | American Literature 1 | × | | 2 | 30 |
| | American Literature 2 | | × | 2 | 30 |
| | American Studies | | × | 2 | 30 |
| | History of English Literature | | × | 2 | 30 |
| | Intercultural communication | × | | 2 | 30 |
| Practicum (2 core units) | Professional development | × | | 2 | 30 |
| | Teaching practicum | × | | 6 | 90 |

# A Need for an EIL/WE-Oriented Materials Development Course

After a thorough examination of the institutional and national contexts and the National Foreign Language Project 2020 in Vietnam, I was motivated, as an EIL/WE-informed researcher, to introduce EIL/WE knowledge and principles into the Materials Development course.

This was the first time that a course on materials was included at that university; hitherto, discussions about materials were included in Methodology. The university staff members agreed that in a setting where English is spoken as a foreign language, considerable time should be spent on investigating teaching materials as they play the role of a guide map or a source of input for classroom teachers. Hence, there was a real need for an independent course to discuss in depth the issues raised by teaching materials.

A close look at the national context further reinforces the need to raise students' awareness of the influence of the sociolinguistic reality of English on the development and implementation of ELT materials. Two important advents are worth mentioning. First, the increasing contact between Vietnamese speakers of English and WE speakers is observed across domains, as can be seen in the increasing number of international tourists to Vietnam (Vietnam Tourism, 2015), economic joint ventures, Vietnamese overseas students in countries other than the USA and England, exported workers globally (Phan, 2009) and joint international training for Vietnamese teachers (Nguyen, 2012). For instance, the latest statistics show that tourists from Finland, Korea, New Zealand, Italy and Singapore were ranked as the top in the 10 countries with the most number of tourists to Vietnam in early 2015 (Vietnam Tourism, 2015). This reality means that some Vietnamese people have the opportunity to communicate in English with speakers from different cultural backgrounds from non-Inner Circle countries, both within and outside the country and on a frequent basis.

The National Foreign Language Project 2020, implemented in Vietnam since 2008, acknowledges the impact of globalization on the need of and the goal for studying foreign languages, among which English is the major one. As Nguyen Ngoc Hung (2008, 2012), the executive manager of the project stated, by 2020 the majority of Vietnamese learners of English are expected to be able to communicate competently with other speakers of English. Even though the project does not explicitly name intercultural communication (IC) as one of the main objectives, such an expectation stated in the project is understood as the ability to communicate across cultures using English as a link language. The role of English in Vietnam today is defined as 'the key to regional and international participation' (Le, 2000). This further signifies the need to be aware of the complex status of English with all its linguistic and cultural variations both on the regional and global scale. An understanding of WE and IC is necessary to open the door to integration.

The nature of the times places more challenging responsibilities on teachers of English. In Vietnam, despite the awareness and understanding of EIL among academics such as Phan (2008) and Ton and Pham (2010), such knowledge remains theoretical and without application, especially in teacher education. This is not only the case in Vietnam but elsewhere. Matsuda (2012a: 6) acknowledges this gap, stating that 'much of the critical examination of ELT vis-à-vis the use of English as an international language remains at the abstract level'.

I took the initiative to respond to this gap. In setting up the course, I drew on the theoretical principles of EIL which, as clarified by numerous EIL scholars such as Matsuda (2012a), Marlina (2014b), McKay (2002), Sharifian (2009, 2013) and Smith (1976), highlight these key aspects:

- English is attached to multiple cultures including various local cultures and is used to express various cultural conceptualizations.
- English is used as a means for international/intercultural communication.
- English is owned by those who speak it, not just by those from Inner Circle countries.
- EIL is represented by different varieties including local varieties.

These points should inform educators of the dire need to revisit their teaching practices and materials. As can be seen, EIL proposes that since the goal of learning English is steering away from native speaker competence, the ELT curriculum should now center on the exposure to, awareness of and sensitivity to diversity in terms of forms, functions, uses and users of English together with communication strategies for negotiating linguistic and cultural differences (Matsuda, Introduction chapter). For those involved in designing the Materials Development course in a teacher education program, they provoke the re-examination of the learning English objectives set in the materials for learning English and material content. Indeed, the selection, evaluation, revision and operationalization of materials in light of EIL/WE need to be highlighted in the TESOL program.

## Overview of the EIL/WE-Oriented Material Course

The course meets for three periods (1 hour 45 minutes) per week for 15 weeks, and covers four sections: the selection and evaluation of teaching materials, the revision of teaching materials, the design of teaching materials and the use of teaching materials. The course is structured as shown in Table 9.2.

**Table 9.2** A snapshot of the Materials Development course syllabus

| Week | Sections | Content | Readings | Assessment |
|------|----------|---------|----------|------------|
| 1 | | Introduction<br>– Introduction to the course<br>– Introduction to ELT materials | Tomlinson (2013) | |
| 2 | Material selection and evaluation | Issues in the evaluation of materials (lecture) | McKay (2002)<br>McKay (2003)<br>Matsuda (2002)<br>Bao (2008)<br>Yuen et al. (2011)<br>McKay (2012)<br>Kiss and Weninger (2013) | |
| 3 | | Textbook selection and evaluation activities | | |
| 4 | | Textbook selection and evaluation activities | | |
| 5 | | Materials evaluation showcase | | Assessment 1: 30% |
| 6 | Material revision | Issues in the revision of teaching materials (lecture and activities) | McConachy (2009)<br>McGrath (2013)<br>Sharifian (2013) | |
| 7 | | Reading and writing task revision activities | | |
| 8 | | Speaking and listening task revision activities | | |
| 9 | Material design | Supplementary teaching materials (lecture and activities) | McGrath (2013)<br>Hino (2010)<br>Matsuda and Friedrich (2011) | |
| 10 | | The design of teaching materials (lecture and activities) | | |
| 11 | | Lesson design showcase | | Assessment 2: 30% |
| 12 | Use of materials | TEIL/TWE issues (lecture and activities) | Hino (2001)<br>Matsuda (2012a) | |
| 13 | | Teaching showcase | | Assessment 3: 40% |
| 14 | | Teaching showcase | | |
| 15 | | Teaching showcase | | |

## The EIL-ness of the course

### Section 1: Material selection and evaluation

In this first section, students are introduced to the sociolinguistic changes affecting English, the implications these have for ELT materials selection/evaluation and current research on the representations of cultures in different sets of textbooks. The aim of the section is to focus the students' attention on the importance of exposing learners to diversity in terms of how English is used and the cultures represented by various Englishes. The advantages of using diverse materials over promoting one variety of English and a group of native English speakers are addressed. Thus, students become aware of the monocentric bias in textbooks, a bias which has been critiqued as idealizing (Basabe, 2006), a form of cultural imperialism (Mineshima, 2008), a misrepresentation (Gray, 2002) and misleading (Arikan, 2005). In addition, this section aims to raise students' awareness of IC. The presence of IC in textbooks, as established by Marlina and Giri (2013), can be examined by raising the question of whether or not conversations among different speakers of English are captured in coursebooks and the way in which they communicate with each other.

Parallel to the introduction of theory and in-class discussions, class time is spent evaluating the English textbooks currently used in the local context. Two categories of English textbooks are focused upon in this course: locally developed English textbooks (*English 10, 11* and *12*) for high school students, and internationally marketed English textbooks used at some high schools, language centers and universities such as *New Headway, New English File* and *New Interchange*. The choice of these textbooks is based on the fact that students will not only do their practicum in the following semesters but will later become English teachers at high schools and language centers where these books are presently in wide use.

Drawing on Crystal (1999), McKay (2012), Marlina (2011, 2014a), Marlina and Ahn (2011), Marlina and Giri (2009) and Matsuda (2012b), I introduce the EIL-based curriculum evaluation framework so that students have some guidelines for their further investigation of the textbooks. The following questions are posed:

LANGUAGE:

- Does the textbook under consideration consider language variation and change?
- Does it respect and promote multilingualism? ('Green Linguistics', see more in Crystal, 1999, 2008; Pupavac, 2012)
- Which variety of English is the textbook based on? Is it the variety that the students should learn?

- Does the textbook provide adequate exposure to or raise awareness of the diversity of English?
- Does it furnish students with the ability to negotiate across differences?

USERS:

- Does the textbook represent a variety of speakers?
- Does it exemplify first language (L1)–second language (L2) interactions?
- Does it exemplify L2–L2 interactions?
- How are the speakers (re)presented?

CULTURES:

- Whose cultures are represented in the textbook?
- Does the textbook raise students' intercultural awareness?
- How are cultures represented? (information/fact-oriented or communication-oriented manner)
- Does the textbook provide opportunities for students to reflect on and to talk about 'their' own cultures?
- Does the textbook create opportunities for students to explore different scenarios and different cultural roles?
- How are cultures from other countries represented? (contesting vs perpetuating stereotypes)

In order to answer these questions, students are reminded to adopt the stance of semiotic analysis, which places emphasis on the investigation of materials across texts, tasks and visuals (Kiss & Weninger, 2013; Weninger & Kiss, 2013). If the analysis and evaluation of the materials is merely based on a single channel of information such as texts or visuals in isolation, the findings will be narrow (Dinh, 2014), since they disregard the negotiation process that is required to fully benefit from the tasks (Kiss & Weninger, 2013).

After theories and activities in class, students work in groups on a material evaluation project. They employ the framework to examine a textbook of their choice and later present their findings in front of class. The focus of this assessment task is on the quality of analysis, the justification for their evaluation with specific examples and suggestions for changes offered by the students.

### Section 2: Material revision

The previous section helps students become aware of issues in the present ELT materials used in Vietnam. These include the overrepresentation of either the local Vietnamese culture or American/British cultures and the narrow language-based tasks that do not foster self-reflection or the skills needed for IC. As a result, this second section aims to stimulate discussion on how to revise the materials, while introducing students to several relevant frameworks and notions such as those developed by McConachy (2009) and Sharifian (2013).

In McConachy's work, the emphasis is placed on sociocultural awareness. Based on Hymes' (1974) framework, McConachy raises different types of questions that encourage learners to engage in linguistic exploration and cultural reflexivity. In particular, attention is placed on the function of language, negotiation across cultures, cross-cultural comparison and reflection on students' own culture. Those questions include:

- Language-based questions.
- Function-based questions.
- Comparative questions.
- General speculative questions. (McConachy, 2009)

Here is an example of how this framework is employed by a group of students in the practice session to revise tasks in a lesson in *Solutions: Elementary*:

> **Clerk**:  Good afternoon, Bronx Zoo.
> **Beth**:  Good afternoon. I'd like some information about the zoo, please.
> **Clerk**:  Certainly. How can I help you?
> **Beth**:  What time do you open?
> **Clerk**:  We open at ten o'clock.
> **Beth**:  Ok. And what time do you close? (Falla & Davies, 2008: 54)

Instead of asking future students to memorize the expressions and conduct controlled conversations based on this model dialogue, my students changed the task by devising these questions and setting scenarios for further practice as follows:

- What does 'how can I help you?' mean? (language-based question)
- In the dialogue, is 'how can I help you?' a question for information? (function-based question)
- In your culture, do people say 'how can I help you?' with customers? (comparative question)
- What are some ways people greet customers in your culture? (comparative question)
- Where do you think the conversation is based? (general speculative question)

As can be seen, the function-based questions stimulate an awareness of 'the potential interactional or social function of an utterance' (McConachy, 2009: 121). Furthermore, comparative questions prompt learners to reflect on their own culture and compare it with the cultures depicted in the materials, while general speculative questions activate interpretations which are based on students' cultural experience rather than seeking a correct answer. Using this question design framework, students are expected to be able to expand upon the available tasks and focus on the functions of language, the relation and interaction between local culture and whatever culture is depicted in a textbook and the diversity in language, context and culture.

Additionally, I introduce Sharifian's (2013) metacultural competence, which, as he argues, has substantial implications for Teaching English as an International Language (TEIL). The notion of metacultural competence acknowledges that English functions as a means to express different cultural conceptualizations and focuses upon the importance of the following aspects in international communication:

- Awareness of cultural conceptualizations.
- Explication strategies.
- Negotiation strategies. (Sharifian, 2013)

A model demonstration was shown in class to illustrate how, in the locally produced English textbook, cultural conceptualizations are entrenched in a lesson. Students then discussed how to integrate Sharifian's notion of competence through revising some texts and activities from the English textbooks. They also created conversations between different speakers of English in which cultural conceptualizations were negotiated to arrive at mutual understanding and designed tasks to practice these strategies.

Students revise the materials with these frameworks and are also encouraged to propose their own criteria/checklist/framework as they revise teaching materials.

### Section 3: Material design

This section focuses on how students can develop their own materials using strategies such as selecting supplementary materials, creating further learning resources and developing/revising activities. According to Tomlinson (2013), the development of teaching materials is a multidimensional process including text collection, text selection, activity development and so forth. TEIL/WE informs educators of the primary objectives underlying such processes so that learners can be exposed to linguistic and cultural diversity, become aware of the changing sociolinguistic landscape of English and exercise IC.

Students were asked to share materials that they found useful and relevant, discuss the advantages and disadvantages of those materials and design EIL/WE-oriented activities. In order to guide students in this practice, I created guidelines for selecting materials and developing activities with reference to Dinh (2015), Hino (2010), Kubota (2001), Kubota and Ward (2000), Matsuda (2002) and Xu (2014). I also provided them with some concrete examples of activities in class.

The guidelines include key aspects such as what materials to consider, how to use the materials, the reasons for using the materials, what activities need to be designed and why those activities are useful. Specific questions were provided to students as follows:

- Do the materials and activities raise students' awareness of the functions of English in different contexts?
- Do they raise students' awareness of linguistic and cultural diversity?
- Do they help expose students to a variety of Englishes across sociocultural contexts reflecting current realities?
- Do they encourage critical examination and reflection on the students' own local context, English variety and culture?
- Do they encourage students to appreciate linguistic innovations and cultural diversity?
- Do they create opportunities for students to experience and discuss issues pertaining to IC?
- Do they allow students to practice IC strategies?
- What are any possible challenges students may face when engaging with the materials and activities?

These questions provoke careful consideration about the selection, design and use of materials and encourage the development of useful activities with those materials. After practicing these skills in class, the students then work in groups and together design a lesson on their own or based on the available textbooks, and present it to the class as their second assessment task.

### Section 4: Use of materials

In this section, the students are offered the opportunity to individually teach using EIL/WE-oriented materials, either of their own design or based on the available materials, for 10–15 minutes. This task helps students 'get a feel' for how practical and easily applicable the principles and frameworks are and how to deal with ELT materials as well as allowing them to experience the roles of both teacher and student in EIL/WE-oriented lessons.

As ELT methodology is a compulsory course for students in the same semester, they have already become informed of and practiced various teaching approaches. Hence, rather than general teaching techniques, this section is restricted to issues producing a more EIL/WE approach. Based on the lesson and the skill(s) they will focus upon in their teaching, students select which chapter to read in Matsuda's (2012a) *Principles and Practices of Teaching English as an International Language*.

The lecturer in charge (myself) conducted a sample lesson and asked students to discuss it in terms of the choice of materials, the 'EIL/WE-ization' of the materials and their feelings about the lesson. They were also encouraged to discuss alternative ways to revise and operationalize the material.

After submitting their lesson plans in advance to me, the students then conducted their own lessons in front of the class and received feedback afterward. The students in the audience were allocated time to give peer feedback, share their reflections/concerns and ask questions after each sample lesson.

## Discussions, Reflections and Directions

The Materials Development course is the first to incorporate EIL/WE at the university where it was conducted, and to my knowledge, it is the first in Vietnam. Issues pertaining to ELT materials are typically included in the ELT methodology courses in TESOL programs, so there is little time for them to be thoroughly discussed in class. Students can merely discuss types of textbooks at different levels and the kinds of supplementary materials that could make classes more interactive and communicative.

The course covers both the key issues surrounding ELT materials/textbooks and introduces the principles of EIL/WE. As can be seen, students discuss aspects of ELT materials including what can be identified as teaching materials, and the evaluation of teaching materials, as well as how to design them and use them in the classroom. These aspects have been widely discussed and their importance emphasized by Gray (2002), McGrath (2013), Nation and Macalister (2010) and Tomlinson (2013). Furthermore, the students are introduced to exploring specific teaching materials-related issues such as the representations of cultures in textbooks, the semiotic approach to textbook analysis and so forth through several articles reporting empirical studies that they are required to read. They are simultaneously introduced to EIL/WE which deepens their understanding of the present sociolinguistic reality of English, linguistic and cultural diversity, IC and the role of the local culture in ELT.

On the basis of my communication with students, evaluation submitted by the students at the end of the course and my own self-reflection, in Table 9.3 I have summarized the main advantages and challenges of integrating EIL/WE into this course.

It is observable that both my students and I recognized the importance of IC, linguistic and cultural diversity and the need for a revised set of materials. Yet, certain limitations were also apparent. First of all, the need to develop knowledge of EIL/WE and teaching materials meant extensive readings each week, which was a challenge for both teacher and students. As there had been no course on EIL/WE before, some students

**Table 9.3** Reflection on the advantages and disadvantages in the post-course stage

| Agents | Advantages | Challenges |
|---|---|---|
| Course designer and teacher in charge | I gained an insight into EIL/WE and their implications for teacher education in material development | The course requires extensive reading on EIL/WE resources |
| | I could transform EIL/WE principles into practice | I was challenged in class when it comes to time constraints, test pressure and the feasibility of EIL/WE-oriented materials |
| | I had interesting classes with lively discussion and innovative lesson plans from students every week | I had to deal with the doubts of some students who did not accept the notion of varieties of English and their legitimacy at first |
| | I am more aware of the active role and power of teacher as a material designer and teacher as a curriculum | |
| Students | Students became aware of English varieties, the importance of intercultural communication (IC) and the misrepresentation of cultures in materials | The course requires an enormous reading workload |
| | | Students face possible challenges about time constraints, grammar-based tests and the practicality of implementing what they learnt given the policies of the schools where they are likely to work in the future |
| | Students grasped specific effective frameworks and principles to revise and develop materials | |
| | Students identified a much wider range of materials and activities | The course requires extensive knowledge and innovation in revising, designing and teaching materials |
| | Students widened their knowledge about both language and culture | |

found it overwhelming and could not fully understand some course readings. Moreover, many concerns and questions were raised around the applicability of EIL/WE-oriented materials. They included questions about time constraints, grammar-based tests in Vietnam, the availability of example lessons and whether high school students would be motivated by the approach. As a result, I believe that there needs to be further EIL/WE courses or more EIL/WE-oriented courses in the whole teacher education program to gradually introduce the field so that students are equipped to discuss these concerns in depth.

However, based on the course evaluation, the majority of students felt extremely satisfied with the course and that is an encouraging initial step for further course development.

## Conclusions

As the course designer, I see the multiple implications of EIL/WE for ELT materials and teacher education. They provide an effective theoretical background and framework for evaluating, revising, devising and teaching ELT materials. The course also brings in related disciplines and introduces ELT frameworks, which illustrates how EIL and WE correspond to and expand other fields in linguistics, applied linguistics and TESOL, which together will inform teachers of English of their responsibilities and help them to establish their teaching orientations. The integration of EIL/WE into this course has insightful implications for not only course materials but also learning English goals, objectives and pedagogy in general.

To conclude, I would like to invite readers to ponder on the applicability of this integration through the following anecdote. In the following semester, I unexpectedly observed a teaching practicum performance by a student from the course. In the lesson, she gave some examples of different speakers of English in various contexts such as a Malay student speaking to a New Zealand teacher, a Chinese employee speaking to an American boss when teaching the topic of making requests. She engaged learners in reflecting on their cultures and performed different scenarios in which they could practice using different expressions and speaking skills and play different cultural roles. She was able to justify her lesson plan in the feedback session, which convinced the supervising teacher. She revealed to me that,

> I think change starts small from practicum session like this. When the observants recognise how effective our lesson is and makes sense of the strong pedagogical principles underlying the way we teach, they will be motivated and later gradually apply in their class. I find it works, so I think others may too, sooner or later. (Personal communication in English, 2014)

Her revelation provokes food for thought for those who are already practicing and will practice the integration of EIL/WE into the teacher education program. It shows that the awareness of and acceptance of TEIL/WE will soon be realized in actual teaching as is required by the changes in society and the sociolinguistic landscape of English. The practice of EIL/WE can start from small initial steps in revising content and tasks in set teaching materials by teachers before being applied on a bigger scale.

## References

Arikan, A. (2005) Age, gender, and social class in ELT coursebooks: A critical study. *Hacettepe Universitesi Egitim Fakultesi Dergisi* 28 (1), 29–38. See http://www.eldergi.hacettepe.edu.tr/200528ARDA%20ARIKAN.pdf (accessed January 2014).

Basabe, E.A. (2006) From de-Anglicization to internationalisation: Cultural representations of the UK and the USA in global, adapted and local ELT textbooks in Argentina. *Profile Issues in Teachers Professional Development* 7 (1), 59–75.

Bao, D. (2008) Dimensions of English Coursebooks in Southeast Asia. *Asian Journal of English Language Teaching* 18, 189–200.

Crystal, D. (1999) From out in the left field? That's not cricket: Finding a focus for the language curriculum. In R.S. Wheeler (ed.) *The Workings of Language: From Prescriptions to Perspectives* (pp. 91–105). Westport, CT: Praeger.

Crystal, D. (2008) *A Dictionary of Linguistics and Phonetics*. Oxford: Blackwell Publishing.

Dinh, N.T. (2014) Culture representation in locally developed English textbooks. In R. Chowdhury and R. Marlina (eds) *Enacting English Across Borders: Critical Studies in the Asia Pacific* (pp. 143–167). Newcastle upon Tyne: Cambridge Scholars Publishing.

Dinh, N.T. (2015) Integrating EIL-oriented activities in class. *English Australia* 31 (1), 60–65.

Falla, T. and Davies, P. (2008) *Solutions: Elementary Student's Book*. Oxford: Oxford University Press.

Gray, J. (2002) The global course in English language teaching. In B. David and D. Cameron (eds) *Globalisation and Language Teaching* (pp. 150–167). London/New York: Routledge Taylor and Francis Group.

Hino, N. (2001) Organising EIL studies: Toward a paradigm. *Asian Englishes* 4 (1), 34–65.

Hino, N. (2010) EIL in teaching practice: A pedagogical analysis of EIL classrooms in action. In N. Hino (ed.) *Gengobunka-kyoiku no aratanaru riron to jissen* [*New Theories and Practice in Education in Language and Culture*] (pp. 93–102). Osaka: Graduate School of Language and Culture, Osaka University.

Hymes, D. (1974) *Foundations in Sociolinguistics: An Ethnographic Approach*. Philadelphia, PA: University of Pennsylvania Press.

Kiss, T. and Weninger, C. (2013) A semiotic exploration of cultural potential in EFL textbooks. *Malaysian Journal of ELT Research* 9 (1), 19–28.

Kubota, R. (2001) Learning diversity through World Englishes. *The Social Studies* 92 (2), 69–72.

Kubota, R. and Ward, L. (2000) Exploring linguistic diversity through World Englishes. *The English Journal* 89 (6), 80–86.

Le, C.V. (2000) Language and Vietnamese pedagogical contexts. In J. Shaw, D. Lubelsk and M. Noullet (eds) *Partnership and Interaction: Proceedings of the Fourth International Conference on Language and Development* (pp. 73–79). Bangkok: Asian Institute of Technology.

Marlina, R. (2011) Critical reflection of teaching English as an international language. A symposium presented at the 17th International Association of World Englishes (IAWE) Conference, Melbourne, Australia.

Marlina, R. (2014a) Teaching English as an international language in Australia: Voices from an Australian university classroom. PhD thesis, Monash University.

Marlina, R. (2014b) The pedagogy of English as an international language (EIL): More reflections and dialogues. In R. Marlina and R. Giri (eds) *The Pedagogy of English as an International Language* (pp. 1–19). New York: Springer.

Marlina, R. and Giri, R. (2009) ELICOS English and curriculum: Perspectives on their internationalisation. A paper presented at the 2009 English Australia Conference, Melbourne, Australia.

Marlina, R. and Ahn, H.J. (2011) 'Internationalised' English teaching materials? Please think again: A Korean case study. A paper presented at the Annual Conference of the Korean Association of Teachers of English (KATE), Seoul, South Korea.

Marlina, R. and Giri, R. (2013) 'We provide the best international education and use international-oriented learning materials': Questioning the 'international' from the perspective of English as an international language. In N.T. Zacharias and C. Manara (eds) *Contextualising the Pedagogy of English as an International Language: Issues and Tensions* (pp. 75–98). Newcastle upon Tyne: Cambridge Scholars Publishing.

Matsuda, A. (2002) 'International understanding' through teaching world Englishes. *World Englishes* 21 (3), 436–440.

Matsuda, A. and Friedrich, P. (2011) English as an international language: A curriculum blueprint. *World Englishes* 30 (3), 332–344.

Matsuda, A. (2012a) Introduction: Teaching English as an international language. In A. Matsuda (ed.) *Principles and Practices of Teaching English as an International Language* (pp. 1–14). Bristol: Multilingual Matters.

Matsuda, A. (2012b) Teaching materials in EIL. In L. Alsagoff, S.L. McKay, G. Hu and W.A. Renandya (eds) *Principles and Practices for Teaching English as an International Language* (pp. 168–185). New York: Routledge, Taylor and Francis Group.

McConachy, T. (2009) Raising sociocultural awareness through contextual analysis: Some tools for teachers. *ELT Journal* 63 (2), 116–125.

McGrath, I. (2013) *Teaching Materials and the Roles of EFL/ ESL Teachers: Practice and Theory*. London/New York: Bloomsbury.

McKay, S. (2002) *Teaching English as an International Language*. Oxford: Oxford University Press.

McKay, S. (2003) Teaching English as an international context: The Chilean context. *ELT Journal* 57 (2), 139–148.

McKay, S. (2012) Teaching materials for English as an international language. In A. Matsuda (ed.) *Principles and Practices of Teaching English as an International Language* (pp. 70–83). Bristol: Multilingual Matters.

Mineshima, M. (2008) Gender representations in an EFL textbook. See http://www.niit.ac.jp/lib/contents/kiyo/genko/13/14_MINESHIMA.pdf (accessed January 2014).

Nation, P. and Macalister, J. (2010) *Language Curriculum Design*. New York/London: Routledge.

Nguyen, H.N. (2008) *National Foreign Language Project 2020*. Hanoi: MoET Publishing House.

Nguyen, H.N. (2012) National Foreign Language Project 2020. Paper presented at the Fourth 'Engaging with Vietnam: An Interdisciplinary Dialogue' Conference, East-West Center, University of Hawaii, Honolulu, HI.

Phan, H.L. (2008) *Teaching English as an International Language: Identity, Resistance and Negotiation*. Clevedon: Multilingual Matters.

Phan, H.T.T. (2009) Impacts of Vietnam's social context on learners' attitudes towards foreign languages and English language learning: Implications for teaching and learning. *Asia TEFL* 73 (1), 169–188.

Pupavac, V. (2012) *Language Rights: From Free Speech to Language Governance*. London: Palgrave Macmillan.

Sharifian, F. (2009) English as an international language: An overview. In F. Sharifian (ed.) *English as an International Language: Perspectives and Pedagogical Issues* (pp. 1–18). Bristol: Multilingual Matters.

Sharifian, F. (2013) Globalisation and developing meta-cultural competence in learning English as an international language. *Multilingual Education* 3 (7), 1–11.

Smith, L. (1976) English as an international auxiliary language. *RELC Journal* 7 (2), 38–43.

Tomlinson, B. (2013) *Developing Materials for Language Teaching.* New York: Bloomsbury.

Ton, N.N.H. and Pham, H.H. (2010) Vietnamese teachers' and students' perceptions of global English. *Language Education in Asia* 1 (1), 48–61.

Vietnam Tourism (2015) International visitors to Viet Nam in April and 4 months of 2015. See http://vietnamtourism.gov.vn/english/index.php/items/8692 (accessed 2 February).

Weninger, C. and Kiss, T. (2013) Culture in English as a foreign language (EFL) textbooks: A semiotic approach. *TESOL Quarterly* 47 (4), 694–716.

Xu, Z. (2014) Teaching and assessing EIL vocabulary in Hong Kong. In R. Marlina and R. Giri (eds) *The Pedagogy of English as an International Language: Perspectives from Scholars, Teachers, and Students* (pp. 143–156). New York: Springer.

Yuen, K.-M. (2011) The representation of foreign cultures in English textbooks. *ELT Journal* 65 (4), 458–466.

# 10 Addressing Culture from an EIL Perspective in a Teacher Education Course in Brazil

Eduardo H. Diniz de Figueiredo
and Aline M. Sanfelici

## Introduction

In Brazil, many teachers of all subject areas work in public schools in spite of the fact that they lack adequate training and formal certification. To address this issue, in 2009, the federal government established the National Plan for Basic Teacher Education (*Plano Nacional de Formação de Professores da Educação Básica*, or PARFOR, in Portuguese), which is an emergency initiative to prepare these educators with combined pre- and in-service training, giving them the certification that is required by law. The need for this project has been particularly strong in the north and northeast regions, which happen to be the poorest areas of the country. According to data from the Federal Ministry of Education, published by the Coordination of Higher Education Faculty/Staff Development (*Coordenação de Aperfeiçoamento de Pessoal de Nível Superior* – best known as CAPES), in 2012 over 48,000 public school teachers from these two regions alone were enrolled in the project as regular students, as opposed to just over 6,000 in the rest of Brazil (Coordenação de Aperfeiçoamento de Pessoal de Nível Superior, 2014).

In this chapter, we describe a course on language and culture, entitled *Culturas Anglófonas* (Anglophone Cultures), which was part of an English language teaching (ELT) program (at undergraduate level) offered through PARFOR at a federal university in the state of Pará, located in the north region of Brazil. The course was prepared by both of the present authors – and delivered by one of them – in 2012, when one of the authors worked at that specific institution. The university where the course was given consisted of 13 campuses until mid-2013, when the one campus where the course reported here took place separated from the rest of the institution to become a federal university of its own. In any case, after this separation,

PARFOR has continued in both institutions, with separate directors, but under the same regulations.

As previously indicated, the students involved in the course described here (19 in total) already worked as English language teachers in public schools at that time. Their ages ranged from early twenties to mid-sixties, and approximately one-third of them lived and worked in rural areas. Many of them taught in more than one school, often three or four, throughout the school year – which in Brazil generally runs from February to June (first semester) and August to December (second semester). With this context in mind, PARFOR was designed as an intensive program with a minimum of seven sections that took place precisely in the months of January to early February and July to early August, in order to ensure that students could attend classes. This usually became a challenge for both instructors and students, since course contents had to be condensed as much as possible in order to meet the strict time frame for each class.

The ELT program in which the course was taught comprised a total of 26 courses, which focused on matters of language use, literature, language teaching and teaching practicum. The program offered through PARFOR was supposed to follow the same guidelines as the regular program (offered to students who are generally yet to become teachers and who have classes following the regular school calendar), with some adaptations based on the specific needs of the program and students.

## Description of the Course

*Culturas Anglófonas* was a 68-hour required course taken by PARFOR students in the later stages of their undergraduate work in the ELT program. The original objective of this course, according to its description in official institutional documents, was to give an overview of the cultures of contexts in which English is a native and/or official language. As stated in the description itself, the goal of the course was for students to understand 'the values, ways of living, codes and symbolic representations of Anglophone countries (or regions)' (Faculdade de Letras Estrangeiras Modernas, 2010, our translation). Although the description also states that this should be done through an intercultural approach, taking into account socioeconomic, political and historical factors, it is important to highlight that the term *anglophone* in Brazilian Portuguese generally has a connotation implying English as a native and/or official language, and is often associated with countries from the Inner Circle (Kachru, 1992) – as evidenced by the fact that the vast majority of the readings in the reading list of the institutional course description (except for one title) centered mainly on the contexts of the United States and Great Britain.

However, as with other disciplines in the ELT program, this course description (and consequently the course itself) is open to reformulation, and the instructor has autonomy to change or adapt it as he or she finds appropriate. In the case reported here, the course was reviewed to fit an English as an International Language (EIL) perspective, based on our understanding of English as a language that 'has spread geographically so as to serve especially as an international lingua franca in various domains, in a way in which no other world language ever has' (Mufwene, 2010: 47), and of the cultural implications that such a role has demanded of its speakers worldwide. More specifically, EIL was interpreted here in two ways: (1) as 'a function of English in international contexts rather than a linguistic variety to be used uniformly in all international contexts' (Matsuda & Friedrich, 2011); and (2) as a new paradigm in teaching English to speakers of other languages (TESOL), second language acquisition (SLA) and applied linguistics which 'calls for a critical revisiting of the notions, analytical tools, approaches and methodologies' within ELT (Sharifian, 2009: 2), bringing a shift to how we understand notions such as the ownership of English and the goals of English learners. The fact that one of the authors specializes in English as a global language, and the other has extensive knowledge of postcolonial theory and literature was also a key factor in determining the shape that the course would take.

The decision to follow an EIL perspective involved a number of modifications to the discipline of *Culturas Anglófonas*. For instance, the objectives of the course were revised, and focused on the following issues: (a) critical reflections on the concepts of culture, and cultural and national identities; (b) the relationship between globalization and cultural manifestations; (c) the global spread of English; (d) the native speaker fallacy in ELT, and its implications in the teaching of culture; (e) the appreciation of students' own cultures, as well as the cultures of the Other; and (f) intercultural communicative competence and the teaching of English. The specific components of the course were thus established based on these issues.

At the end of the course, students were expected to develop a pluralistic understanding of culture, one that is heterogeneous, continuous and not fixed or essentialized. In addition, it was anticipated that they would reflect upon how to treat culture in the English language classroom, including concerns such as: which cultures could be addressed; which cultures and/or cultural aspects are often silenced in teaching materials and the educational environment as a whole, and why; how to overcome matters of cultural overgeneralization and reduction, stereotypes, hegemony and marginalization; and intercultural communicative competence – all of which involve a thorough consideration of the global spread of English, its relation to globalization processes, the cultural encounters that have resulted from globalization and the use of English as a lingua franca (ELF) and the implications that these issues have had upon the roles of teachers of English (such as the students themselves).

Course assignments included student reflections upon the readings and other activities that were being conducted in class (including a final reflection of the course as a whole), and the preparation and presentation of class plans, materials and activities that reflected the theoretical concepts discussed throughout the course. In this way, the learners had the chance to engage with such topics in practice. The fact that they already worked as teachers was particularly interesting in this sense, since they could perform the assigned tasks with a consideration of their own realities and contexts as public school educators, and often had important insights that related closely to their own practices.

## Uniqueness

The course began with an activity that sought to elicit from students their understandings of the term 'Anglophone Cultures', which, as previously stated, was the title of the course. The activity was based on one of the authors' previous classes with a renowned scholar in critical applied linguistics, and it consisted of having students draw pictures of whatever came to mind when they thought about anglophone cultures. After drawing, students were supposed to explain their pictures to the rest of the class, and the instructor asked them questions related to why they had chosen to draw the image, what it conveyed and what their colleagues thought of their illustrations. The objective here was twofold: first, to have students reflect upon the definitions of the terms *anglophone* and *cultures*; and second, to help the instructor understand how these notions were conceptualized by students at the beginning of the course. This was in accordance with the proposal of EIL in teacher education in that it sought to begin with a deconstruction of the notion of *anglophone* (especially within the Brazilian context), in particular, and of the cultures usually associated with it – many of which are also essentialized.

Subsequently (starting in this first encounter, but following up in later classes), each of these two main terms of the discipline's title (*anglophone* and *cultures*) was explored in more detail, with readings, discussions and other activities. The concept of culture and its relation to language was the first one to be undertaken, mainly based on the works of Stuart Hall (2003), Claire Kramsch (1998) and Brazilian anthropologist Roque de Barros Laraia (2009). The main emphasis in class was on the understandings of culture as a multifaceted, non-fixed, constantly changing construct.

In particular, discussions centered on the deconstruction of essentialized notions of national identity and cultural identity. For instance, when discussing these concepts, students were asked to engage in a debate over the idea of a singular Brazilian identity, of how this idea is portrayed both within Brazil and abroad and of how it essentializes and exoticizes what it means to be 'Brazilian', often silencing those from the margins of Brazil itself – most importantly, in this context, cultures from the north of the country, which is exactly where the course was being taught. This was important because it helped students explore the notions being dealt with in class from a personal perspective, and also because it would help us prepare them to address the notion of one's home culture when teaching their own students, something that has been emphasized in the teaching of EIL (Matsuda & Friedrich, 2011). The understandings of imagined communities (Anderson, 1983) and of the role that language plays in the construction of national and cultural identities were particularly relevant here, since they assisted us in addressing cultures (in plural form) from a more locally situated perspective (rather than a singular, over-encompassing national one), and in focusing on how language has served to create stereotypes and nation-based conceptualizations of identity.

A specific activity that was especially interesting in our classes about culture involved the reading of an extract from Gloria Anzaldúa's (2012) *Borderlands/La Frontera: The New Mestiza*. The extract we chose to use (one of the most famous passages from the book, written in verse, and usually referred to as *To Live in the Borderlands Means You* or simply as *Borderlands*) was used as a spark to the discussion on the complex relationships between identity, culture and globalization, including the issues of cultural contact, border epistemology (Moita Lopes, 2008) and cultural clashes. Specific attention was given to the fact that the poem mixes different languages (English and Spanish), and puts different identities in juxtaposition and combination, in an attempt to call attention to the difficulties and pluralism of a broader view of culture. It was particularly curious to see how the poem led students to a discussion about global diasporas and the effects that they have had on people, cultures and languages – including English. This type of discussion is crucial for in-service and preservice teachers of English, since it highlights issues related to our current constructions of *global society* and *culture(s)*, a topic which also needs to be considered in the EIL classroom (Matsuda & Friedrich, 2011).

The treatment of English itself and the notion of anglophone, in turn, was done based on the work of scholars in World Englishes, English as a lingua franca (ELF) and EIL, most notably Braj Kachru (1992), Sandra McKay (2002), Barbara Seidlhofer (2005) and Aya Matsuda and Patricia Friedrich (Friedrich & Matsuda, 2010). Emphasis was given to the historical spread of English, the functions and roles that the language has had in different parts of the world (i.e. Inner, Outer and Expanding Circle countries) and its function as an international language of communication among speakers of different languages. We also gave prominence to concerns of linguistic imperialism (Phillipson, 1992) and disputes over the hegemonic role of the language, and to native speakerism (Holliday, 2006) in ELT.

In addition to the readings that were done by students and regular discussions on these matters, two activities involving videos were conducted.

The first one involved the discussion of an interview with David Crystal in which he talks about the spread of English, its new roles in light of globalization and technology, the increasing number of nonnative speakers of the language and the influence that they have had over the language itself.[1] Students were asked to discuss how such happenings affect the way we look at English-speaking cultures. Our objective was to show students that their teaching of English should not attempt to prepare their pupils to encounter native speakers exclusively, but that it involves a much larger international community of native and nonnative speakers, and that their pupils should be prepared to engage in cross-cultural encounters (both in 'real' and virtual spaces) with people from Inner, Outer and Expanding Circle contexts.

The other activity was an analysis of a campaign by a language school that focused its advertising on the nativeness of its teachers, and on the supposed inadequacy of nonnative teachers to be instructors of the language. Students engaged in debates about the status of different English speakers, and the power relations that are generally implied by these types of discourses. They were then asked to reflect upon how the teaching of culture with a pluralistic perspective on both culture and English would differ from an approach that centered exclusively on native-speaking countries. This discussion was especially meaningful for the class in terms of their self-recognition as authentic English speakers and instructors, who are also part of what is considered English-speaking culture(s), especially in a context where native speakerism and the association of English with the United States and Great Britain are still so pervasive (Diniz de Figueiredo, 2011).

These reflections on the students' roles as instructors and the still prevalent ideology of native speakerism in the Brazilian context led us to the next segment of the discipline (after the more conceptually driven discussions we have just detailed): the actual *teaching* of culture from an EIL perspective. Here, we placed particular emphasis on the discussion of culture in Matsuda and Friedrich's (2011) curriculum blueprint for EIL, on the issues of intercultural awareness and communicative competence in ELT (e.g. Alptekin, 2002; Baker, 2011) and on a more in-depth appreciation of culture from an EIL perspective in Brazilian schools – based on texts such as Gimenez (2001) and Rocha and Silva (2011).

As with other parts of the course, discussions on the teaching of culture from an EIL perspective were based on the assigned readings. Such discussions were then followed up by the most important moment of the discipline: the time when students had the chance to engage in the creation of lesson plans (or course units) that they thought would suit their own classes, and the sharing of such activities with their colleagues. Students worked in groups for the creation of the lesson plans (or units), which had to contain the following elements: objectives; activities and procedures;

materials; and how pupils would be assessed for that particular class or unit. This was one of the activities that served to evaluate students in the course.

We observed that many of the students were able to develop activities that involved non-reductionist perspectives on culture(s) – which is in itself already a great accomplishment of the course – and which also engaged with the teaching of culture from an EIL standpoint (Matsuda & Friedrich, 2011), i.e. taking into consideration at least one of the following aspects (if not more): the notion of a global culture, the cultures of possible future interlocutors and the culture(s) of students themselves. A good illustration of one such plan developed by a group of students was a series of classes comprising the creation of a cultural encyclopedia (in English) about the state of Pará (which, as stated earlier, is where the course was taught), taking as a starting point the experiences of their pupils from this region and its cultures – followed up by their subsequent research on other aspects that they may not have experienced themselves.

After creating this encyclopedia, the students' pupils would conduct further research, this time focusing on the cultures of other regions and/or countries (from the Inner, Outer and/or Expanding Circles, based on their own choices), which would enable them to discuss differences, similarities and to raise questions about what they may not have found, but would still like to know. In this way, they would be using English in order to debate and present their own cultural experiences, and also to think about the cultures of possible future interlocutors that they may encounter. Furthermore, they would understand that cultural information (including that of their own encyclopedia) is not definitive, but is actually only a momentary picture of a complex phenomenon that cannot be reduced or fully catalogued.

At the end of the course, students were asked to elaborate, in a final written individual reflection, on what they had learned, what they considered positive and negative points regarding the classes and the extent to which the discipline might have helped them in their own practices as language educators. In general, their considerations were positive and followed similar patterns of how they had evolved in their thinking of cultures in ELT throughout the course. Yet, one particular aspect raised by a few students captured our attention. It had to do with the difficulty that some of them emphasized in trying to think how a pluricentric understanding of English and of cultures could actually be implemented in classrooms (mainly public school ones) in the Brazilian context. This difficulty, according to the reflections, was mainly caused by matters such as the lack of appropriate resources (such as internet and computers in all classrooms) that could help them guide students in broader understandings of these concepts, or by the fact that Brazilian ELT is still very much guided by entrance examinations that direct what needs to be taught and many times also how. In other words, while students highlighted the importance of a course such as the one presented here, their reflections seemed to underscore the fact that this type of teacher education discipline (i.e. one that pays attention to EIL and a multifaceted view of culture) is only one step for actual change to take place in classrooms. In any case, what was particularly positive here is that most of the students of this class made statements in their reflections that seemed to show an inclination to be part of such change.

## Challenges and Limitations

One of the main challenges during the course had to do with some students' proficiency in English, which was still in the developing stages in a few cases. Such a scenario often resulted in difficulties for these particular students in reading some of the assigned texts and performing some of the required activities. For those not familiar with the context of ELT in Brazil, this may sound odd, given the fact that the students were already teachers of English. However, as explained in previous literature about that context (e.g. Lima, 2011), there are many English teachers in public schools in Brazil who still lack adequate proficiency levels to teach, but who nonetheless are hired in order to fulfill a demand. In order to overcome this challenge in the course presented here, it was necessary to assign some of the more complex readings in Portuguese (for instance, Hall's 2003 text), and to create assisted reading moments for the texts that were assigned in English.

Another challenge that was also related to the readings had to do with the limited time frame for the course – which, as explained previously, was an intensive course over a short period of time. This meant that the instructor of the course had to assign fewer readings than we thought was ideal to address the contents of the discipline. Students were encouraged to find other texts (either suggested by the instructor or on their own) related to the topics discussed, yet this did not often happen – probably due to the very reasons we have just mentioned (i.e. lack of proficiency and time restrictions).

One final limitation refers to the actual impact of the course upon the students' practices over time. Although the students' reflections and the activities they planned for the discipline seemed to show a good understanding of the topics discussed, as well as an inclination to EIL and to complex conceptualizations of culture, it is unknown whether they have been applying such notions to their current teaching. In other words, we do not know the extent of the effect of the course. This type of challenge has also been reported in other accounts of cultural/intercultural content and teacher education (e.g. Smolcic & Katunich, 2015). Based on other authors who have discussed limitations of this kind, we believe that teacher education disciplines need more longitudinal research to track the development of students under such training.

# Conclusion

In concluding this chapter, we emphasize that bringing an EIL perspective to an ELT teacher education course on culture is not only viable, but necessary. When we consider the non-dissociable nature of language and culture, we must integrate a pluralistic view of Englishes with a non-essentialist conception of cultures, especially taking into account that our students in teacher education programs will be the educators of others in our schools.

On that note, we must add that at the time when this discipline was offered by one of the present authors, it was not the only session of this course in which English and culture were conceptualized through an EIL perspective, nor was it the only discipline in which WE, ELF and EIL content was discussed. Other instructors at the institution had also begun to incorporate such standpoint into their classes, and there was a constant exchange of ideas about how to do so in this and other courses. We take these facts as evidence of the growing importance of EIL perspectives in teacher education programs, even if such importance is still only beginning to be understood and recognized.

## Note

(1)  This interview was presented in a series of videos by MacMillan Education. See http://www.macmillanglobal.com (last accessed by the present authors in March 2015).

## References

Alptekin, C. (2002) Towards intercultural communicative competence in ELT. *ELT Journal* 56 (1), 57–64.

Anderson, B. (1983) *Imagined Communities: Reflections on the Origin and Spread of Nationalism*. New York: Verso.

Anzaldúa, G. (2012) *Borderlands/La Frontera: The New Mestiza*. San Francisco, CA: Aunt Lute Books.

Baker, W. (2011) From cultural awareness to intercultural awareness: Culture in ELT. *ELT Journal* 68 (4), 386–396.

Coordenação de Aperfeiçoamento de Pessoal de Nível Superior (CAPES) (2014) *Plano Nacional de Formação de Professores da Educação Básica – PARFOR* [National Plan for Basic Teacher Education – PARFOR], official data. See http://www.capes.gov.br/educacao-basica/parfor (accessed 10 March 2015).

Diniz de Figueiredo, E.H. (2011) Nonnative English speaking teachers in the United States: Issues of identity. *Language and Education* 25 (5), 419–432.

Faculdade de Letras Estrangeiras Modernas (2010) *Projeto Pedagógico do Curso de Letras PARFOR* [Pedagogical Plan of the PARFOR Language Education Program]. Belém: Universidade Federal do Pará.

Friedrich, P. and Matsuda, A. (2010) When five words are not enough: A conceptual and terminological discussion of English as a lingua franca. *International Multilingual Research Journal* 4, 20–30.

Gimenez, T. (2001) *Eles comem cornflakes, nós comemos pão com manteira: Espaços para reflexão sobre cultura na aula de língua estrangeira* [They eat cornflakes, we eat bread and butter: Spaces for reflections over culture in the foreign language classroom]. See http://s3.amazonaws.com/academia.edu.documents/38250081/2001_EPLE_Eles_comem_cornflakes__nos_comemos_pao_com_manteiga.pdf?AWSAccessKeyI d=AKIAJ56TQJRTWSMTNPEA&Expires=1472256640&Signature=IhTlex2l FzwAZEB2xoBr2xFRe0k%3D&response-content-disposition=inline%3B%20 filename%3DEles_comem_cornflakes_nos_comemos_pao_co.pdf.

Hall, S. (2003) *A Identidade Cultural na Pós-modernidade* [*Cultural Identity in Post-Modernity*]. Rio de Janeiro: DP&A.

Holliday, A. (2006) Native-speakerism. *ELT Journal* 60 (4), 385–387.

Kachru, B. (1992) World Englishes: Approaches, issues and resources. *Language Teaching* 25 (1), 1–14.

Kramsch, C. (1998) *Language and Culture*. Oxford: Oxford University Press.

Laraia, R.B. (2009) *Cultura, um Conceito Antropológico* [*Culture, An Anthropological Concept*]. Rio de Janeiro: Zahar.

Lima, D.C. (ed.) (2011) *Inglês em Escolas Públicas Não Funciona? Uma Questão, Múltiplos Olhares* [*Doesn't English in Public Schools Work? One Question, Multiple Views*]. São Paulo: Parábola.

Matsuda, A. and Friedrich, P. (2011) English as an international language: A curriculum blueprint. *World Englishes* 30 (3), 332–344.

McKay, S.L. (2002) *Teaching English as an International Language: Rethinking Goals and Practices*. Oxford: Oxford University Press.

Moita Lopes, L.P. (2008) Inglês e globalização em uma epistemologia de fronteira: Ideologia linguística para tempos híbridos [English and globalization in a border epistemology: Linguistic ideology for hybrid times]. *D.E.L.T.A.* 24 (2), 309–340.

Mufwene, S.S. (2010) Globalization, global English and world English(es): Myths and facts. In N. Coupland (ed.) *The Handbook of Language and Globalization* (pp. 31–55). Malden, MA: Wiley-Blackwell.

Phillipson, R. (1992) *Linguistic Imperialism*. Oxford: Oxford University Press.

Rocha, C.H. and Silva, K.A. (2011) World English no contexto do ensino fundamental público [World English in the context of public elementary education]. In T. Gimenez, L.C.S. Calvo and M.S. El Kadri (eds) *Inglês como Língua Franca: Ensino, Aprendizagem e Formação de Professores* (pp. 253–292). Campinas: Pontes.

Seidlhofer, B. (2005) Key concepts: English as a lingua franca. *ELT Journal* 59 (4), 339–341.

Sharifian, F. (2009) English as an international language: An overview. In F. Sharifian (ed.) *English as an International Language: Perspectives and Pedagogical Issues* (pp. 1–18). Bristol: Multilingual Matters.

Smolcic, E. and Katunich, J. (2015, March) Teachers as Intercultural Learners: A Synthesis of Teacher Education Research and Practices. Paper presented at the American Association for Applied Linguistics/Canadian Association for Applied Linguistics 2015 Conference, Toronto, ON.

# 11 Practicing EIL Pedagogy in a Microteaching Class

## Nugrahenny T. Zacharias

## Introduction

The idea of integrating English as an International Language (EIL) pedagogy into a microteaching course originated from informal observations when I was assigned to teach a microteaching course after completing a PhD in 2010. I was a teacher educator in a four-year preservice teacher department in a private university in Indonesia. From the informal observation as a course instructor, I learned that many mini lessons were informed by student teachers' (STs) understanding of English as belonging to the so-called English-speaking countries of the Inner Circle, to use Kachru's (1986) term. When teaching listening, for example, many STs utilized American songs or texts depicting standard American or British English. Interestingly, although in some songs there was some slang, there was no attempt to highlight the diversity of English uses even within English-speaking countries. The model speakers in the listening texts were native speakers. When teaching English in the era of English as a lingua franca (ELF), many scholars have recommended not to foreground one variety of English as more correct than others, but to focus more on the contextualized English use serving different identitiary and pragmatic functions. Unfortunately, such awareness was not present in the teacher candidates' mini lessons. For instance, when teaching pronunciation, many of the aims were to pronounce English *correctly* rather than *appropriately*. When formulating the objective for teaching speaking, Rin (a pseudonym) wrote that 'students will be able to read with *correct* pronunciation and intonation of a simple text' (my emphasis).

I speculate that there are two primary, yet contradictory, reasons underlying STs' continued beliefs of English as belonging to English-speaking countries. First, STs might not be aware of the pedagogical implications of the current ELF status. Perhaps their previous courses or the curriculum in the present preservice teacher education program continue to use course books depicting English as belonging to the Inner Circle countries. A second possible reason is that STs are indeed aware of ELF but they continue to believe that English belongs to the Inner Circle countries.

Even though the way that STs taught and represented English in the mini lesson was not necessarily 'wrong', it does not seem to justly demonstrate the sociolinguistic changes of English usage and users nowadays. Many EIL scholars have pointed out the need to portray the diversity of English users in teaching English (Kirkpatrick, 2014; Matsuda, 2012b; McKay, 2012). To talk specifically of Indonesia, where the current chapter is based, the need to illustrate the diversity of Englishes is even more significant now than ever before. In 2009, the charter of the Association of Southeast Asian Nations (ASEAN) made English the official lingua franca for ASEAN, which is composed of 10 countries: Indonesia, Malaysia, Singapore, the Philippines, Vietnam, Thailand, Cambodia, Laos, Brunei and Myanmar. Under such a circumstance, then, the purpose of teaching English is to enable learners 'to interact successfully with fellow Asian multilinguals' (Kirkpatrick, 2014: 24) who speak English as an additional language. Consequently, in these lingua franca situations, there is no point in using native speaker varieties of English. Indeed, Canagarajah (2014: 769) maintains that these ELF speakers 'develop another norm that deviates from native speaker varieties'.

For this particular reason, I feel it is necessary to introduce STs to an alternative pedagogy that takes into account the lingua franca role of English and the changing demographic of English usage and users worldwide, which many call 'EIL pedagogy'. In short, the term 'EIL pedagogy' here is used to refer to approaches that appropriate teaching English to its users, contexts and purpose. I consciously used the pluralized form 'approaches' to refer to 'EIL pedagogy' to illustrate McKay's (2012: 122) argument that 'there is no one way of teaching that can meet all the learning contexts of EIL today, nor is there a best method for each particular context'. In other words, EIL pedagogy in this chapter is used to refer to constellations of practices for situating English language teaching and learning in relation to its users and contexts of use. In such, I see EIL pedagogy as embodying a level of openness which can incorporate a wide range of localized teaching practices. By giving the opportunity for STs to enact EIL pedagogy in a microteaching course, I was curious to see how they understand the pedagogy when they are provided with an opportunity to actively engage and practice it.

## Description of the Course

The Microteaching course where the EIL innovation (hereafter, EIL-Microteaching) took place is housed under the English Teacher Education (ETE) department in the Faculty of Language and Literature in a private university in Indonesia. It is a four-year teacher preparation program, and graduates will become English teachers for primary- and secondary-level schools in Indonesia. In the department, English is not only used as the medium of instruction but also the medium of practice in varying proportions (e.g. in staff meetings, announcement boards, student activities). Prior to registering for the Microteaching course, STs need to complete courses in teaching methodologies, such as Language Assessment, Teaching and Learning Strategies, Teaching English as a Foreign Language and Curriculum and Material Development. Each course lasts two hours for 14 weeks with approximately 30–40 students. Each of these courses is theoretical in nature, although there are some courses where assessment includes conducting mini teachings in groups.

Unlike the teaching methodologies classes, the Microteaching course is small, with 14–17 STs in a class. Each meeting lasts 100 minutes (two credits) a week for a total of 14 weeks. The first two weeks of the class usually consist of workshops on lesson planning. Here, STs in groups develop a plan for an imaginary lesson and then present it to the class. Then, they receive feedback from their peers as well as the Microteaching course instructor. The successive weeks of classes consist of mini lessons. Each ST is in charge of teaching three mini lessons of 10–15 minutes depending on the number of students in the class. Each mini lesson will be followed by a five-minute feedback session from peers and the course instructor.

When conducting a mini lesson, STs need to develop a lesson plan, teaching materials and visual aids. There is no requirement for STs to develop original materials. They can use ready-made materials from course books and/or the internet, which are often opted for by many STs. At the end of the mini lesson, STs need to write a self-reflection essay. There is no guideline, other than a word limit, as to what STs should write in the self-reflection essay. For each mini lesson, one student will take turns to be a peer observer. The peer observer, as the name suggest, gives feedback for the mini lesson based on a rubric designed by the course coordinator. The rubric uses a rating scale of 1 (poor) to 4 (outstanding) and includes a space where the observer can give written feedback. Some assessment points in the rubric are teacher preparation, coherence of teaching activities, teaching materials, classroom language, time and class management as well as classroom interaction. A similar rubric is used for the Microteaching course instructor. At the end of the mini lesson, in addition to oral feedback, STs will receive written feedback from the peer observer and the Microteaching course instructor.

## Uniqueness of the Course

The primary aspect differentiating the EIL-Microteaching course from other microteaching classes was the integration of EIL pedagogy into the mini lessons. The ultimate goal was for STs to move toward a greater self-awareness of pedagogical instructional practices that depict the sociolinguistic changes and complexity of English use and users nowadays. Realizing that EIL pedagogy might be new in this context, I implemented several activities that might not be found in the general microteaching classes. Those activities are as follows.

## A presentation on EIL pedagogy

Considering students' lack of, or even no, prior knowledge of EIL pedagogy, I allocated the first weeks to a brief introduction of EIL pedagogy. My challenge was to explain EIL pedagogy in a way that STs could develop a sense of the pedagogy and be able to translate it into teaching strategies for the mini lessons. Also, I was careful not to present it as a one-size-fits-all approach. For that reason, I framed my presentation in a past-and-present format guided by the following themes adapted from Burns (2005a):

- Which models?
- Which standard?
- Which teachers?
- Whose culture?

I added the last theme, 'Whose culture?', not addressed in Burns, because of the traditional assumption that learning English entails learning the cultures of native speakers, which continues to be pervasive in Indonesia (Mukminatien, 2012; Zacharias, 2005). In presenting these principles, I tried my best to present them in a suggestive, rather than a prescriptive, manner.

## Collaborative lesson-planning on EIL pedagogy

This presentation was followed by a lesson planning workshop in the next meeting. A workshop was meant to provide a dialogizing space allowing STs to discuss and learn from one another about the different ways of translating EIL pedagogy theories into teaching steps. To provide a somewhat similar place to start with, I gave students three reading texts entitled 'Everything must go on line!', 'What do you have in your refrigerator?' and 'She was telling me ...,' taken from a course book, *Touchstones* (McCarthy et al., 2006), published by Cambridge University Press. The book was used in the ETE department for an Integrated Course offered to first-year students.

There are two reasons why I chose these three texts. First, the content of these three texts was informed by English-speaking lifestyles and cultures. For instance, the text 'Everything must go on line' discussed a man who sold his hand-me-down clothes online. In many contexts in Indonesia, an internet connection continues to be a luxury and therefore, selling hand-me-downs on the internet might not be possible. Another reason for choosing reading texts from a course book is because during teaching practicums, STs might not have the freedom to choose the teaching materials. Under such a circumstance, I was curious to know the extent to which STs could find creative ways to appropriate available teaching materials to EIL pedagogy.

During the session, STs collaboratively designed a lesson plan based on one of the three reading texts. They, then, presented the lesson plan to the class, particularly highlighting aspects of the lesson plan that demonstrated EIL pedagogy. Some examples of learning activities developed from the texts were assigning students to write a similar topic of the reading text(s) in their own cultures and/or contexts, searching how the topic was addressed in different parts of the world and presenting them to the class. Several groups attempted to teach grammar and used the reading texts as fill-in-the-blank exercises.

## EIL-oriented mini lesson

While in the general microteaching classes, STs had the liberty to select any approaches, in the EIL-Microteaching course, they were expected to accommodate EIL pedagogy into the lesson plan. The time allocation for the mini lesson, the assessment and the format of the lesson plan were the same as the general microteaching classes. After Mini Lessons 1 and 2, I allocated a week for general reflection to discuss STs' evolving understanding of EIL pedagogy as well as addressing their questions, dilemmas and problems. Different from the general microteaching classes, the mini lessons in the EIL-Microteaching were video-recorded to mediate STs' reflection that will be discussed in the next section.

In the general microteaching courses, STs selected teaching materials as well as the teaching focus for the mini lesson. In EIL-Microteaching, I decided to provide a structure to scaffold each mini lesson. In Mini Lesson 1, STs developed a lesson from the lesson plan developed during the collaborative lesson planning session. For Mini Lesson 2, STs taught speaking and/or pronunciation while for the last mini lesson, Mini Lesson 3, they had the liberty to select the teaching focus as well as the teaching materials.

## Action-research (AR) journal

Similar to the general microteaching courses, I utilized a self-reflective journal to mediate STs' reflection after conducting the mini lesson. However, my earlier experiences of assigning students to write a reflection without any specific guidelines or templates proved to be ineffective. STs tended to write an excessive description of the mini lesson rather than providing evaluative or critical comments of their teaching experience. Even if evaluative comments were made (e.g. 'my materials are boring', 'the instruction that I gave was confusing', 'the students were passive'),

**Figure 11.1** Action-research journal template

there were no attempts to analyze how this was mediated by their teaching techniques and preparation.

To understand how STs engaged with the EIL pedagogy, I developed a guideline for the self-reflective journals. The aim of the guideline was to refocus STs' reflection when practicing EIL pedagogy. The guideline was adapted from an action research cycle of plan-action-observe-reflect developed by Burns (2010). At the beginning of the cycle, I added a 'topic' section where students needed to explain what they are going to teach with regard to EIL pedagogy. Figure 11.1 gives the guideline of the self-reflective journal.

In the 'plan' section, STs fleshed out their lesson plan accompanied by some considerations of why such teaching techniques/activities were chosen. In the 'action' and 'observe' sections, STs wrote their reflection of the mini lessons. The difference between the two was in the writing time: the 'action' section should be written after completing the mini lesson whereas the 'observe' section was written after they viewed their video-recorded mini lessons. The 'reflect' section was for STs to give an overall reflection of the mini lesson by taking into account their own reflection written in the 'action' and observe' sections, peer feedback as well as that of the course instructor.

## Challenges and Limitations

In a paper searching for a new paradigm for teaching EIL, Canagarajah (2014: 768) states that changes in pedagogy 'don't always mean that teaching practice is made difficult. Teaching can actually become more creative, interesting and fulfilling, if we only had the patience and tolerance for change'. Canagrajah's comment was echoed by many STs when sharing their experiences of practicing EIL pedagogy in the Microteaching course. Ben (a pseudonym) felt EIL pedagogy made teaching English easier for local teachers since he could bring local contexts into the classroom. Many STs stated that teaching through EIL pedagogy has challenged their creativity as teachers because EIL pedagogy materials were not readily available. Consequently, they needed to create and design their own materials and teaching activities. In other words, through practicing EIL pedagogy there is a shift in the way STs' see teaching – from methodology transmission to methodology construction and appropriation. No ST simply transmitted the knowledge of EIL pedagogy drawn from the workshop; they went the extra mile to construct an understanding of EIL pedagogy through finding outside resources as well as appropriating this knowledge to local contexts. The most encouraging benefit of practicing EIL pedagogy reported by STs is the way it increased the confidence level of beginning teachers. Due to all the benefits they experienced, all STs showed enthusiasm and commitment to practicing EIL pedagogy during the teaching practicum.

Despite the uniqueness and relative success of the EIL-Microteaching course, there continues to be some challenges/limitations that the course needs to overcome. One of the notable challenges when integrating EIL pedagogy into the EIL-Microteaching class is the limited time within the course structure to introduce the EIL pedagogy. From STs' journals and portfolios, the EIL-Microteaching class was their first encounter with the pedagogy although all of them were aware of the role of EIL nowadays. As a result, some STs felt overwhelmed by not being given sufficient time to process and internalize the EIL pedagogy. Several administrative constraints also hindered my suggestion to add another meeting outside the class hour to give a more solid understanding of EIL concepts. In this condition, perhaps, it will be more effective if the EIL-Microteaching class refocuses the mini lesson on one aspect of EIL pedagogy such as 'Which standard?' or 'Which culture?' although during the presentation, the Microteaching course instructor can give a broader overview of the pedagogical implication of the global role of English.

Another challenge written by most STs in the portfolio is the practicality aspect of EIL pedagogy. For the mini lesson, STs were not required to create their own teaching materials and lesson plans. However, it is interesting to note that all STs ended up creating original teaching materials, and some even went as far as creating the entire lesson from scratch, because teaching materials depicting EIL pedagogy were not readily available. Therefore, STs questioned if EIL pedagogy would be applicable to real teaching. I found that STs' concerns about the applicability of EIL pedagogy needed to be given serious attention considering that in real teaching contexts, teachers also need to do many administrative duties. In addition, a microteaching course, while it is not a replica of real teaching (Johnson & Arshavskaya,

2011), aims to prepare STs to teach in real-life contexts. Given this challenge, the preservice teacher education curriculum needs to allocate more time to material adaptation and writing. Ideally, the knowledge and skills of material adaptation can be integrated into a teaching methodology course or in a separate course prior to taking a microteaching course. Publications by Burns (2005b), Matsuda (2012a), McKay (2012), as well as Marlina and Giri (2014) contain some practical ideas and principles that can easily be adapted into courses in material development for EIL pedagogy. Such courses are important considering that preservice teachers will become primary- and secondary-level school teachers and might not have the liberty to design their own courses (also in Lee, 2012).

While the question of which varieties of English should be adopted (Burns, 2005a; Wang & Hill, 2011) is common when adopting EIL pedagogy, the STs in the EIL-Microteaching were certain of which Englishes should *not* be the model, that is, the Englishes of the Outer Circle countries (e.g. Malaysia, India, the Philippines). When asked if the Englishes in the Outer Circle countries could be pedagogical models, many STs seemed to show strong disagreement. They believed that teacher preparation programs in Indonesia need to continue promoting native speaker accents for their graduates due to the marketability value of these varieties. Indeed, their opinions contradict those of EIL scholars, such as Kirkpatrick (2014). Kirpatrick (2014) notes that Englishes in the Outer Circle countries might be more appropriate as pedagogical models for Indonesian learners due to the proximity of these countries.

STs' strong and unanimous opinions for standard English as a pedagogical model need to be appropriately interpreted to inform the integration of EIL pedagogy into preservice teacher education programs in Asia. One obvious interpretation is the need to discuss the sociopolitical and philosophical underpinnings of standard English vis-à-vis the varieties of English. Due to the time constraint, I realized that I mostly focused on developing STs' procedural knowledge of EIL pedagogy (Byram, 2008), that is, translating EIL pedagogy into practical teaching techniques. This may have resulted in STs' hesitancy in bringing varieties of Englishes into the classroom. Second, STs may lack classroom pedagogical techniques to appropriately expose learners to varieties of English in addition to standard English. Finally, STs' strong attachment to standard English may be due to the 'wide currency and prestige' (Gupta, 2012: 256) of standard English. Therefore, some STs might think that using class time to teach other English varieties is a waste of precious class time that otherwise can be allotted to teaching standard English. It would, thus, be interesting to see if STs continue to hold such a strong attachment to standard English if EIL knowledge and pedagogy are given more slots in the curriculum.

Last but not least is the challenge related to the AR journals. While separating the journal into the sections of topic-plan-action-observe-reflect helped STs to write a more focused reflection, I think these sections need to be simplified. Initially, my intention in separating STs' post mini lesson reflection into three sections – action, observe and reflect – aimed to sensitize them to different sources of reflection (own reflection, stimulated-recalled reflection from video-viewing the mini lesson, peer reflection and instructor's reflection). The action and observe sections, in particular, gave STs the opportunity to critically evaluate how their lessons were experienced by their peers and if there was any discrepancy between their own reflection and those of their peers and the course instructor. However, after reading STs' journals, I found many overlaps between these three sections. Therefore, these three sections can be combined into one.

Within the department, EIL pedagogy remains a major challenge due to the continued theory–practice divide where the subject matter knowledge to which teachers are exposed to in the department is often disconnected in any substantive way from the practical, goal-directed activities of actual teaching. Despite these limitations and challenges, however, the EIL-Microteaching course has proven to be successful as seen from STs' mini lessons. In the mini lessons, students no longer associated English with the traditional English-speaking countries but demonstrated a broader view of the pedagogical implications of the international role of English.

## Conclusion

While a journey toward a more holistic understanding of EIL pedagogy might require years, the EIL-Microteaching course shows that this process can begin to take place when an opportunity is given to practice the pedagogy in a carefully structured course. Overall the EIL-Microteaching course suggests that while these STs initially lack sufficient knowledge of EIL pedagogy, the EIL-Microteaching course creates spaces to mediate their thinking as well as opportunities to materialize their evolving understandings of EIL pedagogy both at the conceptual and pedagogical levels in the authentic activities of teaching. Johnson and Arshavskaya (2011) maintain that once a new concept is internalized, it becomes a psychological tool that guides learners in planning and accomplishing future activities. While I may lack empirical support for STs' full internationalization of EIL pedagogy, I do find evidence that EIL pedagogy is becoming much more salient in these STs' thinking as demonstrated by their commitment to continue practicing it during teacher practicum even though there was no requirement to do so. Based on my experience and reflection, I argue that reconceptualizing a microteaching course to include EIL pedagogy may prove to be a powerful first step in creating initial understanding and experiences of EIL pedagogy that support and sustain productive teaching learning in second language (L2) teacher education programs.

# References

Burns, A. (2005a) Interrogating new worlds in English language teaching. In A. Burns (eds) *Teaching English from a Global Perspective* (pp. 1–18). Alexandria, VA: TESOL.

Burns, A. (ed.) (2005b) *Teaching English from a Global Perspective*. Alexandria, VA: TESOL.

Burns, A. (2010) *Doing Action Research in English Language Teaching: A Guide for Practitioners*. New York: Routledge.

Byram, M. (2008) *From Intercultural Education to Education for Intercultural Citizenship*. Clevedon: Multilingual Matters.

Canagarajah, S. (2014) In search for a new paradigm for teaching English as an international language. *TESOL Journal* 5 (4), 767–785.

Gupta, A. (2012) Grammar teaching and standards. In L. Alsagoff, S.L. McKay, G. Hu and W.A. Renandya (eds) *Principles and Practices for Teaching English as an International Language* (pp. 245–261). New York: Routledge.

Johnson, K.E. and Arshavskaya, E. (2011) Strategic mediation in learning to teach: Reconceptualizing the microteaching stimulation in MA TESL methodology course. In K.E. Johnson and P.R. Golombek (eds) *Research on Second Language Teacher Education: A Sociocultural Perspective on Professional Development* (pp. 168–186). New York: Routledge.

Kachru, B.B. (1986) *The Alchemy of English: The Spread, Functions, and Models of Non-native Englishes*. Champaign, IL: University of Illinois Press.

Kirkpatrick, A. (2014) Teaching English in Asia in non-Anglo cultural contexts: Principles of the 'lingua franca approach'. In R. Marlina and R.A. Giri (eds) *The Pedagogy of English as an International Language: Perspectives from Scholars, Teachers and Students* (pp. 23–34). New York: Springer.

Lee, H. (2012) World Englishes in a high school English class: A case from Japan. In A. Matsuda (ed.) *Principles and Practices of Teaching English as an International Language* (pp. 55–69). Bristol: Multilingual Matters.

Marlina, R. and Giri, R.A. (eds) (2014) *The Pedagogy of English as an International Language: Perspectives from Scholars, Teachers, and Students*. New York: Springer.

Matsuda, A. (ed.) (2012a) *Principles and Practices of Teaching English as an International Language*. Bristol: Multilingual Matters.

Matsuda, A. (2012b) Teaching materials in EIL. In L. Alsagoff, S.L. McKay, G. Hu and W.A. Renandya (eds) *Principles and Practices of Teaching English as an International Language* (pp. 168–185). New York: Routledge.

McCarthy, M., McCarten, S. and Sandiford, H. (2005) *Touchstones: Level 3*. Cambridge: Cambridge University Press.

McKay, S.L. (2012) Teaching materials for English as an international language. In A. Matsuda (ed.) *Principles and Practices of Teaching English as an International Language* (pp. 55–69). Bristol: Multilingual Matters.

Mukminatien, N. (2012) Accomodating World Englishes in developing EFL learners' oral communication. *TEFLIN Journal* 23 (2), 222–232.

Wang, H. and Hill, C. (2011) A paradigm shift for English language teaching in Asia: From imposition to accommodation. *The Journal of ASIA TEFL* 8 (4), 205–232.

Zacharias, N.T. (2005) Teachers' beliefs about internationally-published materials: A survey of tertiary English teachers in Indonesia. *RELC Journal* 36, 23–37.

# Part 5

# Independent Units on Teaching EIL

# 12 A Global Approach to English Language Teaching: Integrating an International Perspective into a Teaching Methods Course

Heath Rose

## Introduction

The growth of English as an International Language (EIL) has challenged the fundamental principles of how English is learned and how it is taught. Nowadays, learners of English are likely to use the language in a variety of contact situations with a diverse range of English speakers, many of whom may also be learners of the language or users of English as an additional language. Globalization has been the catalyst for a shift in the ownership of the English language from native English-speaking populations to a global community of speakers. This has changed the fundamental sociolinguistic landscape of English language use from within the Inner and Outer Circles to within and across all three of Kachru's (1985) circles. This shift has clear ramifications for traditional approaches to English language teaching (ELT), which have placed 'native' English norms at the center of classroom practices. Traditionally, many ELT practices are out of sync with the new landscape of English use, such as the practices of using the native speaker as the yardstick for measuring proficiency, positioning the native speaker as the future interlocutor for English learners and assuming that learners will use English in Inner Circle cultures. Thus, old approaches that do not match the current needs of students to use English in an international context are in need of change. Instigating change and innovation in ELT has been the focus of much literature in the field of EIL, which has been critical of the traditional practices that fail to meet the 21st-century needs of their students (e.g. Kumaravadivelu, 2012). Although the field of EIL has also been active in providing recommendations for change, it has been noted that a theory–practice divide exists, where change is campaigned for in academic and research circles, but little is changing in actual English language classrooms (Galloway & Rose, 2015). However, some teacher training programs are beginning to re-evaluate the type of training that they provide to their teachers, so that modern notions of what should be occurring in the classroom are being taught to the future generation of teachers.

As a result, EIL-oriented content is gradually emerging in an increasing number of teacher training programs around the world. Some universities have responded rapidly, and now offer full courses on teaching EIL, or courses where an EIL focus is present throughout the content, as earlier chapters in this volume have shown. In other universities, the programs are more constrained and teacher trainers have worked within existing course structures to provide EIL content in the form of shorter units of study. In this chapter, I will outline one such unit, in which an EIL component is taught within a larger course taken by masters-level students in Ireland. The programs are the Masters of Philosophy (MPhil) in ELT and the MPhil in Applied Linguistics, which are offered by the School of Linguistic, Speech and Communication Sciences at Trinity College Dublin. Both of these degrees are one-year programs, which follow a two-thirds coursework, one-third research dissertation structure.

In terms of the student population, half of the students in these programs tend to be in-service teachers, who are returning to university to further their education after teaching for many years. The other half of the students in the program are early career teachers who are interested in training to become English language teachers based on some, but minimal, experience in the classroom. In terms of the students' country of origin, approximately one-third are from Ireland, one-third are from mainland Europe and one-third are from non-European countries such as Saudi Arabia, China and Brazil. The two programs attract about 20–30 students per year. The position of Ireland as an English-speaking nation within the European Union makes the teaching of EIL in these teacher training programs highly relevant for students, due to the clear implications for the immediate European context, where English is quickly becoming the main lingua franca language (Hoffmann, 2000).

## Description of the Unit

Within the two programs outlined in the previous section, an EIL-related unit is offered as part of a course called Second Language Teaching. This particular course aims to improve the theoretical knowledge base of trainee teachers by providing an overview of the historical and current teaching methods, classroom practices and salient issues surrounding the

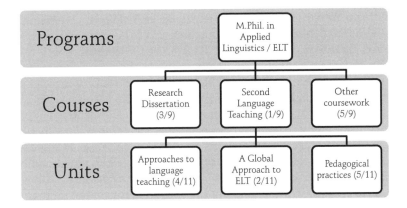

**Figure 12.1** The unit's position in the program structure

profession. The course is elective (made available to students in both the MPhil Applied Linguistics and MPhil ELT), but in reality almost all students choose to take the course. The course involves 22 contact hours over 11 weeks in one academic term, and requires two written assignments – one based on theoretical concepts in teaching approaches, and the other on practical applications to the English language classroom.

The EIL-related unit is called A Global Approach to English Language Teaching, and makes up 2 of the 11 weeks of the course's contact hours, which is almost 20% of the course content (see Figure 12.1). The unit is offered in the middle of the course structure after the theoretical approaches to language teaching are discussed, but before the more practical classroom teaching practices are covered (e.g. the teaching of speaking, or the evaluation of materials for use in the classroom). This structure ensures that students gain an overview of the historical and recent trends in teaching approaches such as grammar-translation, audio-lingualism, communicative language teaching, content-based teaching and content and language integrated learning (CLIL), before looking at the current global context in which English is taught. This leads into the EIL unit, which explores how this global growth of English impacts the way in which we frame our teaching, such as the models taught and tested in international classrooms.

The first hour of the unit provides an overview of the spread of English as a global language, and explores its current position as the global lingua franca. The second hour explores standard language ideology, particularly how it manifests in society, classroom curricula, teaching materials and hiring practices. The second two hours of the unit, which are offered in the following week, examine the incorporation of a global perspective into ELT practices, such as

- raising awareness in the classroom of how English is used as an international language;
- using a student needs analysis to discern the appropriate models of English for our students;
- evaluating, selecting and adapting teaching materials.

The second part of the unit incorporates a more student-centered approach to the course content in the form of discussion-based case studies, discussion of classroom-based academic articles (e.g. Galloway & Rose, 2014), debates based on source material (e.g. Kachru, 1991; Quirk, 1990) and a number of activities taken from chapter nine of *Introducing Global Englishes* (Galloway & Rose, 2015), which includes extra online resources for classroom use.

The unit marks a transition in the course from an exploration of teaching methods to an investigation of current classroom practices; however, teaching English in global contexts remains a framework for discussions on classroom practices. A midterm assignment covers this first part of the course, and while teaching EIL is just one of the four possible assignment topics, it is by far the most popular one.

## Uniqueness of the Unit

The unit is driven by the Global Englishes Language Teaching (GELT) framework, which was created by Galloway (2011, 2013), and then further developed by Galloway and Rose (2015). GELT is a framework that 'focuses on diversity and the function of English as an international lingua franca, rather than traditional approaches to ELT which aim to teach people to speak with native English speakers' (Galloway & Rose, 2015: 208). For more detail on the use of GELT as a teacher training framework, please see Galloway (this volume). It is important to note that the term Global Englishes is defined for students as an umbrella term to unite the work of World Englishes, English as a lingua franca (ELF) and EIL. Therefore, the concept of GELT mirrors the definition of teaching EIL provided by Matsuda (this volume), which she also describes as an umbrella term.

The GELT framework is underpinned by six key notions that have emerged from various calls within the fields of EIL, ELF and World Englishes, regarding changes in ELT classrooms, including:

(1) Increasing World Englishes exposure (e.g. Mastuda & Friedrich, 2012; McKay, 2012).
(2) Emphasizing respect for multilingualism (e.g. Friedrich, 2012; Kirkpatrick, 2012).
(3) Emphasizing respect for diverse and fluid culture and identity (e.g. Baker, 2009, 2012; Friedrich, 2012).

(4) Raising awareness of Global Englishes, including EIL (e.g. Galloway, 2013; Seidlhofer, 2004).
(5) Changing English teacher hiring practices (e.g. Braine, 2010; Kirkpatrick, 2011, 2012; McKay, 2012).
(6) Raising awareness of interaction strategies for using ELF/EIL (e.g. House, 2012; McKay, 2012).

These six proposals form the basis of the uniqueness of the EIL unit, and differentiate the course from traditional courses which often take more static views of ELT. The unit ends with the presentation of the GELT framework as a visual summary of the differences between a global approach to ELT and traditional approaches to ELT (see Galloway, this volume, for framework). The course content of the unit, therefore, can be best explained using these six notions that inform the GELT approach.

First, the unit introduces trainee teachers to the importance of providing diverse models of English in the language curriculum in order to expose their learners to a wider variety of dialects. This is a departure from traditional approaches that have often posited received pronunciation (RP) British English and General American English as the models of spoken English, and as a result, these models saturate language teaching classrooms and materials. The unit argues that greater exposure is essential to meet student needs: by not exposing learners to the diversity of English, teachers are doing their learners a disservice by ill-equipping them to use English in the future with a wide variety of speakers who will not conform to the unrepresentative standards promoted in traditional English as a foreign language (EFL) classrooms. This generally leads to a discussion of which models to use, and students are encouraged to read literature in the area (e.g. D'Souza, 1999; Matsuda & Friedrich, 2012). This aspect of the content concludes with the notion that needs analysis is essential to reveal the varieties that are most salient to learners in their classes, which will depend on the learners' goals and future communities of practice. Trainee teachers are taught that curriculum choices should always be led by student needs, and selecting models of English to use in the classroom is no exception. For example, for a group of business students studying in Indonesia, it might be more appropriate to focus on exposure to Australian and Singaporean varieties of English than the further afield British or American varieties. When needs are not apparent, the unit encourages the teachers to be innovative, and present learners with autonomous learning tasks where they can select the varieties of English most relevant to them. The unit refers to the Galloway and Rose (2014) study for ideas of how this can be done in the classroom. In the seminar component of the unit, classroom models are returned to in a case study for which students pre-read the famous articles in *English Today* (Kachru, 1991; Quirk, 1990), in which legitimate models of English are fiercely debated.

Second, trainee teachers are taught about the benefits of embracing multilingualism in their classrooms. While traditional ELT approaches may have discouraged the use of other languages by following an 'English-only' classroom policy, the trainee teachers in this unit are encouraged to view knowledge of other languages as a resource. Moreover, it is explained to be more representative of students' future use of English. In the unit, the trainee teachers often engage in heated debate on the benefits of an 'English-only' policy in language classrooms, and supporters of English-only classrooms argue that the policy creates a second language (L2) environment in EFL contexts, where opportunities to use the language are rare. The trainee teachers usually come to a compromise that languages other than the target language can serve purposes for some learning activities, but if students are able to perform, explain or understand a task in the L2, that it should be reinforced as it is the subject of study. For further reading, we explore research that highlights the benefits of code-switching in the language classroom (e.g. Tian & Macaro, 2012).

Third, the unit emphasizes respect for other cultures and identities, which is also important in challenging the monocultural ideology that underpins many classroom resources. Textbooks, for example, often depict the goal of language learners as being to join an Inner Circle culture (Syrbe & Rose, 2016). The target interlocutor is almost always an Inner Circle speaker, therefore perpetuating an idea that the ownership of English is within the Inner Circle. To illustrate this point, I often provide examples of well-known texts that focus solely on a learner travelling to an Inner Circle country to use the language. In the unit, trainee teachers are encouraged to challenge this concept and discuss ways in which they can shift this ideology while using the Inner Circle resources that they are given to teach from.

Fourth, raising awareness of the global use of English is seen as an essential part of any modern curriculum in a globalized context. Awareness raising involves directly teaching students about the current global use of English, the ownership of the language, language diversity and issues surrounding standard language ideology. Studies in the past (e.g. Galloway, 2013) have shown awareness raising to have a confidence-boosting effect for students. Raising awareness in the learner body can also make students more open to the benefits of being taught by a 'nonnative' expert user of the language, who may not share their first language (L1) (see Galloway & Rose, 2013). In the unit, I have also seen awareness raising to have a confidence-boosting effect for trainee teachers who are nonnative speakers of English and who have taken a deficit view of their abilities as a teacher due to their nonnative identities. These identities have often been reinforced in traditional ELT practices, which posit 'nativeness' rather than 'expert use' as the goal of language learning.

This changing of awareness is also essential to facilitate the changing of hiring practices in the ELT industry, which posit nativeness as a more desirable characteristic in an English teacher than teaching credentials. The unit explores notions of nonnative English-speaking teacher discrimination, which have restricted access to many high-profile teaching positions around the world (Ali, 2009). During the final part of the unit, trainee teachers discuss a case study taken from Tollefson (1995), which discusses the difficulties experienced by a highly qualified English teacher from the Philippines when finding an English teaching job in the US. This teacher had grown up bilingually, using a Filipina variety of English as her primary language of schooling. The case is used as a discussion point to raise broader issues surrounding the native–nonnative divide in other teaching and learning environments. It is teacher education like the unit described here, or larger components of teacher training programs as described in previous chapters, which are essential in breaking down the native–nonnative divide that is rife in the ELT industry worldwide.

The teaching of communication strategies for use in lingua franca environments is a final element to the unit. While the building of learners' strategic competence has been an important goal in communicative language teaching since the 1970s, and remains an important component in proficiency measures such as the Common European Framework for Reference, the GELT framework pushes this concept further. In the unit, trainees are exposed to the need of future learners to interact with a wider variety of speakers from diverse linguistic backgrounds. The need for students to develop strategies to 'shuttle between communities' (Canagarajah, 2005: xxv) of different speakers is made apparent to the students. It is emphasized that ELF research has shown that linguistic norms emerge in each instance of communication, rather than being bound by national boundaries – 'language and culture are created in each instance of communication, and are fluid and unfixed' (Galloway & Rose, 2015: 229). It is impossible for teachers and students to predict what these localized norms of language use are, thus, rather than teaching them, learners need to develop strategies to negotiate meaning, accommodate speakers and successfully take part in communication across these cultures. We concur with Baker (2009) that, for learners of English today, the ability to negotiate, mediate and adapt to emerging communicative practices is at least as important as a systematic knowledge of the English language itself, and thus strategies to facilitate this negotiation, mediation and adaptation need to be emphasized in English language classrooms.

## Challenges and Limitations

Although many students choose to follow up concepts in their final assignments, the unit is clearly limited in its ability to cover a broad amount of content in just four hours of lectures. Moreover, as the unit addresses many issues that are still being fiercely debated at a theoretical level, trainee teachers often have difficulty translating these ideas into classroom practices.

In the first year of implementation, the unit took a largely lecture-style format. End-of-course feedback revealed that while students were professionally and personally engaged with the content of the unit, they were left perplexed as to how to use this information to inform their teaching. As an instructor, I was concerned that the unit was too theoretically, politically and ethically driven, rather than providing trainee teachers with concrete ideas of how to initiate change in their classrooms. In the second year of implementation, the class took more of a seminar approach, with lectures reduced to two of the four hours, and the remaining time devoted to expanding on issues in the form of real case studies and discussions, where trainee teachers could examine the issues of connecting EIL ideas to classroom practice. In its new format, the unit gave voice to a rich variety of ideas from some of the more experienced teachers in the classroom, who could share their experiences in a variety of teaching contexts. It also gave a voice to nonnative English-speaking students in the course – many of whom had studied and taught within more traditional approaches to ELT. These students could provide an 'insider' account of exactly what needed to change.

The unit raised a number of problems that students felt were unresolved in terms of implementing EIL-oriented ideas into the classroom. One of the biggest issues was the timing and degree of exposure to variation in English. While all students saw the benefits of exposing students to variation in English, some of them felt that it might detract from the teaching of the mechanics of the language in the earlier stages of learning development, and thought it best left until later. I referred students to D'Souza's (1999: 273) point that exposing students 'to as many varieties of English as possible would do more to ensure intelligibility than trying to impose a single standard on everyone'. That is, even if classes showcase a limited variety of Englishes, I argued that it would be more ethical to let learners know that the models presented were only used by a small portion of the English-speaking population. By doing this, learners would not be surprised later to discover that the English they were learning was not representative of most speakers. While students were somewhat placated by this response, the unit did not fully resolve this issue by providing a definitive answer.

Furthermore, the unit was very idealistic in nature, and students felt that it might cause frustration when they entered the workforce and had to conform to teaching in environments which favored native English-speaking teachers, native speaker models and ideas of standard language. This is an issue that often occurs in teacher training programs, where the learning of new pedagogical practices can be the cause of later feelings of futility when teachers enter jobs where these practices are not followed. In Japan, for example, I was involved in in-service teacher training where

English language teachers would become excited over learning about student-centered, communicative approaches before then returning to their exam-oriented, grammar-led teaching contexts, where integrating these new approaches proved difficult. It is hoped, however, that the dissemination of new ideas within existing teacher training programs, whether it be teaching approaches or the teaching of EIL, will be the first step in a wider conversation between graduates of these programs and their students, peers and the stakeholders of the institutions where they will go on to teach.

A final limitation of the unit was its lack of connection to actual materials that could be used to implement the proposals into the classroom. At the end of the unit, I made available to students some English for academic purposes (EAP) materials that I had created in a business school in Japan, which had a global element throughout the curriculum. I also gave them links to an extensive bank of online resources as part of the *Introducing Global Englishes* (Galloway & Rose, 2015) textbook. However, as many of the trainee teachers were going into teaching lower-proficiency classes, the unit did not provide materials or material ideas for this common teaching context. Although commercial textbooks are only one resource used in language classrooms, they remain the most prevalent source for curriculum design, and as such assert a major influence on the way language is taught and the way students view the language (Matsuda, 2002). EIL research has highlighted an appalling lack of materials for the teaching of EIL, and this remains a significant challenge to implementing change in ELT. It is important to note, however, that textbooks by their very nature represent an uncontroversial, idealized view of the world that is often culturally biased (Crawford, 2002), and thus teachers will often need to supplement them with more authentic materials. Nevertheless, the lack of EIL-related content in existing textbooks remains a major limitation for students to put a global approach to ELT into practice.

## Conclusion

The global spread of English has changed the sociolinguistic landscape of how the language is used, and how learners need to use English in the future. In recent decades, we have seen the growth of English as *the* international language, and English language learners are witnessing the emergence of a new need to use English on this global platform – a shift that must then be reflected in teacher training programs. The unit outlined in this chapter is an example of this initial step of integrating EIL material into an existing teacher training course. It is hoped that it serves as an example of a way language educators can work within existing program structures to deliver the important ideas emerging from EIL research. Lecturers are often required to work within fixed courses and programs, which have been approved at university council level (and in some institutions at the national level). As a result, in can be difficult or impossible to introduce new courses quickly, or add new dimensions to these pre-approved programs. However, lecturers will almost always have the autonomy to develop and change content within their own assigned course, and this is where the power of an EIL unit lies. In a course title as generic as 'Second Language Teaching', it was easy to add a unit which focused on the teaching of EIL. The same can be said for courses typical in most programs, such as 'curriculum design', 'language testing' or 'teaching speaking'.

The other advantage of encasing EIL content within a unit is that units are easily transplantable to other course structures. In September 2015, I moved from Trinity College Dublin to take up a position at the University of Oxford to teach on a postgraduate teacher training program, called the MSc in Teaching English Language in University Settings. In my new position, I had to take over the lecturing of pre-approved courses within an existing program, none of which reflected my previous course title of 'Second Language Teaching' where the EIL unit was placed. However, as a unit is transplantable into other courses, I could take the Teaching English as an International Language (TEIL) unit and place elements of it within two new courses, which were Understanding and Teaching Grammar and Evaluating and Designing English Language Teaching Materials for University Settings. Because of the flexibility given within the course structure, I could expand the unit and adapt it according to the different aims of the two courses – something I could not have done with an entire EIL course. Thus, the unit offers more flexibility than an entire EIL course can provide. In addition, I believe that units offer more opportunity to reach more students, because they are more easily integrated into mandatory core courses compared to many EIL courses that are often offered as elective courses, and viewed as *additional* rather than *essential* in teaching English to speakers of other languages (TESOL) programs.

In conclusion, while I have found great success in the unit, it is still a work in progress, which develops each year as my own ideas develop, and my learners raise new issues and challenges to consider in the next cycle of the course syllabus. Our job as teacher educators is to constantly try to improve teaching practices to better serve our students. Change, however, is often very slow – as teacher training programs can only reach new teachers, or those returning to education. It may be decades before elements of teaching EIL filter down to mainstream classrooms, curricula and materials. In reality, ELT is constrained by the contexts in which we teach, and it will take time for these contexts to adjust to the changes suggested in academic circles. However, with the emergence of EIL-related content in teacher training programs, we are engaging in an important initial step in disseminating these ideas to future teachers, who may then carry them further afield to international, national or regional teaching conferences, organized staff development workshops or even informal staffroom conversations. EIL is fast becoming an important component of TESOL training programs, thus the methods to integrate this important concept within existing programs are becoming increasingly relevant. Without knowledge of EIL, newly trained teachers would emerge from institutions without the necessary skills to teach their students to use English in the 21st century.

## References

Ali, S. (2009) Teaching English as an international language (EIL) in the gulf corporation council (GCC) countries: The brown man's burden. In F. Sharifian (ed.) *English as an International Language: Perspectives and Pedagogical Issues* (pp. 34–57). Bristol: Multilingual Matters.

Baker, W. (2009) The cultures of English as a lingua franca. *TESOL Quarterly* 43 (4), 567–592.

Baker, W. (2012) From cultural awareness to intercultural awareness: Culture in ELT. *ELT Journal* 66 (1), 62–70.

Braine, G. (2010) *Non-native Speaker English Teachers. Research, Pedagogy, and Professional Growth*. New York: Routledge.

Canagarajah, A.S. (2005) Introduction. In A.S. Canagarajah (ed.) *Reclaiming the Local in Language Policy and Practice*. Mahwah, NJ: Lawrence Erlbaum Associates.

Crawford, J. (2002) The role of materials in the language classroom: Finding the balance. In J.C. Richards and W.A. Renandaya (eds) *Methodology in Language Teaching: An Anthology of Current Practices* (pp. 80–95). New York: Cambridge University Press.

D'Souza, J. (1999) Afterword. *World Englishes* 18 (2), 271–274.

Friedrich, P. (2012) ELF, intercultural communication and the strategic aspect of communicative competence. In A. Matsuda (ed.) *Principles and Practices of Teaching English as an International Language* (pp. 44–54). Bristol: Multilingual Matters.

Galloway, N. (2011) *An Investigation of Japanese Students' Attitudes Towards English*. Unpublished Doctoral Dissertation. University of Southampton.

Galloway, N. (2013) Global Englishes and English Language Teaching (ELT) – Bridging the gap between theory and practice in a Japanese context. *System* 41 (3), 786–803.

Galloway, N. and Rose, H. (2013) 'They envision going to New York, not Jakarta': The differing attitudes toward ELF of students, teaching assistants, and instructors in an English-medium business program in Japan. *Journal of English as a Lingua Franca* 2 (2), 229–253.

Galloway, N. and Rose, H. (2014) Using listening journals to raise awareness of Global Englishes in ELT. *ELT Journal* 68 (4), 386–396.

Galloway, N. and Rose, H. (2015) *Introducing Global Englishes in ELT*. Abingdon: Routledge.

Hoffmann, C. (2000) The spread of English and the growth of multilingualism with English in Europe. In J. Cenoz and U. Jessner (eds) *English in Europe. The Acquisition of A Third Language* (pp. 1–21). Clevedon: Multilingual Matters.

House, J. (2012) Teaching oral skills in English as a lingua franca. In L. Alsagoff, S.L. McKay, G. Hu and W.A. Renandya (eds) *Principles and Practices for Teaching English as an International Language* (pp. 186–205). New York: Routledge.

Kachru, B.B. (1985) Standards, codification and sociolinguistic realism: The English language in the outer circle. In R. Quirk and H. Widdowson (eds) *English in the World: Teaching and Learning the Language and Literatures* (pp. 11–30). Cambridge: Cambridge University Press.

Kachru, B.B. (1991) 'Liberation linguistics and the Quirk concern'. *English Today* 7 (1), 3–13.

Kirkpatrick, A. (2011) English as an Asian lingua franca and the multilingual model of ELT. *Language Teaching* 44 (2), 212–224.

Kirkpatrick, A. (2012) English as an Asian lingua franca: The 'Lingua Franca Approach' and implications for language education policy. *Journal of English as a Lingua Franca* 1 (1), 121–139.

Kumaravadivelu, B. (2012) Individual identity, cultural globalization and teaching English as an international language: The case for an epistemic break. In L. Alsagoff, S.L. McKay, G. Hu and W.A. Renandya (eds) *Teaching English as an International Language: Principles and Practices* (pp. 9–27). New York: Routledge.

Matsuda, A. (2002) International understanding through teaching world Englishes. *World Englishes* 21 (3), 436–440.

Matsuda, A. and Friedrich, P. (2012) Selecting an instructional variety for an EIL curriculum. In A. Matsuda (ed.) *Principles and Practices of Teaching English as an International Language* (pp. 17–27). Bristol: Multilingual Matters.

McKay, S.L. (2012) Teaching materials for English as an international language. In A. Matsuda (ed.) *Principles and Practices of Teaching English as an International Language* (pp. 70–83). Bristol: Multilingual Matters.

Quirk, R. (1990) Language varieties and standard language. *English Today* 6 (1), 3–10.

Seidlhofer, B. (2004) Research perspectives on teaching English as a lingua franca. *Annual Review of Applied Linguistics* 24, 209–239.

Syrbe, M. and Rose, H. (2016) An evaluation of the global orientation of English textbooks in Germany. *Innovation in Language Learning and Teaching* 10 (1), 1–12.

Tian, L. and Macaro, E. (2012) Comparing the effect of teacher codeswitching with English-only explanations on the vocabulary acquisition of Chinese university students: A lexical focus-on-form study. *Language Teaching Research* 16 (3), 361–385.

Tollefson, J. (1995) *Power and Inequality in Language Education.* Cambridge: Cambridge University Press.

# 13 English as a Lingua Franca in an Online Teacher Education Program Offered by a State University in Brazil

Michele Salles El Kadri, Luciana Cabrini Simões Calvo and Telma Gimenez

## Introduction

It has been widely accepted that the understanding of English as a lingua franca (ELF) should have an important role in the education of English language teachers in order to allow for the recognition of the diversity inherent in its use in the world today. In Brazil, only recently has this naming been introduced as an important topic for discussion (El Kadri, 2010; Siqueira, 2008, 2011; Souza et al., 2011). This does not mean that the recognition of English as a global language has received scant attention, but rather that the ELF perspective is relatively new in our context. While international studies on ELF and its consequences have evolved to analyze specific instances such as teacher education schemes (Dewey, 2012) and textbooks (Takahashi, 2014), or to suggest approaches to teacher education (Sifakis, 2014), in Brazil, research engaged with the so-called 'ELF project' is still at the early stages (Bordini & Gimenez, 2014; El Kadri & Gimenez, 2013).

A partial explanation can be found in the commonly held assumption that the teaching of English as a foreign language is not incompatible with that perspective, suggesting that misconceptions about ELF may be in place.[1] Since the dominant models of language development in the country are based on discursive notions of language, largely focused on native speakers' norms, teacher education programs are faced with the challenge of deconstructing historical understandings that associate English solely with native speakers. As a consequence, there are few publications reporting how an ELF perspective is being included in preservice English language teacher education (Gimenez et al., 2015) and even fewer have provided practical examples of how to implement a curriculum that is sensitive to those points of view (Calvo *et al.*, 2014). Thus, one can conclude that one of the big challenges for English language teacher education is how to deal with the critical analysis of the assumptions underlying historically persistent practices in the teaching of English.

In this context, this chapter describes one initiative to raise awareness about the new linguistic realities of lingua franca encounters: a unit dedicated to ELF as part of an online program for preservice English language teachers in a public university in the state of Paraná, Brazil. First, we describe the specific components of the teaching unit; then, we present an analysis based on a criteria list in order to demonstrate its distinctiveness. Finally, we discuss the challenges and limitations of such a unit based on the participants' questionnaire and the analysis carried out.

# Teaching Unit: 'English in the Contemporary World'

## Overview of the unit

The context of our work is a five-year online teacher education program offered by a state university located in Maringá, Paraná state. The program aims at preparing schoolteachers who can teach Portuguese and English in secondary schools. The program is funded by the Brazilian Federal Agency for Higher Education Professional Development (CAPES) through the Brazilian Open University System (Universidade Aberta do Brasil – UAB). UAB was created in 2006 to support the expansion of the public higher education system via distance learning. The partner universities offer undergraduate courses to low-income students thanks to the funding provided by CAPES, as well as providing educational opportunities to those living in remote areas, with little access to universities and colleges. According to the UAB official website, its aim is to expand the offer of university education by enhancing the universality of high education, to qualify teachers, to strengthen school education in remote areas and to minimize the concentration of undergraduate courses in big cities and thus avoid internal migration.

For this context, the materials follow an instructional dialogic language, bearing in mind the target audience (in our case, preservice English teachers in their first contact with the ELF perspective) and the fact that it will rely mainly on self-study.

Two teacher educators who are also the coauthors of this chapter produced the unit. One of them had already had some experience with materials design for distance education and the other had her first experience in producing an online teaching unit. Both were 'content teachers'. Content teachers, in online education, are the experts on a specific subject. When designing materials, these experts not only draw on their knowledge about the topic but also consider the potential audience's needs. Content teachers, then, are not necessarily the teachers who will be with the group of preservice teachers.

The teaching unit entitled 'English in the Contemporary World' (ECW) (El Kadri & Calvo, 2015) is one of the four units that make up the book *Teacher Education: Linguistic-Communicative Skills and English as a Lingua Franca* (Calvo, Freitas & Alves, 2015), specifically directed at preservice students enrolled in the online teacher education program. The other units are: (1) Oral Skills and Foreign Language Teaching, (2) Foreign Language Reading and (3) Foreign Language Writing. The book is used in the course 'Methodological Practice of English Language Teaching', whose syllabus comprises topics such as the teaching and learning of language skills (speaking, listening, reading, writing), the status of English nowadays and its implications for the teaching and learning of the language and textual genres in the teaching and learning of a foreign language (especially English). This 68-hour course is offered for students in the fifth year of the Language Arts undergraduate program and it lasts one semester.

The ECW unit aims at discussing beliefs and attitudes toward the English language, inviting reflections on the objectives, perspectives and didactic materials for the teaching of English as well as the main implications of considering ELF. Its central purpose is to raise awareness about the spread of English and the linguistic changes resulting from its relocation (Saraceni, 2011). It is divided into four sections: (1) English expansion in the world, (2) linguistic implications, (3) political and social linguistic implications and (4) educational implications. This last section is subdivided into five subsections: (i) English varieties, (ii) pronunciation: intelligibility issues, (iii) articulation between the local and global: planetary citizenship, (iv) the teaching of culture and (v) teaching objectives. There are 20 tasks in total, with different resources for mediation: videos, texts, audios, excerpts from newspapers, sites from the internet, etc.

## Detailed description of the unit

The unit aims at raising awareness about ELF. As suggested by Bayyurt (2014) and Llurda (2014), aiming at raising awareness has the potential to empower teachers and enhance their confidence since they have more realistic goals for their teaching (Sifakis, 2014), especially in those contexts where teachers have the power to make local decisions about teaching.

The reflective approach guided the production of the unit in order not only to raise awareness of the issues regarding ELF but also to connect to what prospective teachers understand about it, based on their own experience as learners and student teachers.

The unit follows a pattern in which the authors' views on ELF, supported by references to the literature (e.g. Crystal, 1997, 2003;

El Kadri, 2010; Gimenez, 2001, 2006, 2009; Graddol, 2000, 2006; Jenkins, 2000, 2012; Rajagopalan, 2003, 2009, 2010; Seidlholfer, 2001, 2009, among others) are interspersed with the tasks.

It begins with two excerpts from Brazilian newspapers highlighting the status of English. Both excerpts emphasize that English is the most spoken language in the world and if people want to be included in the worldwide society (and if they want their country to be noticed around the globe), they need to learn English. Students are expected to express their perceptions in relation to the status of English in our country.

Then, the unit explores some of the reasons why English is considered a global lingua franca. Firstly, historical aspects are presented (including the colonial expansion of Great Britain and the power of the USA after the Second World War); then, there is the recognition of the role of globalization in promoting ELF. Some aspects of globalization are mentioned and its connection to English is emphasized, although without questioning of the consequences of such relationship, a limitation that was only noticed when writing this chapter. To conclude this first part, Kachru's circles for representing the expansion of English are introduced.

After that, ELF becomes the focus, together with its linguistic, political/social and educational implications. In the linguistic implications section, the multiplicity of users as well as the notion of language ownership are briefly discussed. Some examples of the corpus available through the Vienna Oxford Corpus of English (VOICE) project are brought to exemplify some of the linguistic changes in language that would not prevent communication. The section finishes with an activity for the preservice teachers to analyze a short text by India's prime minister, in which he describes some characteristics of Indian English. The students are then directed to a website (http://www.hawaii.edu/satocenter/langnet/descriptions/index.html) to describe some of the characteristics of Singlish and any other variety of their choice.

Regarding the political and social implications, the students are asked to consider to what extent English is part of exclusionary processes, as well as its functioning as a social gatekeeper. Considerations about linguistic policies to ensure access to English learning for all students are also pointed out. There are five subsections under educational implications:

(i)   English varieties – it highlights the importance of students being exposed to different English accents and varieties.
(ii)  Pronunciation: intelligibility issues – it presents different points of view regarding the pros and cons of having a central core of intelligibility.
(iii) Glocalization and planetary citizenship – it discusses the possibility of having access to and participating in English discussions or global social movements around the world through the English language.

(iv) The teaching of culture – it highlights the importance of developing intercultural competence in ELT.

(v) Teaching objectives – it addresses topics such as communication with native speakers versus communication with nonnative speakers; students learning English according to their own needs; effective use of the language.

In order to sum up the issues raised in the unit, the students are required to analyze a teaching unit (Matos *et al.*, 2009) according to a set of given parameters, as proposed by Gimenez *et al.* (2015). Finally, students are presented with the view that ELF is already finding spaces for institutional recognition due to the example of a question in a university entrance exam in which a literary text in 'non-standard' English is selected to check understanding of the 'lyric self'.

## Unique Characteristics of the Teaching Unit

In order to establish the distinctiveness of the unit, we also designed a checklist with features reflecting an ELF approach, as discussed in the literature already mentioned. The results of this analysis are shown in Table 13.1.

Having the opportunity to look at the unit retrospectively, we can observe that some of the fundamental topics in an ELF perspective were partially or not addressed (e.g. a comparison of standardized proficiency tests and other parameters for the evaluation of linguistic proficiency/ language use; pragmatic strategies), thus revealing a need for revision. The criteria list may help us in this endeavor.

In addition to our own evaluation, we also wanted to listen to the instructor and to the tutors involved with the course and so we created a questionnaire that was sent to all of those involved. As at the time of writing, the instructor and two of the four tutors had responded to a questionnaire probing into their experience with the unit. Both the instructor and the tutors considered the unit relevant. According to tutor A, it enabled both students and teachers to reflect on their practices in order to improve them. According to tutor B, this was a relevant unit because it is contemporary in terms of language teaching issues in the 21st century and also because it presents to the future teacher not only the perspective of teaching but also of learning English (as they are also students of English in the online course). According to the instructor/teacher, the unit is relevant because it deals with beliefs regarding the English language and the implications of considering it a lingua franca. Also, all of them believe that the unit achieved its goals as the objectives are addressed clearly (tutor A) in a pedagogical way through the national and international literature and exercises about it (instructor).

**Table 13.1** ELF criteria list applied to the unit

| Does the unit... | Yes | Partially | No | Where in the unit |
|---|---|---|---|---|
| – encourage reconceptualizations of the reasons for learning English, i.e. does it ask the future teacher to rethink why he/she and his/her students are studying English? | √ | | | Educational implications – learning objectives and Activity 18 |
| – enable understandings of the spread of English in the world and its connection with globalization? | √ | | | English and globalization |
| – help with the recognition that English can no longer be associated only with native speakers? | √ | | | ELF implications |
| – discuss questions of the ownership of English? | √ | | | Linguistic implications of ELF and Activities 6–7 |
| – raise awareness of the different varieties of English other than standard American or standard British? | √ | | | Educational implications – varieties of English and Activities 12–14 |
| – raise awareness about intelligibility and different English accents? | √ | | | Educational implications – intelligibility and Activity 15 |
| – include tasks to help preservice teachers reflect on the concept of culture and the intercultural dimension in language teaching/use? | √ | | | Educational implications – teaching of culture and Activity 17 |
| – help preservice teachers reflect on the advantages and disadvantages of the nonnative teacher? | √ | | | Activity 10 |
| – include tasks for future teachers to analyze didactic materials considering the ELF perspective? | √ | | | Activity 19 |
| – challenge traditional language assumptions? | √ | | | The whole unit |
| – help future teachers reflect on the identity stances of English users? | √ | | | Activity 6 |

**Table 13.1** (*continued*)

| | | |
|---|---|---|
| – discuss the concept of 'mistakes'/'errors' in communication versus standard norms? | √ | Linguistic implications |
| – compare standardized proficiency tests and other parameters for the evaluation of linguistic proficiency/language use? | √ | |
| – discuss the importance of addressing topics and themes covering a wider range of social and global issues, connecting the global and the local? | √ | Educational implications – glocalization and planetary citizenship and Activity 16 |
| – include a topic on pragmatic strategies? | √ | |
| – give teachers an opportunity to see how ELF is appropriate in the context of the expansion of English? | √ | Linguistic implications |
| – propose an integration of the perspective into English classes? | √ | Only in a reflective way (Activities 14(a), 16(b)) |
| – allow teachers to engage in action research projects that use ELF-related concerns in ways that are appropriate for their context? | √ | |

Both the teacher and the tutors pointed out positive points about the unit: (a) the information on ELF, which is unknown by many of the undergraduate students (tutor A); (b) the topic addressed; the theoretical approach; the organization of the unit (the studied topics and the way they were distributed in the unit); the EFL linguistic, political and educational implications and the proposed activities that gave a didactic character to the unit (tutor B); and (c) the proposed exercises (which makes the understanding of the subject easier), the topic structure used (which helps to spot the information needed) and the pedagogical implications (which not only inform but also guide the teachers' positioning and role during their practice).

In relation to the difference between the unit and more traditional ways of teaching English, they answered that they valued the opportunity of being in touch with a 'different' perspective. Specifically, tutor A highlighted that several pedagogical implications for the teaching of ELF are considered and the fact that bringing other accents to her practice is not a common thing, although she does think this is important. Tutor B reports the most interesting points for her: the implications. She considers that this perspective suggests how to work with English as a lingua franca and not as a foreign language (as it is still traditionally taught in Brazil). Tutor B also points out the differences between the perspectives, including the decentralization of privileged varieties and the valorization of intelligibility. The instructor stresses the fact that the unit depicts (a) the idea that teachers also have to be researchers because this is the way to be aware of new concepts regarding language education and the transformation they engender, (b) the issue of 'empowerment' brought by the perspective and (c) the issue of 'standard' English and the misconception of having 'the correct and unique' English. To her, discussing these issues provides the opportunity to have a broader view of what it means to teach English in her context. The instructor also highlights the fact that the unit depicts concern with the specific situation of each country, suggesting that English should be taught according to the needs of each context.

The consultation revealed that the tutors expressed positive attitudes toward the implementation of the unit, emphasizing not only the need to incorporate such discussion for undergraduate teachers but also stressing that the unit also influenced their views.

Besides the unit potential presented here, we also identified some challenges and some of its limitations, which will be discussed in the next section.

## Challenges and Limitations

In addition to assessing the teacher and tutors' perceptions, we also wanted to evaluate the reflective nature of the unit. For this purpose, we looked at the rubrics of the tasks to be developed by the prospective teachers in terms of their cognitive skills, as shown in Table 13.2.

**Table 13.2** Learning skills encouraged by the tasks

| Activities | Rubrics | Cognitive skills |
|---|---|---|
| 1 | Read the following excerpts from two leading newspapers in Brazil. How are the points of view connected to the current status of English? | Comparing and contrasting Arguing |
| 2 | Before reading the first parts of the text, try to answer the following questions: what is a lingua franca? Why is English a lingua franca? What factors contribute to consider a language a lingua franca? | Defining Explaining Arguing |
| 3 | Watch the video 'Global English' (David Crystal), available at https://www.youtube.com/ watch?v=WZI1EjxxXKw, and write down the aspects related to the reasons why a language becomes a global language and the different meanings of power 'at different times in history'. | Active listening |
| 4 | Do research and identify countries where English is used as a (a) first language/mother tongue, (b) second language, (c) foreign language. | Information seeking Classifying |
| 5 | Read the quotations below and match the implications that they refer to. Use (1) for political implications; (2) for educational implications and (3) for linguistic implications. | Classifying |
| 6 | Read the talk of India's prime minister – Manmohan Singh – in 2005 and answer the following questions: | Locating information |
| 7 | Visit the website Hawaii.edu- available at http://www.hawaii.edu/satocenter/langnet/descrip- tions/index.html and describe the main characteristics of SINGLISH (the English variety of Singapore) and of another chosen variety. | Locating information |
| 8 | Based on the ideas presented in El Kadri's (2010) bibliographical review, answer the ques- tions. (The questions ask about the authors' perspectives and suggestions regarding the implications and the way in which foreign languages have been dealt with in Brazil. Students are asked to take part and discuss the teachers' role in this scenario.) | Locating information Arguing |

(continued)

**Table 13.2** (continued)

| Activities | Rubrics | Cognitive skills |
|---|---|---|
| 9 | **Part A:** Identify in the following sentences the differences between English as a foreign language and English as a lingua franca. | Comparing and contrasting |
| | **Part B:** Now, put the main idea of the sentences from the last exercise in its appropriate space in the table below and compare the differences between the perspective of English as a foreign language and English as a lingua franca. | Comparing and contrasting |
| 10 | Watch Sávio Siqueira's video in *Portal Sala* (http://www.sala.org.br/index.php/tv/ entrevistas/390-o-ingles-do-mundo-uma-lingua-franca) and summarize the author's main ideas concerning the current position of English in the world. | Identifying key ideas<br>Listening actively<br>Summarizing |
| 11 | Read Leffa's (2002) text 'Teaching English as a multinational language', available at http:// www.leffa.pro.br/textos/papers/multinational.pdf, and list the main priorities in English teaching suggested by that perspective. | Locating information<br>Identifying key points |
| 12 | Watch David Crystal's talk 'Should English be taught as a global language?' on YouTube, available at https://www.youtube.com/watch?v=tLYk4vKBdUo, and explain what he says about: (a) Global English in the classroom; (b) Global English in teaching production; (c) Global English in teaching comprehension; (d) Global English and pronunciation. | Active listening<br>Locating information |
| 13 | Watch another video from David Crystal (http://www.youtube.com/watch?v=0XT04E05RSU). What is the author's position in relation to the question: Which English should we teach students? | Active listening<br>Locating information |
| 14 | (...) describe what would be the choice of varieties to be taught in your context in a perspective that considers the status of English as a lingua franca.<br>Search on the web for three different English varieties (try to expand you search for beyond the Inner Circle countries!). Then, describe your reaction in listening to these varieties. Are you used to listening to them? What are the difficulties? What can you do to improve this language skill? | Describing<br><br>Information seeking<br>Describing<br>Problem-solving |

| Activities | Rubrics | Cognitive skills |
|---|---|---|
| 15 | Watch the video 'The Pink Panther' (http://www.youtube.com/watch?v=dphayJDCzog) and answer the questions: (a) As a student, or even as a teacher of English, would you feel more confident knowing that 'native-like' pronunciation wouldn't have the same importance or stress anymore? (b) Can we keep our accent and identity while still being intelligible? Are there limits? (c) What does the video tell us about learning and teaching English? | Reacting<br><br>Explaining<br><br><br>Active listening |
| 16 | Answer the following questions: (a) Why do the authors believe that developing planetary citizenship is one of the implications of ELF? and (b) Brainstorm and write examples showing how it could be implemented in English classes. | Locating information<br>Problem-solving |
| 17 | Read [a text] and write a paragraph positioning yourself in relation to the ideas presented by the author. | Arguing |
| 18 | **Part A:** Go to YouTube (http://www.youtube.com/watch?v=8t5tEFyCTno) and watch the video about students' experiences and goals in learning English. Choose two of them and take notes of their objectives for learning English.<br>**Part B:** What about you and your students? What are the objectives for learning English in Brazil? | Active listening<br><br><br>Explaining |
| 19 | **Part A:** Analyze a didactic unit from the material below, using the given criteria list.<br>**Part B:** Would you say these materials approach any of the implications of ELF for English teaching? If so, which one(s)? Justify your answer. | Analysing<br>Evaluating<br>Comparing<br>Arguing |
| 20 | Read the question below from the entrance examination of UEL – this question seems to recognize the ELF position. (…) Based on the reading of text I, explain the relation between the 'lyric self' and the English language in the poem. Justify your answer with examples from text II. | Identifying argument. |

Although we recognize that the unit invites some problem-solving and arguing, we also identify a limitation in proposing an articulation of the ELF concept with didactic practices, that is, tasks in which student teachers could elaborate lesson plans or didactic units articulating some of the implications of ELF. If this aspect were considered, the future teachers would have the chance to think more about the English classroom and their roles as teachers.

Another point to notice is that the activities were elaborated upon to get student teachers cognitively engaged with ELF without questioning its assumptions. If the course had more hours, it would be relevant to include tasks to check understandings by asking the students to plan lessons or course units taking an ELF perspective into account, or even to pose problems (in vignettes, for instance) and ask them to provide solutions.

Other missing aspects we could add to improve the unit are (i) to write it in English (totally or partially); (ii) to create opportunities for 'ELFing', that is, provide contexts for intercultural encounters among students and teachers from different countries so they experience ELF; and (iii) to provide more agentic tasks, i.e. those which would encourage students to play a more active role in their learning.

## Concluding Remarks

Our retrospective stance toward the unit highlighted aspects of an ELF perspective that were successfully addressed and others that would deserve further development. We hope this unit may contribute to the practice of English teacher educators (as it contributed to ours) in a way that when implementing ELF in their classes, they can analyze and reflect on the assumptions that guided their implementation.

## Note

(1)    The literature on ELF has abundant references to terminological issues that reveal it is a paradigm under construction (Jenkins, 2015). We share the understanding that ELF is 'any use of English among speakers of different first languages for whom English is the communicative medium of choice, and often the only option' (Seidlhofer, 2011: 7).

## References

Bayyurt, Y. (2014) ELF7 interview: Getting started with ELF. See http://elfpron. wordpress.com/2014/09/21/elf7-interview-getting-started-with-elf/ (accessed 5 March 2015).

Bordini, M. and Gimenez, T. (2014) Estudos sobre inglês como lingua franca no Brasil (2005–2012): Uma metassíntese qualitativa [Studies on ELF in Brazil (2005–2012): A qualitative meta-synthesis]. *Signum: Estudos Da Linguagem* 17 (1), 10–43.

Calvo, L.C.S., El Kadri, M.S. and El Kadri, A. (2014) ELF in Teacher Education Programs: Mapping the Proposal Presented in ELF5 and ELF6. A paper presented at the 7th International Conference of English as a Lingua Franca. Athens, Greece.

Calvo, L.C.S.C., Freitas, M.A., and Alves, E.F. (Org.). (2015) *Formação inicial de professores: habilidades linguístico-comunicativas e inglês como língua franca*. Maringá: Eduem.

Crystal, D. (1997) *English as a Global Language*. Cambridge: Cambridge University Press.

Crystal, D. (2003) *English as a Global Language* (2nd edn). Cambridge: Cambridge University Press.

Dewey, M. (2012) Towards a post-normative approach: Learning the pedagogy of ELF. *Journal of English as a Lingua Franca* 1 (1), 141–170.

El Kadri, M.S. (2010) Atitudes sobre o estatuto do inglês como língua franca em curso de formação inicial de professores. MA thesis, Universidade Estadual de Londrina.

El Kadri, M.S. and Gimenez, T. (2013) Formando professores de inglês para o contexto do inglês como língua franca [Educating English language teachers for the English as a lingua franca context]. *Acta Scientarium, Language and Culture* 35 (2), 125–133.

El Kadri, M.S. and Calvo, L.C.S. (2015) English in the contemporary world. In L.C.S. Calvo, M.A. Freitas and E.F. Alves (eds) *Formação inicial de professores: Habilidades linguístico-comunicativas e inglês como língua franca* Maringá: Eduem.

Gimenez, T. (2001) English language teaching and the challenges for citizenship and identity in the current century. *Acta Scientiarum* 23 (1), 127–131.

Gimenez, T. (2006) English in a new world language order. In L.T. Machado, V.L.L. Cristóvão and V. Furtoso (eds) *Aspectos da linguagem: Considerações teórico-práticas* (pp. 59–72). Londrina: EDUEL.

Gimenez, T. (2009) Antes de babel: Inglês como língua franca. In *Proceedings of the 7th Encontro de Letras: Linguagem e ensino – ELLE*. Londrina: UNOPAR. ISSN é 2176-3372.

Gimenez, T., Calvo, L.C.S. and El Kadri, M.S. (eds) (2011) *Inglês como língua franca: Ensino-aprendizagem e formação de professores*. Campinas: Pontes Editores.

Gimenez, T., Calvo, L.C.S. and El Kadri, M.S. (2015) Beyond Madonna: Teaching materials as windows into pre-service teachers' understandings of ELF. In Y. Bayyurt and S. Akcan (eds) *Current Perspectives on Pedagogy for English as a Lingua Franca* (pp. 225–238). Berlin: De Gruyter Mouton.

Graddol, D. (2000) *The Future of English?* London: British Council.

Graddol, D. (2006) *English Next*. London: British Council.

Jenkins, J. (2000) *The Phonology of English as an International Language*. Oxford: Oxford University Press.

Jenkins, J. (2012) English as a lingua franca from the classroom to the classroom. *ELT Journal* 66 (4), 486–494.

Jenkins, J. (2015) Repositioning English and multilingualism in English as a lingua franca. *Englishes in Practice* 2 (3), 49–85.

Jordão, C.M. (2011) A posição do inglês como língua internacional e suas implicações para a sala de aula. In T. Gimenez, L.C.S. Calvo and M.S. El Kadri (eds) *Inglês como língua franca: Ensino-aprendizagem e formação de professores* (pp. 221–252). Campinas: Pontes Editores.

Llurda, L. (2014) ELF7 interview: Getting started with ELF. See http://elfpron.wordpress.com/2014/09/21/elf7-interview-getting-started-with-elf/ (accessed 15 June 2015).

Matos, A.M., del Rio, A.A., Aparicio, N., Mobilia, S. and Martins, T. (2009) Intercultural resource pack: Latin American perspectives. See http://www.teachingenglish.org.uk/sites/teacheng/files/icrp-july07.pdf (accessed 15 June 2015).

Rajagopalan, K. (2003) A geopolítica da lingual inglesa e seus reflexos no Brasil: Por uma política prudente e positiva. In Y. Lacoste (ed.) *A Geopolítica do Inglês* (pp. 135–159). São Paulo: Parábola.

Rajagopalan, K. (2009) Maria Nilva Pereira pergunta/Kanavillil Rajagopalan responde: O inglês como língua internacional na prática docente. In D.C. Lima (ed.) *Ensino e aprendizagem de língua inglesa: Conversas com especialistas* (pp. 39–46). São Paulo: Parábola.

Rajagopalan, K. (2010) O lugar do inglês no mundo globalizado. In K. Silva (ed.) *Ensinar e aprender línguas na contemporaneidade: Linhas e entrelinhas* (pp. 21–24). Campinas: Pontes Editores.

Saraceni, M. (2011) Reflections on the rhetorics on the (re-)location of English. *Changing English* 18 (3), 277–285.

Seidlhofer, B. (2001) Closing a conceptual gap: The case for a description of English as a lingua franca. *International Journal of Applied Linguistics* 11 (2), 33–58.

Seidlhofer, B. (2009) Common ground and different realities: World Englishes and English as a lingua franca. *World Englishes* 28 (2), 236–245.

Seidlhofer, B. (2011) *Understanding English as a Lingua Franca*. Oxford: Oxford University Press.

Sifakis, N. (2014) ELF awareness as an opportunity for change: A transformative perspective for ESOL teacher education. *JELF* 3 (2), 317–335.

Siqueira, D.S.P. (2008) *Inglês como língua internacional: Por uma pedagogia intercultural crítica*. PhD thesis,Universidade Federal da Bahia.

Siqueira, D.S.P. (2011) Inglês como língua franca: O desafio de ensinar um idioma desterritorializado. In T. Gimenez, L.C.S. Calvo and M.S. El Kadri (eds) *Inglês como língua franca: Ensino-aprendizagem e formação de professores* (pp. 87–115). Campinas: Editora Pontes.

Souza, A.G.F., Barcaro, C. and Grande, G.C. (2011) As representações de alunas-professoras de um curso de Letras sobre o estatuto do inglês como língua franca. In T. Gimenez, L.C.S. Calvo and M.S. El Kadri (eds) *Inglês como língua franca: Ensino-aprendizagem e formação de professores* (pp. 193–220). Campinas: Editora Pontes.

Takahashi, R. (2014) An analysis of ELF-oriented features in ELT coursebooks. *English Today* 30 (1), 28–34.

# 14 WE, EIL, ELF and Awareness of Their Pedagogical Implications in Teacher Education Programs in Italy

## Paola Vettorel and Lucilla Lopriore

## Introduction

Preservice teacher education in Italy has witnessed over the last few years the implementation of new forms of training programs, modeled on the basis of previous ones.[1] Since 2012, the training of teachers has been carried out within university-run courses directed at novice teachers (*Tirocinio Formativo Attivo*/TFA) as well as teachers with a few years of teaching experience but without any previous formal background preparation (*Percorso Abilitante Speciale*/PAS). Both programs encompass a general part on pedagogical approaches (18 ECTS[2]), and a more specific disciplinary one (18 ECTS) dedicated to language and language teaching; TFA novice teachers also have a considerable practicum period (19 ECTS) to complete. A final individual reflective report, which generally includes a sample of a teaching unit, concludes the training path. Both TFA and PAS programs are elective, but are a necessary qualification to teach in state schools: at the end of the course, attendees are required to pass a teaching qualification exam entitling them to become teachers of English in secondary state schools.

This chapter will illustrate the implementation of the above-mentioned programs as carried out in two Italian universities, where one or more components of the training courses for prospective English teachers focused on introducing participants to English as an International Language (EIL) and, more specifically, to World Englishes (WE) and English as a lingua franca (ELF), while enhancing their awareness on how to plan and devise their English lessons with a new perspective on the emerging uses of English/es. We will first delineate the experience at the University of Verona, where the initial three out of six units were wholly dedicated to the introduction of WE, ELF and their pedagogical implications. We will then illustrate the experience at Roma Tre University where EIL, WE and ELF were integrated throughout the program components. The potential implications of both approaches for teacher education aimed at fostering a plurilithic, WE- and ELF-informed didactic approach to teaching English today will then be discussed.

## Case 1: WE, EIL and ELF as Course Components of the 'English Language' Module

Within the TFA and PAS training courses for secondary school English as a foreign language teachers run at the Department of Foreign Languages and Literatures at the University of Verona (Italy) in the academic years from 2012–2013 to 2015–2016, the module related to the English Language (6 ECTS/36 hours for PAS and 3 ECTS/18 hours for TFA) included some units connected to the global spread of English, focusing on EIL, WE and ELF, as well as their pedagogical implications.[3] These units were placed at the beginning of the course, so that they would represent a reference framework for the whole module, and also for the following lessons dealing, respectively, with lesson planning, material evaluation and the development of language skills.

The general structure of the PAS English Language module was as follows:

- Units 1–3: The changing world of English: English, Englishes, ELF.
- Units 4–6: Methodological tools for EFL teachers: textbook evaluation, lesson planning, developing skills and dealing with vocabulary and grammar.

The first two units of the module were aimed at providing an overview of the focal points for English in its international function (EIL), WE and ELF (spread of English, language variation, standard language ideologies, main research findings from both areas), including exemplifications and reflection based upon the attendees' experience. The last unit, 'Pedagogical Implications of WE and ELF', starting with examples from literature, textbook materials and pedagogic projects (e.g. Vettorel, 2010, 2014a), provided a basis for reflection and for developing teaching ideas, that were carried out individually and in groups both during the lessons and in the virtual Moodle class dedicated space.

The topics introduced and discussed in Unit 1 were intended first of all to foster reflection upon what the trainees already knew about the spread of English across the world in different historical periods, and consequently to familiarize them with the plurality into which English has developed nowadays. A brainstorming phase partly based on an initial questionnaire,[4] was followed by some factual information about the first and the second dispersals of English (Crystal, 2003; Jenkins, 2009; Schneider, 2011) with exemplifications and the main characteristic traits of different WE varieties, from American, Australian and New Zealand English to Indian and Singaporean ones. Language variation at different levels (phonology, lexicogrammar, syntax, idiomatic expressions) was specifically dealt with and exemplified, first of all in order to foster reflection on how language naturally changes, adapting to different contexts and being adapted by its speakers. Secondly, it also allowed a parallel with the processes of language change involved in ELF and the demographics related to speakers of English across the world, and the main models of categorization that have been developed for the spread of English – from Kachru (1992) to Modiano (1999a, 1999b) – were also illustrated, alongside focal issues such as the problematic aspects in conceptualizing native/nonnative/bilingual speakers of English in today's multilingual and linguistically superdiverse societies.

Two short video interviews with David Crystal were shown as an illustrative résumé of the main points, followed by small-group and class discussion. In the 2014–2015 and 2015–2016 PAS program, an article by Seidlhofer (2009) was also used in order to introduce the commonalities and differences in WE and ELF discourse. The first unit of the module closed with the video of Dizraeli reciting his 'The 21st Century Flux' rap poem and with an examination of the proposed class activities in small groups, to foster reflection on how the latter may be relevantly used with lower and upper secondary school students.

The second unit in the module dealt specifically with ELF, exploring issues like the ownership of English (Seidlhofer, 2011; Widdowson, 2003), the relationship between second language acquisition (SLA) and ELF (Cogo & Dewey, 2012; Jenkins, 2006a; Seidlhofer, 2011), English-knowing bilingualism (Jenkins, 2009) and multicompetence (Cook, 2008) as well as the complex relationship between second language (L2) learners and ELF users (e.g. Seidlhofer, 2011; Vettorel, 2014b: Chapter 7). Characteristics of ELF contexts and communication, together with reasons for the functional language 'difference' in ELF, were also explored, setting them within a perspective of exploitation of the plurilingual and pluricultural language repertoires of ELF users. Personal and professional reflection was fostered through discussion in small groups, taking into account the trainees' and their students' first-hand experiences of ELF.

The third unit focused entirely on the pedagogical implications of WE and ELF. Starting from an overview of the presence of English in formal education in Europe, as well as Europeans' self-perceived competence in English (EACEA/Eurydice/Eurostat, 2012; Eurobarometer, 2006, 2012), the possibility of students' out-of-school extensive contact with English was set forward. Attention was drawn to the fact that this contact nowadays increasingly takes place not only through the media, advertising, music, etc., but with an 'active' use of the language, too, for example in internationally oriented communication settings either face to face or through Web 2.0 social media. This constituted a starting point for reflection on the implications that the plurality and the extended presence of English can have in, and for, English language teaching (ELT), with a redefinition of the priorities in teaching practices within an inclusive and plurilithic perspective (e.g. Alsagoff et al., 2012; Matsuda, 2012; McKay, 2002, 2003; Seidlhofer, 2011). Attention was also focused on the role that communication strategies play in effective interaction, both in language and in (inter)cultural terms, as well as on language variation and the processes of adaptation and appropriation in WE and ELF. These concepts were then seen in practice in the examination of ELT textbooks: this activity was aimed at scrutinizing whether a more inclusive perspective is present in any way in existing materials, and coursebook exemplifications incorporating such a plurilithic approach were provided. Finally, trainees were invited to reflect upon and devise possible didactic activities that could be planned and carried out in class, and to discuss them in small groups.

Personal views, as well as proposals resulting from group work, were then shared on the Moodle e-learning virtual classroom, in forums where trainees responded to the input for reflection provided by the teacher trainer after each unit, such as the following:

---

*WE- and ELF-aware textbook analysis and planning*
   As a follow-up to our work on textbook analysis related to the inclusion of a pluralistic perspective on WE and ELF, and to our class discussion, this week's task is as follows:

- Does your textbook (or the textbook you looked at yesterday) have a reference website?
- If so, does the website include any (downloadable) resources that are inclusive of a WE- and ELF-related perspective?
- Is there an accompanying DVD? If so, does it include in any way a WE- and ELF-related perspective?
- How could the above, or your findings in the textbooks you analyzed yesterday, be used as a starting point in classroom activities to raise awareness of the current role and spread of English?

---

The virtual class proved an important area for discussion and for sharing views, opinions and challenges related to the issues examined in class, as well as a repository for pedagogic and lesson ideas. Further resources, either in the form of links to research articles or multimedia material available on the web, were also part of this repository on which participants could draw both for their knowledge and as a point of reference for lesson planning.

To sum up, the units, each focusing on different but complementary aspects of the spread of English, proved fundamental not only to familiarize trainee teachers with research into the plurality of Englishes, EIL and ELF, but, most importantly, to make them reconsider their teaching practices by taking into account WE- and ELF-related issues. Most answers to the questionnaire survey, as well as the comments by the participants in the Moodle forums, highlighted that the units constituted a valuable opportunity to acquaint them with the pluralization of English, both in terms of WE and of EIL and ELF. Most trainees, in fact, stated that before attending the course their knowledge of the issues that were dealt with during the module was of a general kind, and that the three units provided a fundamental contribution particularly in terms of a more inclusive perspective, not least of the need to take into account their students' experience of the plurality of the English language today and to promote an awareness of this aspect in ELT classroom practices.

In fact, several of the individual reports that had to be produced as part of the final exam focused on WE/ELF/EIL-informed lesson plans, including topics related to both cultural and linguistic aspects (see Lopriore & Vettorel, 2016[6]), showing that the issues discussed in the course had positively been taken on board by the trainee participants.

## Case 2: EIL, WE and ELF as Course Embedded Notions

The second experience described here was at Roma Tre University where WE, EIL and ELF have been integrated into the ELT components of the four training programs – both TFA and PAS – offered by the university since 2012.[7]

Choosing to focus on current instantiations of English – EIL, WE or ELF – as a cross-curricular notion to be referred to throughout most of the course components, was meant to engage the participants in a reflective process (Freeman & Johnson, 1998; Johnson, 2006, 2009) as well as to challenge their beliefs about and views of English. Participants were asked to reconsider their perspectives on English, as multilingual speakers, as learners and as teachers of English, a language whose borders are becoming increasingly mobile and difficult to label (Canagarajah, 2013; Pennycook, 2012; Pennycook & Otsuji, 2015).

Each program lasted approximately 18 weeks and had an average of 60 to 80 participants, mostly Italian native speakers holding a degree in foreign languages. Within the two PAS groups there were smaller groups (15%) of native English speakers with temporary teaching jobs for 'English conversation' classes in Italian schools. This presence added a new perspective to the course, particularly in the group discussions about the role and function of native and nonnative speakers in the English language classroom (Lipovsky & Mahboob, 2010).

Each TFA and PAS program was subdivided into two main parts: the pedagogical part (18 ECTS) run online only, and the blended ELT part (18 ECTS) where participants attended face-to-face classes while regularly using the university Moodle platform to access resources and materials for their individual study and discussions.

The English language part was subdivided into different components where WE, EIL and ELF were embedded to different degrees: one component on English culture and literature, one on language teaching methodology, one on ELT and one on information and communications technologies (ICT). While the English culture and literature component mainly aimed at providing exposure to English literary and cultural studies inclusive of samples of literatures in English, the short language teaching methodology focused on SLA and on different teaching approaches, and the ELT component – From English to English/es – was organized into six modules. Each of the modules, subdivided into units, was geared at exploring different aspects of English language development within the perspective of current uses of English in different world contexts.

English grammar, lexis, phonology and phonetics, communicative activities development, assessment, coursebook and material evaluation were introduced and discussed in light of the current status of English. In the last two modules – From Language Planning to Assessment and Evaluation – participants were required to devise English lesson plans, using the Common European Framework of Reference (CEFR; Council of Europe, 2001) and within an EIL, WE and ELF perspective.

In order to introduce course participants to WE, EIL and ELF, the aim was for trainees to notice different instantiations of English in a variety of contexts as well as to reflect upon the implications for teaching English nowadays. This was achieved by exposing them to video stimuli and by engaging them in group discussions on the basis of specific readings and tasks presented either in class or during their individual and group work on the Moodle platform. During the group meetings and their individual study hours, the course participants would watch brief videos available on YouTube, such as David Crystal's 'World Englishes', 'Which English?' or 'Global English'; Dizraeli's 'The 21st Century Flux', 'The English Language in 24 Accents'; and brief extracts from TV series, such as *The Big Bang Theory, Grey's Anatomy* or *The Simpsons*, which are very popular among Italian students. The tasks elicited their reflections about their beliefs and understanding of English as it is currently used in the media, on TV and on social media. They were also asked to read articles or extracts from books on the current state of English, e.g. David Graddol's (2006) *English Next,* and on WE, EIL or ELF (Cogo & Dewey, 2012; Jenkins, 2006b; Matsuda, 2003; Seidlhofer, 2005; Widdowson, 2012). They had to complete tasks to trigger their attention and reflections on the English that they and their students were currently exposed to in a sort of loop input (Woodward, 2003), whereby they would consider the issue both from their perspective as learners and as teachers of English.

This approach served as a springboard to revisit their beliefs and understanding of English grammar, lexis, phonology and phonetics. This was done through focused readings (Cogo & Dewey, 2006; Jenkins, 2006b, 2009; Larsen-Freeman, 2009; Lipovsky & Mahboob, 2010; Seidlhofer, 2011) or the exploration of specific websites, e.g. The Speech Accent Archive or the ELF section of Speech in Action http://www.speechinaction.org. They were also involved in discussions about the way coursebooks presented aspects of English grammar, pronunciation or lexis. In the following weeks, they were first engaged in small-group discussions aimed at sharing their thoughts about ways to include WE, EIL and ELF within some of the currently used coursebooks. Specific tasks asked them to revisit traditional presentations of English grammar or vocabulary as well as to devise new types of ELT activities.

Later on in the course, in the last two modules, the course participants were asked to plan teaching–learning paths at different levels (A2, B1 and B2 of the CEFR) devising ways that different instantiations of English could become part of the English syllabus. The following is an extract from the first task.

---

*From English to Englishes: Norms, uses and varieties*

*Objectives:*

- To learn about English, its varieties and its current state at global level (*Global English, WE, EIL, ELF*).
- To discuss learning and teaching implications.
- To identify ways to take the current state of English into account when planning English teaching paths, lessons and forms of assessment.

English has definitely changed its role and function all over the world. Besides its well-known varieties, English has become a global language while its emerging and most diffused use is in interactions among nonnative speakers. This poses several questions for teachers of English: *What English to teach? What varieties? What standards to bear in mind? How has the role of non-native teachers changed?* Let's explore these issues through the following tasks.

*Tasks:*

- Read David Graddol's *English Next* and write a brief summary of the main ideas highlighting what you think could be relevant for you as a teacher of English.

- Watch David Crystal's videos: The Biggest Challenges for Teachers; World Englishes.
- Jot down two things you did not know before watching these videos and write four main points relevant for you as a future teacher of English.
- Choose three of the four articles provided[8] and then answer the questions (max 500 words).

*Questions for group discussions*

(a) What are the main implications for English language teachers?
(b) Has the role of nonnative speakers changed in the last two decades? How? What about that of native English teachers?
(c) How could WE, EIL and ELF be taken into consideration and/ or included in English language manuals, materials, lessons or activities? Ideas?

The participants' reactions to the first section tasks showed surprise. Many of them had never realized how different the language that they were going to teach was from the language that they were currently exposed to. Some wrote in the task:

> It's not enough to understand what teaching materials and tools to be used, but HOW teachers should use them. (Donna)

> Another thing I did not know before was that even a native speaker of English can consider himself a foreigner in a country where a new variety of English is spoken because of its culture. (Lucrezia)

As a consequence, they also became more critical of the coursebooks that they were asked to analyze since one of the tasks was to focus on what they thought was missing in the coursebooks.

In the last module, participants were engaged in planning lessons referring to the CEFR level descriptors (Council of Europe, 2001) and within an EIL, WE and ELF perspective. They focused on aural and oral skills development not only because these skills are often neglected in coursebooks, but also because it is in spoken language that changes in English are more noticeable by learners, as stated in the example of the lesson plan *English around the world*, produced by two course participants.[9]

Not all lesson plans were Teaching English as an International Language (TEIL) oriented, though; some participants proposed very traditional grammar-oriented lessons, while others designed either short discrete activities or lesson plans whereby learners would be exposed to varieties of English and ELF. In the English literature and culture component where they were also asked to produce lesson plans, quite a few produced lessons with a focus on literatures in English.

## Shared Key Elements and Challenges

Although trainee teachers may have some familiarity and general knowledge of the global spread of English and of its international role (EIL), the inclusion of key elements in relation both to the pluralization of this language and the characteristics of its role as a lingua franca constituted fundamental aspects in the dedicated modules of both training courses. Particularly for teachers who graduated some time ago, the examples introduced in both programs allowed the trainee teachers to critically explore issues related to the plurality of English, and to start reflecting upon the possibility of taking them into account in their actual teaching experiences, sharing reflections, ideas and resources in class and on the Moodle e-learning space.

Dealing with research findings and sample literature on EIL, WE and ELF also provided these trainee teachers with the opportunity to reflect on the implications for teaching, both in general and in their own context and experience, critically looking at existing materials in a 'new light' and planning locally relevant activities within a WE and ELF-informed viewpoint.

Shifting perspectives in English language teacher education is certainly not an easy task and it may be characterized by resistance and contradictions. It is a slow path to be followed jointly by trainers, teachers, future teachers, students and publishers, not to mention school authorities. Challenges are inherent in the multiple roles and functions of English in everyday life, in nonnative teachers' professional profile, in the standards set by public institutions, in the curriculum guidelines, in learners' linguistic education in the language of schooling, as well as in the initial education of future teachers of English. These challenges have inevitable implications not only for teacher education and material design, but also for the constructs in terms of the language to learn/teach, language standards as well as types of assessment. Furthermore, teachers – both tenured and temporary – are nowadays confronted with so many tasks and duties that, despite their willingness to do so, they may not be able to consistently incorporate in their actual classroom practices aspects related to the plurality of English today – like those that were dealt with during both teacher education programs illustrated above. ELT materials still remain mainly anglophone oriented, although aspects related to the diversity of Englishes and to the development of intercultural communication skills are increasingly being incorporated (e.g. findings in Vettorel & Lopriore, 2013, for Italy).

The shift illustrated above has represented a challenge for us trainers as well because we set out on an unsettling journey, we reshaped our training routines, to revisit our training materials, to adopt an approach, to develop a perspective for teaching English that has not yet been officially accepted and implemented at an institutional and publishing level. We have been so far sustained in adopting this approach by the enthusiastic response we have received from our trainees – both novice and experienced – who found this perspective truly reflective of the surrounding reality where English has *de facto* 'mobilized' and is now inclusive of a multifaceted role.

## Conclusions

Teachers should be encouraged to seize the opportunity to further develop aspects related to the current plurality of English starting from existing materials and from their own environment, using pedagogical approaches and tasks that are locally tailored and locally meaningful both for them and their students (e.g. Lopriore & Vettorel, 2015), as the two teacher education programs illustrated in this chapter have sought to foster.

Resistance is certainly hard to dismantle, but it is through raising awareness and individual and group actions that more consistent changes can occur. Teacher education is the first and most important step to sensitize present and future generations of English teachers to the inevitable implications of EIL, WE and ELF for ELT. The examples from the two institutional teacher education programs illustrated above seem to have fostered a change toward a more inclusive perspective, one that could also work well within in-service teacher education. Indeed, if teachers' attitudes change, responses toward a more inclusive and less monolithic approach may also more consistently come from publishers and materials developers.

## Notes

(1) Preservice courses at university level for teachers of all subjects were first established in Italy in 1999 and were implemented at the national level in 2009. The two-year teacher training programs called SSIS for teachers of all subject matters consisted of a face-to-face course and a practicum component supervised by expert school teachers (Freeman, 2003; Lopriore, 2003). This program was subsequently changed at the national level into shorter six-month courses, respectively, called TFA and PAS. PAS participants are not required to do the practicum at school since they have all had previous teaching experiences.

(2) In the Italian university system, 1 credit in the European Credit Transfer System (ECTS) usually corresponds to 25 working hours for the students, 6 of which are class hours and the rest individual student work.

(3) In the 2014–2015 TFA course, 12 out of the 18 hours of the English Language course, that is, the first two units, were dedicated to WE and EIL/ELF, and the third to lesson planning and textbook evaluation. The remaining 18 out of the total 36 hours covered topics related to the teaching of English literature, as required by the upper secondary school curriculum. A module focusing on more

practical teaching aspects was also part of both PAS (36 hours) and TFA (18 hours) courses.

(4)   The questionnaire is part of an ongoing larger research project on trainee teachers' views and opinions about the inclusion of WE, EIL and ELF in ELT practices; for preliminary findings see Vettorel (2016).

(5)   See Note 4.

(6)   See also the presentation at the Colloquium 'ELF Aware Classroom Practices and Teaching Materials: Issues and New Perspectives in ELT', ELF7 Conference, Athens, September 2014. See https://www.youtube.com/watch?feature=player_embedded&v=8MVGrI_yK7A (accessed 28 April 2015).

(7)   Between 2012 and 2015, a total of four courses were run at Roma Tre University: two TFA and one PAS blended courses and a second PAS course that was totally run online and whose components were subdivided differently. Since the introduction of preservice teacher education programs in 1999, Roma Tre University has regularly offered pre- and in-service courses for teachers of different subject matters including foreign language teachers, and, more recently, the new model courses – TFA and PAS.

(8)   (1) Jenkins (2006b); (2) Matsuda (2003); (3) Seidlhofer (2005); (4) Widdowson (2012).

(9)   Lesson Plan: *English around the world* (Paola and Daniele). *Rationale:* The module is aimed at raising students' awareness of the different varieties of English spoken around the world, focusing on the different slang variations. Slang is an essential skill in today's society as it occurs in everyday social interactions. Therefore, being exposed to it, the students are provided with the tools to develop 'real' foreign language interactions, getting in touch with the language of songs, films and the language spoken by their peers in English-speaking countries. For this purpose, the teacher provides the students with authentic materials like American videos, a film trailer (on Indian-English), an Australian song, etc.

# References

Alsagoff, L., McKay, S.L., Hu, G. and Renandya, W.A. (eds) (2012) *Principles and Practices for Teaching English as an International Language*. London: Routledge.

Canagarajah, S. (2013) *Translingual Practice*. London: Routledge.

Cogo, A. and Dewey, M. (2006) Efficiency in ELF communication: From pragmatic motives to lexico-grammatical innovation. *Nordic Journal of English Studies* 5 (2), 59–93.

Cogo, A. and Dewey, M. (2012) *Analysing English as a Lingua Franca*. London/New York: Continuum.

Cook, V. (2008) *Second Language Learning and Language Teaching*. London: Routledge.

Cook, V. (2010) Multi-competence. See http://www.viviancook.uk/Writings/Papers/MCentry.htm (accessed 24 August 2016).

Council of Europe (2001) *Common European Framework of Reference for Languages. Learning, Teaching, Assessment*. Modern Language Division Strasbourg. Cambridge: Cambridge University Press.

Crystal, D. (2003 [1997]) *English as a Global Language*. Cambridge: Cambridge University Press.

EACEA/Eurydice/Eurostat (2012) *Key Data on Teaching Languages at Schools in Europe 2008*. Brussels: Eurydice.

European Commission (2006) *Special Eurobarometer 243. Europeans and their Languages*. Brussels. See http://ec.europa.eu/public_opinion/archives/ebs/ebs_243_en.pdf (accessed 28 April 2015).

European Commission (2012) *Special Eurobarometer 386. Europeans and their languages*. Brussels. See http://ec.europa.eu/public_opinion/archives/ebs/ebs_386_en.pdf (accessed 28 April 2015).

Freeman, D. (2003) Building common knowledge in the SSIS. In A. Graziano and L. Lopriore (eds) *PERSPECTIVES. A Journal of TESOL Italy. Special Issue on SSIS – Pre-Service Training* 30 (1), 51–63.

Freeman, D. and Johnson, K. (1998) Reconceptualising the knowledge-base of language teacher education. *TESOL Quarterly* 32, 397–417.

Graddol, D. (2006) *English Next*. London: The British Council.

Graziano, A. and Lopriore, L. (eds) (2003) *PERSPECTIVES. A Journal of TESOL Italy. Special Issue on SSIS – Pre-Service Training* 30 (1).

Jenkins, J. (2006a) Points of view and blind spots: ELF and SLA. *International Journal of Applied Linguistics* 16 (2), 138–162.

Jenkins, J. (2006b) Current perspectives on teaching World Englishes and English as a lingua franca. *TESOL Quarterly* 40 (1), 157–181.

Jenkins, J. (2009 [2003]) *World Englishes* (2nd edn). London: Routledge.

Johnson, K. (2006) The sociocultural turn and its challenges for second language teacher education. *TESOL Quarterly* 40, 235–257.

Johnson, K. (2009) *Second Language Teacher Education: A Sociocultural Perspective*. New York: Routledge.

Kachru, B.B. (ed.) (1992) *The Other Tongue. English across Cultures*. Urbana, IL: University of Illinois Press.

Larsen-Freeman, D. (2009) Teaching and testing grammar. In M. Long and C. Doughty (eds) *The Handbook of Language Teaching* (pp. 518–542). Oxford: Wiley-Blackwell.

Lipovsky, C. and Mahboob, A. (2010) Appraisal of native and non-native English speaking teachers. In A. Mahboob (eds) *The NNEST Lens: Non Native English Speakers in TESOL* (pp. 154–179). Newcastle upon Tyne: Cambridge Scholars Publishing.

Lopriore, L. (2003) Didattica della lingua inglese. *PERSPECTIVES. A Journal of TESOL Italy. Special Issue on SSIS – Pre-Service Training* 30 (1), 167–186.

Lopriore, L. and Vettorel, P. (2015) Promoting awareness of Englishes and ELF in the English Language classroom. In H. Bowles and A. Cogo (eds) *International Perspectives on English as a Lingua Franca. Pedagogical Insights* (pp. 13–34). Basingstoke: Palgrave Macmillan.

Lopriore, L. and Vettorel, P. (2016) A shift in ELT perspective: World Englishes and ELF in the EFL classroom. In N. Tsantila, J. Mandalios and M. Ilkos (eds) *ELF: Pedagogical and Interdisciplinary Perspectives. Proceedings of the Seventh International Conference of English as a Lingua Franca*, Deree – The American College of Greece. Athens, Greece.

Matsuda, A. (2003) Incorporating World Englishes in teaching English as an international language. *TESOL Quarterly* 37 (4), 719–729.

Matsuda, A. (ed.) (2012) *Principles and Practices of Teaching English as an International Language*. Bristol: Multilingual Matters.

McKay, S.L. (2002) *Teaching English as an International Language*. Oxford: Oxford University Press.

McKay, S.L. (2003) EIL curriculum development. *RELC Journal* 34 (1), 31–47.

Modiano, M. (1999a) International English in the global village. *English Today* 15 (2), 14–19.

Modiano, M. (1999b) Standard English(es) and educational practices for the world's lingua franca. *English Today* 15 (4), 3–13.

Pennycook, A. (2012) *Language and Mobility: Unexpected Places*. Bristol: Multilingual Matters.

Pennycook, A. and Otsuji, E. (2015) *Metrolingualism. Language in the City*. London: Routledge.

Schneider, E.W. (2011) *English around the World. An Introduction*. Cambridge: Cambridge University Press.

Seidlhofer, B. (2005) English as a lingua franca. *ELTJ* 59 (4), 339–341.

Seidlhofer, B. (2009) Common grounds and different realities. World Englishes and English as a lingua franca. *World Englishes* 28 (2), 236–245.

Seidlhofer, B. (2011) *Understanding English as a Lingua Franca.* Oxford: Oxford University Press.

Vettorel, P. (2010) English(es), ELF, Xmas and trees: Intercultural communicative competence and English as a lingua franca in the primary classroom. *Perspectives* XXXVII (1), 25–52.

Vettorel, P. (2014a) Connecting English wor(l)ds and classroom practices. *TEXTUS* XXVII (1), 137–154.

Vettorel, P. (2014b) *English as a Lingua Franca in Wider Networking. Blogging Practices.* Berlin: De Gruyter Mouton.

Vettorel, P. (2016) WE- and ELF-informed classroom practices: Proposals from a pre-service teacher education programme in Italy. *Journal of English as a Lingua Franca* 5 (1), 107–133.

Vettorel, P. and Lopriore L. (2013) Is there ELF in ELT course-books? *Studies in Second Language Learning and Teaching* 3, 483–504.

Widdowson, H.G. (2003) *Defining Issues in English Language Teaching.* Oxford: Oxford University Press.

Widdowson, H. (2012) ELF and the inconvenience of established concepts. *Journal of English as a Lingua Franca* 1 (1), 5–26.

Woodward, T. (2003) Loop input. *ELT Journal* 57 (3), 301–304.

## Online materials

Crystal, D. (2009) Which English should we teach? Global-MacMillan Education ELT. See http://www.macmillanglobal.com/blog/teaching-tips/which-english-should-we-teach-david-crystal (accessed 28 April 2015).

Crystal D. (2009) Why is English a Global Language? Global-MacMillan Education ELT. See http://www.youtube.com/watch?v=WZI1EjxxXKw (accessed 28 April 2015).

Crystal, D. (2013) Will English always be the Global Language? British Council Serbia. See https://www.youtube.com/watch?v=2_q9b9YqGRY&app=desktop (accessed 28 April 2015).

Crystal, D. (2013) The biggest challenge for teachers. Interview, British Council Serbia. See https://www.youtube.com/watch?v=ItODnX5geCM (accessed 28 April 2015)

Crystal, D. (2013) World Englishes. Interview, British Council Serbia. See https://www.youtube.com/watch?v=2_q9b9YqGRY (accessed 28 April 2015).

Dizraeli, R.S. (2010) The 21st Century Flux, poem. See http://www.macmillandictionary.com/external/pdf/21st%20Century%20flux.pdf?version=2013-03-11-1344 (accessed 28 April 2015).

*Grey's Anatomy.* See http://www.greys-anatomy.com/ (accessed 1 May 2015).

Speech in Action (1998). See www.speechinaction.org (accessed 1 May 2015).

*The Big Bang Theory.* See http://the-big-bang-theory.com and http://www.cbs.com/shows/big_bang_theory/ (accessed 1 May 2015).

The English Language in 24 Accents. See www.youtube.com/watch?v=dABo_DCIdpM (accessed 28 April 2015).

*The Simpsons.* See https://www.youtube.com/watch?v=ItODnX5geCM and http://www.tv.com/shows/the-simpsons (accessed 1 May 2015).

The Speech Accent Archive (1999). See http://accent.gmu.edu/about.php (accessed 1 May 2015).

# Part 6

# Lessons, Activities and Tasks for EIL Teacher Preparation

# 15 Lessons, Activities and Tasks for EIL Teacher Preparation

This chapter presents a collection of pedagogical ideas that have been developed and implemented by teacher educators across the world who incorporate the English as an International Language (EIL) perspective into their teacher preparation courses. These ideas address various issues identified in previous chapters as crucial in preparing teachers to teach EIL. Some activities focus on the understanding of relevant theories and research, the paradigm shift called for and the critical examination of current practices and pedagogical implications. Others focus on raising awareness about different varieties of English, cultural diversities associated with the language or student teachers' own biases toward various forms and users of English.

And just like the previous chapters in this book, the activities presented in this chapter vary in their scope, collectively providing a wide range of options for teacher educators. Some are short, focused and easily adoptable in any teacher preparation courses, while others can be a long-term project that can serve as the backbone for one entire course and beyond.

These ideas, although they were originally created for a particular context that the contributors were working with, are flexible enough to be adapted to a variety of contexts and audience – preservice and in-service teachers, 'native' or 'nonnative' English-speaking teachers and a context where English may or may not be used extensively outside the classroom. Each contributor identified the kind of courses they believed that the suggested activity will be particularly suitable for, in order to give readers a sense of the nature of the activity, but these ideas are by no means limited to those instructional contexts.

In addition, the curricular descriptions and pedagogical activities presented in Matsuda (2012) include ideas that can be adopted for English language courses for preservice and in-service teachers whose first language (L1) is not English.

## Think Local, Write in English: Writing across Cultures

### Goal

This activity aims to promote multiculturalism and the development of intercultural awareness in EIL pedagogical materials through identifying the multiplicity of cultures constructed and reflected in English today.

By the end of this activity, students will be critically aware of and recognize cultural schemas and conceptualizations in writing across cultures (Sharifian, 2011).

**Appropriate Courses**:   World Englishes (WE); EIL; English Language, Identity and Culture
**Class Time**:            60–75 minutes

## Procedure

(1) *Warm up and introduction to World Englishes literature* (10–15 minutes). Teachers introduce the activity by beginning with the following warm-up discussion questions: Have you read any book, novel or poem lately? What was it about? Which culture(s) was represented in the text? What elements (words or sentences) led you to think about that particular culture in the text? Drawing upon the comments from the students, teachers can move onto discussing WE literature – which explores the culture(s) of the people and the country where the text is written, usually employing the English of that place (to a lesser or greater degree) (Dawson, 2011). For a detailed description, teachers can provide examples of WE literature from across the globe; one such example can be an excerpt from the novel *The Mistress of Spices* (1997) by Chitra Banerjee Divakaruni, which exhibits the Indian culture through the variety of English used in the novel.

(2) *Group work* (20–25 minutes). Distribute handouts about the source culture and the international target culture literary texts (Cortazzi & Jin, 1999), both focusing on a common theme like the celebratory events of a wedding, New Year, cultural celebrations or even world issues like education. Such texts can also be obtained from the country's local newspaper. To appreciate the reflection of culture in the diverse varieties of English, the text from the source culture – which is the students' own culture – will not only foster an appreciation of their own representation of culture in English, but will further enable respect and acceptability of the Englishes of international target cultures, involving a mixture of cultures from Inner, Outer and Expanding Circle countries. For instance, if this activity were to be performed in the context of Pakistan, teachers can select one literary text from the students' source culture (Pakistan), namely, *Wedding in the Flood* by Taufiq Rafat (1947–1978), and compare it with the international target culture of Thailand through the literary text 'The wedding' in *My Boyhood in Siam* (Chandruang, 1970). In groups, students are encouraged to read and highlight the discourse variations

(at lexical, thematic or stylistic level) from both the texts, and discuss their possible meanings and purpose for utilization.

(3) *Class discussion* (30–35 minutes). Encourage the students by leading the discussion with questions like 'What did you think about the texts?' and 'Which words, statements or concepts in the texts sparked your interest?' This will eventually lead the students to point out and discuss the lexical, thematic or stylistic variations in both the texts, such as the use of code-switching and metaphoric expressions, which will enable the students to understand how English is nativized (Kachru, 1986) and appropriated (Canagarajah, 1999) to reflect various cultural schemas and conceptualizations. For example, in the sample text described above (*Wedding in the Flood* by Taufiq Rafat), the use of the metaphoric expression 'the girl has been licking too many pots' in Pakistani culture means that if it rains on the wedding day, it is due to the bride licking the remnants of curry from a pot. But, on a deeper level, it signifies the cultural norm of holding a bride responsible for the good or ill fate of her husband. This indicates that English may have become de-anglicized (Kachru, 1992), but it does not necessarily mean that it has become 'de-culturalized' (Marlina, 2013).

## References

Canagarajah, A.S. (1999) *Resisting Linguistic Imperialism in English Teaching*. Oxford: Oxford University Press.

Chandruang, K. (1970) *My Boyhood in Siam*. London: Andre Deutsch Limited.

Cortazzi, M. and Jin, L. (1999) Cultural mirrors: Materials and methods in the EFL classroom. In E. Hinkel (ed.) *Culture in Second Language Teaching* (pp. 196–219). Cambridge: Cambridge University Press.

Dawson, E. (2011) Beyond the postcolonial. *Transnational Literature* 3, 1–9.

Divakaruni, C.B. (1997) *The Mistress of Spices*. London: Black Swan.

Kachru, B.B. (1986) *The Alchemy of English: The Spread, Functions and Models of Non-native Englishes*. Oxford: Pergamon Press.

Kachru, B.B. (1992) Models for non-native Englishes. In B.B. Kachru (ed.) *The Other Tongue: Englishes across Cultures* (2nd edn) (pp. 48–75). Urbana, IL: University of Illinois Press.

Marlina, R. (2013) *Teaching English as an International Language: Voices from an Australian University Classroom*. PhD thesis, Monash University, Australia.

Rafat, T. (1985) *Arrival of the Monsoon: Collected Poems, [1947–78]*. Lahore: Vanguard Books.

Sharifian, F. (2011) *Cultural Conceptualisations and Language*. Amsterdam: John Benjamins.

## Contributor

Zahra Ali is a Doctor of Philosophy candidate at Monash University, Australia. Her research areas include teaching EIL and intercultural communication.

# Foods and Englishes

## Goals

By the end of the lesson, students have a basic understanding that (1) variations of a language like English are common because it spreads globally; and (2) English influenced by the local acceptance or flavors is usually an outcome when there are existing local languages and cultures.

**Appropriate Courses**: Sociolinguistics, Introduction to Linguistics, History of the English Language, Teaching English as a second language (ESL)/English as a foreign language (EFL)

**Class Time**: 30 minutes

## Procedure

(1) Show students a picture of one food item that can be easily found in your local area, for example, pizza, sandwich, taco or curry. Alternatively, you may show three or four pictures of the same food but they contain different colors and ingredients. For example, if you choose pizza, you may have pictures of pizza with different toppings such as peperoni pizza, pizza with seafood topping, veggie pizza and Hawaiian pizza.

(2) Ask students if they have eaten the type of presented food in other cities, countries or regions. Ask them to share their experiences of having and tasting the food in different places. The guiding questions are: 'Are they similar to or different from the ones in your local area?', 'How are they similar or different?', 'Which one do you prefer?' and 'Why?'

(3) Ask students why they think this type of food varies in different places. The answers possibly include local preferences, local ingredients, different cultural orientations and interpretations, food restrictions based on beliefs and the like.

(4) Encourage students to think about these answers as if the food were a language. Lead a discussion about how a language like English could vary when it spreads or travels to different places, countries and regions. The details of the discussions may also include attitudes toward accents and dialects. For example, when asked about food preferences, students might like the ones served in their area because they are familiar and comfortable with them but not those in other cities. Or, they may prefer the ones from other cities or countries where the food is believed to be originally from. Discuss how the same thing can be said about English. There would be one's favorable and unfavorable English varieties. But, the important point is that we cannot expect English to be the same everywhere. The local preferences and resources

inevitably shape the way English sounds and forms differently from its origin.

(5) Conclude the lesson by emphasizing that language variations are a typical phenomenon, especially with a global language like English.

## Contributor

Chatwara Suwannamai Duran is Assistant Professor of Applied Linguistics at the University of Houston. She teaches and researches in the field of sociolinguistics, social literacy, transnationalism and multilingualism.

# Variations of English Grammar

## Goals

(1) Students are introduced to a number of examples presenting international variations of English grammatical structures that are different from standard American English and/or British English.
(2) Students understand that English linguistic norms can be multiple depending on multiple factors such as the English users' local languages.
(3) Students will be more open to different English variations.

| | |
|---|---|
| **Appropriate Courses**: | Sociolinguistics, Introduction to Linguistics, History of the English Language, Teaching ESL/EFL |
| **Class Time**: | 30 minutes |

## Procedure

(1) Present some English sentences used by or collected from the local and international communities. To achieve the lesson objectives successfully, include grammatical structures that are different from the standard English that is commonly introduced in British or American grammar books, textbooks or usage dictionaries.

Here are some examples:

(a) You must be knowing him.
(b) I'm understanding you.
(c) Do you know where is he going?
(d) You are going home soon, isn't it?
(e) You are joking, isn't it?
(f) Children these days they misbehave.
  (a)–(d) are from Börjars and Burridge (2010); (e)–(f) are from Kamwangamalu (2001)

(2)  Ask students what they think about the grammatical features in the sentences above and how these sentences are different from the English grammatical features that they have learned. Ask them to identify those differences.

(3)  The instructor may discuss those differences using the grammatical concepts that the students have learned. For example, (a)–(b) present stative verbs – in this case, the stative verbs 'to know' and 'to understand' – that are followed by –ing, which is found more often with an action verb; (c) presents a clause within a question without moving the verb back to form a declarative clause; (d) and (e) present a tag question with 'isn't it' regardless of what verb is used in the main clause; and (f) presents a repetition of the subject.

(4)  Explain to students that these grammatical features are commonly used in Global/World Englishes such as Indian English, Singaporean English and South African English. They represent systematic variations of English grammar that have been influenced by language contact and/ or the local languages of the speakers. They are not necessarily a wrong form of English.

(5)  Building on the steps above, the instructor may facilitate a discussion about teaching and learning English for intercultural/international communication that consists of speakers from different linguistic backgrounds.

## Additional information

During the discussion about the grammatical differences, avoid using such words as 'correct' and 'incorrect', 'grammatical' and 'ungrammatical' and 'lacking' or 'missing'. These words reinforce the belief that the Englishes different from the traditional British and American English are inferior.

## References

Börjars, K. and Burridge, K. (2010) *Introducing English Grammar Second Edition*. London: Hodder Education.
Kamwangamalu, N. (2001) Linguistic and cultural reincarnations of English: A case from Southern Africa. In E. Thumboo (ed.) *The Three Circles of English: Language Specialists Talk about the English Language* (pp. 45–66). Singapore: UniPress.

## Contributor

Chatwara Suwannamai Duran is Assistant Professor of Applied Linguistics at the University of Houston. She teaches and researches in the field of sociolinguistics, social literacy, transnationalism and multilingualism.

# Becoming an International Lingua Franca User through the Negotiation of Meaning

## Goals

The lesson aims to (1) raise awareness of the nature of English as a lingua franca (ELF) users' interaction; and (2) understand how ELF users are able to come to a mutual understanding through the negotiation of meaning.

What is of significance in this activity is the successful evidence that will result from the participants' use of various procedures to negotiate meaning for mutual understanding. By the end of the activity, the students will be encouraged and have tools to improve interactional communication skills.

> **Appropriate Courses**: This pedagogical idea and activity was originally designed for a discussion-based class for university students who want to engage in teaching English. However, it can be adapted in a variety of contexts and also adjusted according to the students' proficiency level.
>
> **Class Time**: 180–270 minutes

## Procedure

(1) *Preparation*. This activity requires a recording and viewing device for each pair of students and a viewing device for students to share their video clips with the entire class.

(2) *Introduction* (10 minutes). The teacher informs students that they will experience ELF interactions in this lesson. The students are asked to make a pair with another student who does not share their L1, and they engage in an interaction. They are not assigned a topic to discuss but rather are encouraged to explore possible topics and talk freely about whatever topic they decide on, all in English. The teacher assists students to set up a video camera with a microphone to record their interaction.

(3) *Conversation activity* (20 minutes). Students engage in conversation, which is video recorded.

(4) *Conversation analysis activity* (60 minutes). After step 3, each pair watches and listens to the video recording of their own interactions. They identify places where they experienced communication difficulties, transcribe the exchanges and analyze the exchanges in terms of what linguistic and paralinguistic features they noticed, sources for communication breakdowns and why they acted in certain ways. [Note: Depending on the time availability, this step can be completed outside the class time. It can also be expanded to cover sections where

communication was successful, in which case students can identify successful use of communication strategies.]

(5) *Group discussion about the interaction* (60–100 minutes). Students share a section from their interaction (what they analyzed in step 4) with the entire class (The more interactions they can watch the better, but the number will depend on the time availability.) Students are encouraged to take notes and ask questions as needed. After reviewing interactions, students attempt to identify key issues in ELF communication by responding to such discussion questions as *What did you learn from the interaction? What aspect is important for ELF communication? Why? Did you see any differences or similarities among the pair groups?* Students share their responses on the board.

(6) *Additional conversation activities* (as desired, 20 minutes). Students will find a new partner and engage in conversation again. This gives students an opportunity to apply what they have identified in step 5 as well as to practice using English for international communication. [Note: this section can be repeated as desired if time allows.]

(7) *Reflection and conclusion* (30–60 minutes). Students discuss and reflect on their own effectiveness and challenges in ELF interaction. Discussion questions may include: *What did you learn from both interactions? Did you have trouble understanding? Why did the troubles happen? How did you overcome the communication troubles?* The students may find that differences in phonology or lexicon trigger the need for the negotiation of meaning, or that other areas such as minimal responses or different uses of discourse markers and non-verbal actions cause ambiguity for interlocutors. In addition to encouraging students to make the interaction intelligible for diverse ELF users, the teacher may need to explain that there are varieties of English around the world, that English interactions take place more often between nonnative speakers (NNS) of English and that gaining interactional communication skills may be more important for ELF communication than linguistic accuracy.

## Contributor

Hanamoto Hiroki is a full-time Lecturer in the Department of Science and Engineering at Tokyo Denki University in Japan. His interests include mutual intelligibility studies from EIL and ELF perspectives.

# Language and Literacy Self-Assessment

## Goals

To have preservice and/or in-service teachers understand their own language proficiency in order to help them better understand their students' ongoing language learning. Part I of the assignment is designed to help teachers evaluate their L1 and all additional languages in terms of the four domains (reading, writing, speaking, listening) as well as how their proficiency in each language may change over time depending on the opportunities that they have to use each language. This will enable teachers to empathize with their students as well as to understand the complexities of developing an individual student's language(s) across the four domains. Part II of the assignment is designed to help teachers apply both the information learned in Part I and the knowledge that they have gained throughout the course to their role as a teacher.

**Appropriate Courses**: Any teacher preparation course involving a multicultural perspective where students need to understand what it means to be multilingual. The activity can be completed by participants who speak any language as their L1 and have even minimal knowledge of additional languages.

**Class Time**: 30–45 minutes to explain Grosjean's Language Grid (2011) and the WIDA Consortium's (2012) English language development standards or another development framework that students can use to explore their own language proficiency.

## Procedure

This assignment consists of two parts, both of which are individual writing assignments completed out of class. Part I is completed early in the semester so teachers are mindful of their own language and literacy development throughout the course. Part II is completed near the end of the course to allow teachers to reflect on their own language learning experiences as well as the knowledge gained in the course, and how these can inform their understanding of their students' language and literacy development.

## Part I:

(1) In class, introduce Grojean's (2011) Language Grid to explore language fluency and how it can change over time. Use the instructor's own language proficiency and usage in multiple languages, or use Grosjean's example.
(2) Demonstrate in class how to use a language standards framework for second language (L2) learners such as the WIDA (2012) to rate the languages they know (other than their L1). Explain to teachers the levels of language proficiency using the WIDA performance indicators.

Explain that this is a tool to help teachers understand their students' language proficiency in elementary and secondary education with which they should be familiar and that the performance indicators can help us to understand our own language proficiency. Provide an example using the instructor's own second and, if possible, additional languages, even those in which the fluency is limited, in order to show the range of proficiency levels one person may have across multiple languages. If appropriate, give the option of using a different tool such as the Common European Framework of Reference for Languages (Council of Europe, 2011).

(3) Explain to teachers that they will write a reflection on their own language and literacy development describing the language(s) they know, how and when they learned each one and rating their levels of proficiency across the four domains (speaking, listening, reading and writing).

(4) Provide a sample language and literacy self-assessment using the instructor as an example. This may be necessary in courses where teachers have a limited knowledge of multilingualism. Teachers will not copy the sample since each self-assessment will be highly personal and individualized.

## Part II:

(1) Near the end of the semester, remind teachers that they will apply both the information learned in Part I and the knowledge they have gained throughout the course to their role as a teacher for Part II.

(2) Direct teachers to refer back to their writing in Part I to analyze their self-assessments and evaluate which tools helped them understand their own language proficiency. They will write a reflection of this process and then explain how it helped them determine what information they need to gather to understand their own students.

(3) Explain to teachers that they will also write a description of how they will use their knowledge of their students' languages and proficiencies in their teaching. Their paper will include the theory, methods, strategies and activities they will use to motivate students and to scaffold the learning process for their multilingual learners, citing readings from the course.

## Additional information

In courses designed to teach students about multiliteracies, students can also describe how they use multiliteracies in their daily lives. In order for students to experience multiliteracies firsthand, their language and literacy self-assessments can be written as a blog and can include photos, music, video and other multimedia supports. The blog access should be limited to the professor and students in the course since some information may be personal.

## References

Council of Europe (2011) Common European Framework of Reference for Languages: Learning, Teaching, Assessment. See http://www.coe.int/t/dg4/linguistic/Cadre1_en.asp (accessed 24 August 2016).

Grosjean, F. (2011) Visualizing One's Languages. See https://www.psychologytoday.com/blog/life-bilingual/201112/visualizing-ones-languages (accessed 24 August 2016).

WIDA Consortium (2012) The 2012 Amplification of the English Language Development Standards, Kindergarten-Grade 12. Madison, WI: Board of Regents of the University of Wisconsin System. See https://www.wida.us/standards/eld.aspx (accessed 24 August 2016).

## Contributor

Tracy Hodgson-Drysdale teaches courses in literacy and bilingualism part-time at the University of Ottawa and her research focuses on teaching writing across content areas in multicultural educational settings.

# Design, Implementation and Evaluation of ELF-aware Lesson Plans

## Goal

To have the teacher candidates in preservice teacher education acquire comprehensive ELF-related pedagogical experience through microteaching and practicum.

**Appropriate Courses**:    ELF, EIL, WE, Methodology, Practice Teaching, School Teaching, Internship

**Class Time**:    For the presentation and evaluation of each ELF aware lesson plan: 60 minutes. The rest of the activity will be completed outside the class.

## Procedure

The lesson will be introduced in four steps: preparation, implementation, evaluation and follow-up.

(1) *Preparation for the lesson*: The teacher candidates read articles on ELF theory and pedagogy, reflect on them and discuss them. Following this, they are asked to design an ELF-aware lesson which may focus on several ELF-related subjects like English used by NNS from different L1 backgrounds, communication strategies in NNS–NNS interactions and

students' own use of English and their ELF user identity dependent on their linguistic and cultural sources. ELF can be integrated into the English classroom by:

(a)  using videos that show interactions between NNSs from different L1 backgrounds for awareness raising, analysis, reflection and discussion;

(b)  encouraging the productive use of L2 by allowing the students to speak with their own accents and L1 sources if need be and not making corrections on variations that do not deteriorate intelligibility;

(c)  incorporating the students' and other ELF users' own cultures into the class through discussions and examples.

(2)  *Implementation: The actual lesson.* In each class, a prospective teacher implements his or her lesson plan in the form of microteaching, i.e. he or she presents and tries out what he or she has planned with his or her colleagues.

(3)  *Evaluation.*

(a)  Following each microteaching session, the classmates of the teacher candidate and the instructor give feedback about the content and presentation of the lesson. The session together with the feedback is video-recorded.

(b)  After the session, the prospective teacher revises his or her lesson plan using the feedback and submits it with a self-assessment report to the instructor.

(c)  The instructor checks it and sends back his or her comments.

(4)  *Follow-up.*

(a)  If the teachers are doing their practicum, this microteaching session can pave the way for an ELF-related lesson to be applied in their real teaching practice. That is, the instructor can ask each candidate to adapt the final form of their ELF-aware lesson and any other relevant ELF-related ideas acquired in the course to their practicum class and work with the mentor teacher and the practicum supervisor collaboratively to guide the teacher candidate.

(b)  If it is not time for the practicum in the teacher education curriculum, the prospective teachers can be recommended and regularly reminded to apply this microteaching experience to their future practicum and/or any real teaching practice available.

**Note:** This lesson design has been inspired by the ELF Aware Teacher Education Project for in-service teachers initiated by Bayyurt and Sifakis (2015) and modified and adapted to a preservice language teacher education program at a state university in Turkey as a part of the contributor's PhD thesis.

# Reference

Bayyurt, Y. and Sifakis, N. (2015) Developing an ELF-aware pedagogy: Insights from a self-education programme. In P. Vettorel (ed.) *New Frontiers in Teaching and Learning English* (pp. 55–76). Newcastle upon Tyne: Cambridge Scholars Publishing.

# Contributor

Elif Kemaloglu-Er has extensive work experience as an English instructor and is currently teaching and writing her dissertation supervised by Yasemin Bayyurt and Nicos Sifakis on ELF-aware preservice teacher education at Bogaziçi University in Istanbul, Turkey.

# Past and Present: Role of English and Culture in English Language Teaching

## Goal

This lesson aims to develop students' awareness of their attitudes toward the role of English varieties and cultures in English classes and their ability to explain the major shift in the approach to English and culture in English language teaching (ELT).

This lesson allows students to assess/review their attitudes toward a traditional and new view of English and culture in language teaching and identify key principles associated with each of these views.

**Appropriate Courses**: General introductory teaching English to speakers of other languages (TESOL) courses, Continuing teacher education courses (current trends in ELT)

**Class Time**: 90 minutes

## Procedure

(1) The teacher writes the word 'English' on the board and tells students to draw a picture or write a word on a piece of paper that symbolizes the word for them. Students leave the sheet of paper with their answer on the desk and walk around to see what others have created. After they have looked at all the answers, they work in groups, explain to each other their symbol of English and share how they perceived their peers' answers while walking around. After they finish, the teacher tells students to put their sheets away for the time being for a later activity.

(2) The teacher provides each group with an opinion worksheet. Students read out each statement, explain their opinions about it and share their

level of agreement with it in their groups. Students record their group answers. Meanwhile, the teacher creates a spreadsheet on the board (numbers from 1 to 10, levels of agreement) in which representatives of each group record their group answers. The teacher scans students' opinions and challenges those that are in favor of traditional native speaker models by posing additional questions. The teacher transits to the next activity by saying that some of the statements that were just discussed are associated with the traditional view of English whereas some reflect the new function of English in the world which will be further explored next.

(3) The teacher hands out a past and present worksheet. Students work individually. Then, they compare their answers with their group peers (traditional approach – 1, 6, 7; current approach – 2, 3, 4, 5, 8). The teacher checks if they have any questions about their answers before he or she briefly discusses the state of ELT in their context (region, country) with the whole class.

(4) The teacher tells students to return to their symbols of English from the beginning of the lesson and consider whether they would keep/add/change anything to their symbol or their explanation of it. The teacher encourages students to share their answers again in their groups. Any member of the group should be able to summarize their answers for the whole class. The teacher elicits summaries from each group by selecting random students. The teacher uses the summaries as an informal assessment of the lesson goals.

## Appendix

*Opinion worksheet*

Write your level of agreement with the following statements (SA – strongly agree, A – agree, D – disagree, SD – strongly disagree)

(1) In general, I prefer native English teachers to XXXX (name of students' nationality, e.g. Czech) teachers of English.
(2) I don't like when XXXX (name of students' nationality, e.g. Czech) people speak with a strong XXXX (name of students' L1, e.g. Czech) accented pronunciation in English.
(3) Mainly native speakers of English should be heard in recorded/audio teaching materials.
(4) In speaking English, it is not important to have native speaker-like pronunciation or flawless language but getting your message across.
(5) School excursions to English-speaking countries provide the best opportunity for students to use English in real-life communication.

(6)  I wish I could pronounce English just like a native speaker so people would think that I am a good language learner.
(7)  In English classes, students need to hear native speakers of English to develop good listening skills.
(8)  It is the task of the English language teacher to contribute to the understanding of English-speaking countries.
(9)  NNSs do not need to internalize the cultural norms of native speakers of the English language.
(10) Language teaching should contribute to students' understanding of their own national identity.

### Past and present worksheet

(Adopted from Byram *et al.* [2002] and Pulverness [2003])

Mark if the following statement describes the traditional view of English and culture teaching or a current approach to ELT.

(1)  Share cultural information – life and institutions of English-speaking countries.
(2)  Enable learners to understand and accept people from other cultures as individuals with other distinctive perspectives, values and behaviors.
(3)  Teach language to effectively communicate with any speaker of English.
(4)  Prepare learners for interaction with people of other cultures.
(5)  Help learners to see such interaction as an enriching experience.
(6)  Use cultural texts and visuals as contextual backdrops to language tasks.
(7)  Teach language to effectively communicate with native speakers of English.
(8)  Develop learners' intercultural communicative competence.

## References

Byram, M., Gribkova, B. and Starkey, H. (2002) *Developing the Intercultural Dimension in Language Teaching: A Practical Introduction for Teachers*. Strasbourg: Council of Europe.
Matsuda, A. (ed.) (2012) *Principles and Practices of Teaching English as an International Language*. Bristol: Multilingual Matters.
Pulverness, A. (2003) Materials for cultural awareness. In B. Tomlinson (ed.) *Developing Materials for Language Teaching* (pp. 426–438). London: Continuum.

## Contributor

Gabriela Kleckova teaches TESOL methodology courses to preservice and in-service teachers in the English Department, College of Education at the University of Western Bohemia in Plzen, the Czech Republic.

# World Englishes and Computer-Mediated Communication (CMC): Developing an Awareness of EIL via Videoconference

## Goals

This lesson aims to:

(1) expose teacher trainees to several varieties of Expanding Circle Englishes found on videoconference;
(2) raise the awareness of English varieties (e.g. English usage and functions) among teacher trainees; and
(3) discuss and explore the pedagogical implications that may help teacher trainees consider how and to what extent they can integrate insights from this lesson into their own teaching context.

**Appropriate Courses**: WE; Computer-Mediated Communication (CMC)
**Class Time**: 180 minutes

## Procedure

(1) *Warm-up* (5 minutes). The teacher educator (i.e. the instructor of the course) introduces the day's lessons by activating the teacher trainees' prior knowledge based on the following questions:

- What is your definition of globalization?
- How has globalization changed the English language?
- How is English used in many different ways throughout the world today?
- What kind(s) of English are taught as legitimate varieties of English in local contexts?
- What is the attitude toward the status of EIL in local contexts?

(2) *Mini-lecture* (30 minutes). The teacher educator gives brief answers to the aforementioned questions that take into account its historical, cultural and sociolinguistic factors. Then, he or she narrows down his or her focus to EIL usage and its roles in local contexts (with special attention on Outer Circle contexts).

(3) *YouTube Video: Exposure to varieties of English usage and functions* (70 minutes).
   (a) The teacher educator makes a transition to a YouTube video, which features a 50-minute panel discussion among ELT scholars (from the US, Japan, South Korea and Indonesia) via five-way Skype video calls from the fall semester of 2014 (available at https://www.youtube.com/watch?v=TwkKoRZOVpE).

(b) The teacher educator explains that this videoconference addresses important issues such as the impacts of globalization on English language policy, English teachers' practices in the classroom and attitudes toward EIL in Inner Circle (the US) and Outer Circle countries (Japan, South Korea and Indonesia) that were briefly discussed in the warm-up and mini lecture stages.

(c) This time, the teacher educator introduces the notion of 'the ownership of English' by using English speakers on the video conference video as prime examples: The fact that presenters, except for one American professor, are neither from North America nor England, challenges the assumption that English speakers come from the 'western world.'

(d) Now, the teacher educator draws trainees' attention to language itself, today's main objective(s), by mentioning that the four participants (three panelists and one moderator) are Expanding Circle speakers of English.

(e) The teacher educator plays the video clip for one minute and checks trainees' understanding of the discussion in terms of intelligibility (word or utterance recognition) and comprehensibility (word or utterance understanding) by asking a few comprehension questions.

(f) The teacher educator invites the trainees to share their reactions to the other varieties of English by asking 'How is it different from the standardized spoken English?'

(g) After discussing briefly that they do not speak in a way that corresponds to common perceptions of 'native speakers', the teacher educator distributes the handouts. Then, the teacher educator asks trainees to write down similarities or differences among these varieties of English in comparison to American/British English in terms of pronunciation, grammar, vocabulary, idioms and communication style while watching the video clip for 50 minutes.

(4) *Small/Whole Group Discussion: Critical reflection about language* (30 minutes).

(a) While watching the video clip, the teacher educator splits the whole class into groups of five and discusses the similarities and differences among Englishes as possible. The additional discussion topics may include:

- What did you learn from the lesson?
- What was interesting or surprising for you?
- Which language feature is most interesting for you? Why?
- Which variety is most interesting for you? Why?

(b) They are then asked to present/share their findings to the whole class.

    (c) The teacher educator emphasizes that each of five individuals on the video speaks English differently in accents, vocabularies, idioms, sentence structure, non-verbal clues and other linguistic features (which are commonly known as 'variations').

    (d) Then, the teacher educator leads the discussion into the deeper (and more critical) level by asking questions:

- Do nonnative English speakers have to learn English so as to communicate with native English speakers?
- Why do you think setting a single target variety (e.g. American English) is problematic for your English instruction?

(5) *Small-Group Discussion: Pedagogical implications and application* (30 minutes).

    (a) Teacher trainees are asked to write their perspectives on EIL issues and write ideas on how and to what extent they can incorporate EIL into their own teaching context. Once they are done, they are free to read their ideas and receive feedback from colleagues.

    (b) Finally, teacher trainees in each group are given three minutes to present their ideas. For a more engaging class activity, teacher trainees in the group may vote for the best pedagogical applications that can be feasibly adapted in their school context.

(6) *Wrap-up* (10 minutes).

    (a) The teacher educator draws the conclusion that varieties of English are common in that people of different cultures experience/think/feel/speak the same language differently.

    (b) The teacher educator also emphasizes that English learners/speakers in Outer Circle countries do not necessary interact with native speakers of English. The teacher trainees should thus take EIL into account when teaching English in their local classrooms.

    (c) Finally, the teacher educator gives a homework assignment in which teacher trainees write up one reflective journal using one of the following three prompts:

- Have I changed my attitude to English(es) in any way as a result of today's lesson?
- In class, am I teaching WE or mainly focusing on one particular variety of English (e.g. US/UK English)?
- How can I create an environment where my students can get exposed to varieties of English, not one particular English variety? (e.g. utilizing CMC)

## Additional Resource

A video of the second English for speakers of other languages (ESOL) Online Roundtable: Globalization and Teaching EIL (http://eslweb.wixsite. com/esol-roundtable).

## Contributor

Ju Seong (John) Lee is a doctoral student in Curriculum and Instruction (C&I) at the University of Illinois at Urbana-Champaign (UIUC). His research interests include WE, technology-integrated learning in foreign language classroom (via videoconference, telecollaboration, wearable devices), NNEST issues and self-directed teacher professional development.

# John Agard's 'Half-Caste': Standard English and Englishes

## Goal

This lesson aims to (1) raise students' awareness of varieties of English; (2) enable students to understand their own attitudes toward Englishes; and (3) make connections between language, English and identity.

This lesson makes use of video clips, literary texts and classroom discussions to introduce and discuss the idealization of standard English and the development of English varieties as well as exploring the complex interrelationship between language, culture and identity.

**Class Time:**  90 minutes

## Procedure

(1) *Preparation.* Before class, prepare the two poems by John Agard (without putting the author's name on the sheet): 'Half-Caste' and 'Flag' ('Half-Caste' is written in Caribbean English and 'Flag' is written in the so-called standard English).

(2) *Peer discussion* (10–15 minutes). Distribute the two poems and ask the students to read them. Ask the students to compare the language of the two poems along with some guiding questions for peer-discussion such as:

- What are your impressions of the two poems?
- How do the two poems differ from one another (in terms of grammatical structure, vocabulary, accent and other linguistic features)?
- Do they use the same language? Why? Why not?
- What are the two poems about?
- Why do you think poem one is written that way? What are the purposes?
- Where do you think the author of poem one comes from?
- Where do you think the author of poem two comes from?

(3) *Audio recordings of English variations* (10 minutes). Tell the students to hold the answers among themselves and lead them to listen to the audio

recordings of the poems read by the author (extracted from YouTube, do not show the video in full view to allow students to only focus on the voice of the author reading the two poems). Then, the teacher asks the students whether they notice anything special from the two audio recordings (possible answer: similar English pronunciation or accent; one poem is read out using standard English and the other is non-standard; one poem is more formal than the other; both poems are read out by NNS). After listening to the two audio recordings, the teacher can give some discussion questions: Do you understand what the speakers are saying? Is the English intelligible enough for you to attain the message of the read out poems? What do you think about the two speakers' English speech?

(4) *Class discussion* (30 minutes). Using their own answers, ask students to further elaborate on what they understand as a (non)native speaker of English, (non-)standard English and English(es). This step aims to find out about their understanding of each concept and the associated imagination of each concept (e.g. non-standard English is often associated with uneducated English, incorrect grammatical structure and heavy accent, produced by NNS of English).

(5) *Problematizing native speakerism and the idealization of standard English* (5 minutes). Explain to the students that the two poems are written by the same person and display the author's picture and biography or background (or play the complete video clip from YouTube). From here, the teacher can lead the discussion to the issue of native speakerism, standard English and how very often the idealization of native speakerism is based on assumption and ideological motives about a particular language and culture.

(6) *Reflection and further discussion on English and Englishes* (30 minutes). Ask the students to discuss their reaction when they find out that the two poems were written by the same person, in terms of English and Englishes, written and spoken English, language and identity and communication:

- Review your earlier comments about your impression of poem one and two. What is your opinion about the author now?
- What can you learn about the author?
- What do you learn from this activity?

Then, the teacher can lead the discussion to the use of EIL, English as the medium of multilingual and multicultural identity and English as the medium of self-actualization (as what the author did through his poems).

(7) *Journal reflection questions.* As a follow-up activity, the teacher can give out a set of questions for student's reflection journal entry such as

- What English variety do you think you tend to speak in? Why do you think so?
- Have you ever experienced coming into contact with another English variety? When (what was the occasion)? Who was your interlocutor? What were you talking about? Was it a (in)formal communicative setting? How did you feel at that time when you heard that English variety?
- How do you want other people to view you as an English user? (I want people to understand that as an English speaker, I am ..........)
- Knowing all of the information you learned in this session, how do you think English should be taught? What should be the goal of ELT today?

## Resources

John Agard's 'Half-Caste': http://www.intermix.org.uk/poetry/poetry_01_agard.asp

## Video clips links

John Agard's 'Half-Caste' video: https://www.youtube.com/watch?v=zDQf2Wv2L3E
John Agard's 'Flag': https://www.youtube.com/watch?v=1tYHpMHtaGE

## Resources

Lippi-Green, R. (1997) *English with an Accent: Language, Ideology, and Discrimination in the United States*. New York: Routledge.
McKay, S. (2002) *Teaching English as an International Language: An Introduction to the Role of English as an International Language and Its Implications for Language Teaching*. Oxford: Oxford University Press.

## Contributor

Christine Manara lectures at the MA TESOL Department of Payap University, Thailand. Her research interests include teaching methodology, EIL pedagogy, teacher's professional learning and identity and the use of literature in ELT.

# An English-as-an-International-Language Case Study

## Goal

The goal of this case study project is to provide teacher candidates with an opportunity to demonstrate their understanding of the EIL framework through an analysis of the history and status of ELT in another country.

**Appropriate Courses**:   Special Topics in ESL, Methods in Teaching ESOL, Practicum in TESOL

**Class Time**:   This case study project can be completed in one month with each class session meeting approximately 3 hours each week.

## Procedure

### Preparation

In preparation for the case study, teacher candidates will:

(1) Read McKay's (2002) *Teaching English as an International Language* and engage in discussions around concepts central to the EIL paradigm. Topics may include:
   (a) Re-analysis of Kachru's Inner, Expanding and Outer Circles.
   (b) Reconsideration of the notion of 'native speakerism'.
   (c) Analysis of ELT textbooks and materials through the 'sphere of interculturality'.
   (d) Understanding of the political, economic, social, cultural and institutional dimensions that influence ELT in a variety of contexts.
(2) Compare two different ELT contexts listing a teaching position and analyze both contexts from the political, economic, social, cultural and institutional dimensions. McKay and Bokhorst-Heng (2008) include two contrasting case studies from private language institutions in Japan and Spain. Teacher candidates can read the responsibilities of each and determine which position they would consider. Alternatively, they can search for two teaching positions online and provide a rationale for their selection based on the dimensions listed above.

### Case study project

(1) *Directions*. Using the following criteria as a guide, teacher candidates can create a presentation (iMovie or PowerPoint) about ELT in a country of their choice. They can select countries that they have taught in prior to enrolling in the program, countries that many of their students are from in their current classrooms or countries that they hope to teach in in the future.

Each project should at minimum include the following three components:
   (a) a meaningful rationale with thoughtful reasons for the selection of the country;
   (b) research on the political, economic, social, cultural and institutional contexts that influence ELT in the country;

    (c)  a reflective analysis of how they plan to incorporate and approach teaching English using the EIL paradigm.
(2) *Presentations.* Each teacher candidate will have 10 minutes to show their movies or narrate their presentations in class.
(3) *Assessment.* A sample grading criteria has been provided below.

A sample project of this assignment conducted by a student from Hong Kong, who wishes to teach in Hong Kong upon completion of her program can be viewed through the following link: https://www.youtube.com/watch?v=vDKGMZV2qYo.

## References

McKay, S.L. (2002) *Teaching English as an International Language: Rethinking Goals and Approaches.* Oxford: Oxford University Press.
McKay, S.L. and Bokhorst-Heng, W. (2008) *International English in its Sociolinguistic Contexts: Towards a Socially Sensitive EIL Pedagogy.* New York: Routledge.

# Appendix

| | Achievement | | |
| Criteria | Performance Level 1 | Performance Level 2 | Performance Level 3 |
| --- | --- | --- | --- |
| **Introduction (10%)** | The introduction includes a rationale for the selection of the country for the case study, which is superficial (e.g. beautiful beaches). | The introduction includes a rationale for the selection of the country for the case study and includes some thoughtful reasons for the selection, but with some superficial reasons. | The introduction includes a meaningful rationale with thoughtful reasons for the selection of the country for the case study. |
| **Case Study (50%)** | The case study includes research on one or two of the five contexts that influence ELT in the country. | The case study includes research on three of the five contexts that influence ELT in the country. | The case study includes research on the political, social, economic, cultural and institutional contexts that influence ELT in the country. |
| **Conclusion (15%)** | The conclusion does not present any evidence of reflective thinking about where the student would like to teach in the future. | The conclusion presents a thoughtful, but not deeply reflective analysis of where the student would like to teach in the future. | The conclusion presents a thoughtful and deeply reflective analysis of where the student would like to teach in the future. |
| **Presentation (20%)** | The presentation is not clear or is not visually appealing and does not include a discussion of two or three of the criteria listed above. | The presentation is visually appealing and clear, but is missing one criterion listed above. | The presentation is visually appealing, clear and includes at minimum all three of the criteria listed above. |
| **Mechanical Issues (5%)** | The case study exhibits major mechanical issues. | The case study exhibits minor mechanical issues. | The case study is free from mechanical issues. |

## Contributor

Sarina Molina serves as a faculty member and coordinator of the MEd in TESOL, Literacy and Culture program at the University of San Diego.

# Devil's Advocate and Debate: Reflecting on EIL

## Goals

Learners will be able to:

(1) Highlight and problematize various issues in teaching EIL.
(2) Articulate personal positions on topics including language teaching, native speakerism and 'standard English'.
(3) Problematize the notion of 'standard English'.

**Appropriate Courses**: Teacher education, WE, ELT, Sociolinguistics, general conversation courses for preservice teachers who are not L1 speakers of English

**Class Time**: 60 minutes

## Procedure

(1) *Warm-up: Partner devil's advocate* (5 minutes). Learners are divided into sets of partners. One controversial statement is presented. In Round 1, each Partner A talks continuously for one minute, explaining to their Partner B the merits of the statement, expressing support for the position. Then the instructor says, 'Switch', and Partner A continues speaking, but switches perspective to explain why they oppose that statement. In Round 2, Partner B follows the same format, but with a different topic. Suggested examples of topics:

- English instruction should begin in the first grade of primary school.
- All language teachers should be required to be fluent in at least two languages.
- English language courses should be taught using 'English Only'.

(2) *Partner debate* (15 minutes). Learners are shown the following information, are given two minutes to prepare and then spend five minutes debating back and forth about who they would prefer to hire as a language instructor at their institution. Following the debate, a whole-class discussion on the learners' true thoughts and reasons is facilitated.

| | CONNECTIONS You are both on the hiring committee for a new English language instructor at your institution. The final two candidates are the following. Discuss who you would prefer to hire. | |
|---|---|---|
| | **Samuel Smith** | **SuMin Kim** |
| Citizenship | America | South Korea |
| Major | Finance | English education |
| Experience | Worked at a bank in the US for 10 years and taught one year at language institute in Korea | Taught English 10 years at a University in Korea |
| Languages spoken | 1st-English | 1st-Korean 2nd-English, Chinese |

- Speak with your partner about who to hire. Partner 1 wants to hire Samuel Smith.
- Partner 2 wants to hire SuMinKim. Each try to convince each other.
- Which instructor would you really prefer?

(3) *Whole class debate* (30 minutes). Divide the class into two teams. Learners may begin by self-selecting sides and the instructor can then even out the sides as needed, so some learners will be arguing 'devil's advocate' style. The debate topic is announced, for example, 'All speakers of English should work toward speaking the same variety of "standard English"'. Teams are given 10 minutes to prepare for the debate. In that time, learners cooperate to do the following:

- Create their main arguments, specific arguments and supporting evidence for their position.
- Identify counterarguments that the opposing team might have.
- Develop responses to the counterarguments.

A formal style debate is then conducted. One person on Team 1 begins by stating their team's 1-minute introduction. Team 2 follows. Another person on Team 1 then gives one argument supporting their side. Team 2 offers a response and either extends the counterargument or introduces a new argument, to which Team 1 responds. After a few rounds of debate, teams are given one minute to regroup and prepare a final conclusion statement to present. (Note: To encourage more balanced participation, I recommend that each person must contribute at least once before others are allowed to speak multiple times to ensure that everyone has a chance to contribute before dominant speakers take over.)

(4) *Follow-up: Individual written reflections* (outside of class). Learners can blog or write a written reflection on their own personal beliefs and

experiences with the debate topic, which can also be extended to a discussion in the next class.

## Contributor

Shannon Tanghe, an Assistant Professor at Dankook University, has 15 years of teaching experience in Korea. Her major research interests include WE, teacher development and education and teacher collaboration.

# Confronting Linguicism in the Teacher Education Classroom

## Goals

(1) To simulate classroom-based linguistic discrimination.
(2) To initiate a discussion on linguistic discrimination.
(3) To elicit and develop pedagogical practices that will confront linguistic discrimination.

**Appropriate Courses**:   WE, ELT
**Class Time**:                  Approximately 90 minutes (flexible)

## Procedure

(1) *Pre-activity*. In the class prior to the language discrimination simulation, learners are asked to individually brainstorm and create lists of ways people discriminate or are discriminated against vis-à-vis language.
(2) *Linguistic Discrimination Simulation Implementation*. The class is randomly divided. Half are told that the language variety they are using is 'ideal' and will be privileged, while the other half's language is judged as less acceptable. The instructor then intentionally enacts the discriminatory practices that the students had brainstormed in the pre-activity, and adds others, clearly privileging one group and their linguistic forms while marginalizing the other. Some specific examples include:

Ways the Two Groups were Treated Differently

| Classroom | Privileged group | Marginalized group |
|---|---|---|
| Seating | Sat at front of room | Sat at back of room, desks crammed together |
| Comprehension checking | Paraphrased, asked for clarification | 'I have no idea what you are talking about' 'Are you speaking English?' |

| Wait time | Sufficient wait time | Rushed to finish answers<br>Short pause, sigh and redirect to other group |
|---|---|---|
| Circulation | Circulated around students, knelt beside, some to chat | Ignored back half of room |
| Eye contact | Always focused eyes here | Almost non-existent eye contact |
| Noise | Encouraged to discuss ideas with partner | Criticized for speaking too loudly to others |
| Student answers | Guidance offered<br>Usually selected to answer questions | No support<br>Incredulity at correct answers 'Did you think of that by yourself?' |
| Feedback | Widely praised for volunteering any answers | Very short, if any acknowledgment of correct answers |
| Vocal tone | Friendly, enthusiastic voice | Gruff, short voice |
| Speaking speed | Normal pace | Spoke very quickly and impatiently |
| Naming | Addressed students by name | Grouping all together 'you guys', appearance-based 'you, green shirt' Mispronounced names, gave English names, 'Sorry JuYeon is too hard to say, I'll call you Julie' |

Students remain in these assigned roles for half of the activity's allotted time, then the two groups are reversed, repositioning their levels of privilege.

The actual class proceeds as a seemingly regular class meeting, discussing concepts of language discrimination (specific content included discussions of discriminatory language practices in the media, discriminatory language education policies, hiring/housing practices, personal experiences, representation, race issues in the classroom and key studies in the field plus reflections on local English education and language policies) while implementing the discrimination simulation.

(3) *Post activity.* A short reflective debriefing session immediately follows the activity, with the following questions discussed:

- How did you feel when you were in each of the groups?
- What other implications, possibly classroom related, can you draw from this simulation in addition to linguistic discrimination?
- Do you think it is important to talk about discrimination-related issues in the classroom?
- To what extent does linguicism exist in the world? Local area? Your classroom?

Learners are first given time to individually reflect on their responses prior to a group discussion.

(4) *Extension*. All students are asked to further reflect on a course blog detailing their personal reactions to the activity or further thoughts.

**Note:** This activity needs to be implemented with care, as it can be quite powerful. Brief learner reflections are included below:

**JooYeon**: 'Even though all these were just simulation activities, the students who were discriminated felt insulted, embarrassed, got hurt and mad and became less motivated as if it were a real situation…I realized language learning and psychological issues are stronger related and language linguicism can affect students more negatively than I expected'.

**Suyoung**: 'As an educator, I would like to…make my students realize how cruel linguistic discrimination can be. I hope my students find their rights to not be discriminated and also set their minds not to discriminate for any reason'.

## Recommended Related Resources

### Texts (Books and articles)

Hammond, K. (2006) More than a game: A critical discourse analysis of a racial inequality exercise in Japan. *TESOL Quarterly* 40 (3), 545–571.

Lippi-Green, R. (1997) *English with an Accent: Language, Ideology, and Discrimination in the United States*. London/New York: Routledge.

### YouTube videos

'Accents' (Fair Housing PSA) Simulation video to show effects of linguicism, highlights unfair housing rental practices. See http://www.youtube.com/watch?v=84k2iM30vbY

Disney Dialects – Examples of how animated characters in Disney movies often use certain dialects associated with negativity and evil. See http://www.youtube.com/watch?v=5hCTI6JYtuo

Jane Elliott on the Oprah Winfrey Show (1992) Blue Eyes Brown Eyes Exercise – Elliott describes her discrimination experiments and their effects.

## Contributors

Shannon Tanghe is an Assistant Professor of TESOL at Dankook University. Her major research interests include WE, teacher development and education and teacher collaboration.

Jooyeon Cho, a graduate student at Dankook University's Graduate School of TESOL in South Korea, majored in Education and has been teaching English since 2006. Major interests include critical pedagogy, teaching methods and WWE.

Suyoung Ahn has been taking TESOL master courses in Dankook University in South Korea. She has 12 years language teaching experience. Her major research interests include WE, native speakerism, the ownership of English and linguicism.

# Who Uses English? Awareness of English as an International Language

## Goal

To familiarize teachers and students with pertinent information about English in the world. This introductory lesson will help provide students with a wider perspective about English use in the world, particularly those students who use English as their mother tongue.

**Appropriate Courses**:   English, Geography, English Education, Comparative Cultures
**Class Time**:   30–90 minutes

## Procedure

### Activity One

(1)   The teacher explains how English in the world can be characterized by three concentric circles (Kachru, 2003) consisting of the Inner Circle (where English is learned as L1), the Outer Circle (English is used as L2 and has historic or official importance) and the Expanding Circle (English is used as a foreign language [EFL] and has no official role but has some importance).

(2)   The teacher elicits examples of countries from each of the three circles and writes them on the board.

(3)   Students place the following countries in the appropriate column, L1, L2 or EFL: Ireland, South Africa, Canada, the Philippines, China, Russia, Australia, India, Germany, Pakistan, Hong Kong, Singapore, Nigeria, New Zealand, Spain, Turkey, Kenya, Vietnam, Russia, Brazil, Ghana.

(4)   Students (together or in small groups) add 10 more countries to the list, including countries from all three categories.

(5)   The teacher concludes the activity by asking students: Of the approximately 224 countries in the world, how many do you think

use English as L1? L2? After eliciting estimates, the teacher informs students of the answers.

## Activity Two

(1)  Building on Activity One, the teacher instructs students to make a pie chart, dividing it into English L1 users, L2 users and EFL users.
(2)  Students activate their prior knowledge and estimate the percentage of each of the three areas.
(3)  Students examine each other's charts and estimates and compare the ranges.
(4)  Teacher provides the correct answers. Students compare their own answers with the correct answers, and discuss what they learned.

## Activity Three

(1)  The teacher first asks student to give an estimated world population.
(2)  Teacher gives the answer (about 7 billion) and asks students to activate their knowledge from Activities One and Two and estimate the number of English L1 speakers, L2 speakers and EFL speakers.
(3)  Students look up the answers, or the teacher provides the answers. Students compare their answers with the correct answers, and discuss what they learned, or what surprised them in this activity.
(4)  (This could also be used to introduce Activity One.) The teacher elicits guesses for the number of different languages spoken in the world today, and the number in danger of extinction. As a follow up, students guess the top 10 L1 languages spoken in the world today.
(5)  After lists are made and students' guesses recorded, the teacher gives the correct answers or assigns students to look up the correct answers. If students look up the answers, they must provide a source for their research.
(6)  Students gain awareness of the wide variety of the world's languages and develop an understanding of the importance of English in world communication as well as the varieties of English that are available.

# Answers and discussion

## Activity One

(3)  L1:   Ireland, South Africa, Canada, Australia, New Zealand.
     L2:   India, Pakistan, Nigeria, the Philippines, Ghana, Kenya, Singapore, Hong Kong.
     EFL:  China, Egypt, France, Germany, Indonesia, Japan, Korea, Spain, Turkey, Vietnam, Zimbabwe, Russia, Brazil.

(5) According to Crystal (2003), English has a special status in 70 countries, and is taught as an L2 in 100 more.

### Activity Two
L1 is about 23%, ESL 27% and EFL about 50%.

### Activity Three

(2) By weighing various sources, Crystal (2003) estimates English L1 speakers are between 320 to 380 million, ESL speakers between 300 and 500 million and EFL speakers between 500 million and 1 billion.
(4) There are more than 6000 languages, and 2500 are in danger of extinction in the 21st century (Crystal, 2003).

The most widely spoken L1 languages are

(1)  Chinese (1.197 billion)
(2)  Spanish (399 million)
(3)  English (335 million)
(4)  Hindi (260 million)
(5)  Arabic (292 million)
(6)  Portuguese (203 million)
(7)  Bengali (189 million)
(8)  Russian (166 million)
(9)  Japanese (128 million)
(10) Lahnda (88.7 million) (Lewis *et al.*, 2014)

Chances are that students will be surprised by many parts of this awareness exercise. This could be the starting point for further EIL discussion and debate, or could be used as a stand-alone exercise. Students can better understand how widely English is used for communication by people of different nations, and that L1 speakers are in the minority of English users.

## References

Crystal, D. (2003) *English as a Global Language*. Cambridge: Cambridge University Press.
Kachru, B.B. (2003) Liberation linguistics and the Quirk concern. In B. Seidlhofer (ed.) *Controversies in Applied Linguistics* (pp. 19–33). Oxford: Oxford University Press.
Lewis, M.P., Simons, G.F. and Fening, C.D. (eds) (2014) *Ethnologue: Languages of the World* (18th edn). Dallas, TX: SIL International. See http://www.ethnologue.com (accessed 24 August 2016).

## Contributor

Paul Tanner has been teaching EFL in Japan for more than 25 years.

# Englishes, ELF and Teacher Education: How to Foster Awareness and Plan Pedagogic Activities

## Goal

To foster an awareness of the pedagogic implications of the pluralization of English (WE, EIL/ELF).

**Appropriate Courses**: Teacher training courses
**Class Time**: Equivalent of eight 1-hour lessons: one hour to set the scene, one-hour discussion, three hours for group work 3, two for activity (a) and one for activity (b); three hours for group work 4 (that may also partly be carried out as a home assignment)

## Procedure

(1) *Introduction to the spread of English.* Main concepts to be introduced include language variation and change, first and second diasporas, WE, nativized varieties and characteristic differences; ELF – demographics, spread of English, characteristics and contexts of use.

(2) *Implications of WE and ELF in ELT.* Main concepts and issues include native/bilingual speakers, cross/intercultural interactions, communication strategies, exemplifications of possible points for lesson plans and 'positive' examples from recent ELT material (textbooks, additional materials).

(3) *Group work 1*

    (a) Analysis of ELT textbooks currently used by the trainee teachers in the local context. During group work, textbooks are scrutinized in order to analyze whether, and to what extent, a pluralistic perspective for WE and EIL/ELF is included. The activity can be carried out with the help of a template including the following main points for analysis:

        • Range of speakers: Are only native speakers presented as language models, or are bi-/plurilingual speakers included, too?
        • Range of settings: Do they include also plurilingual settings, or are they only anglophone, Inner Circle ones?
        • Cultural representations: Are only anglophone countries represented (traditional 'target culture') or are activities aimed at fostering intercultural awareness in international settings included? Is reflection upon the learner's own culture and 'other' cultures promoted? (This point may also be organized by theme, e.g. looking at representations of food, school and

festivals, even within a content and language integrated learning [CLIL] perspectives.)
- Communication strategies: Are they explicitly dealt with and how?
- Learners' experience: Is reflection on the learners' experience with English included?

(b) Sharing of findings in class discussion both in person and in the course online platform (e.g. Moodle) and main reflection points.

(4) *Group work 2*
  (a) Exploration of 'positive' findings from textbooks (see *Group work 1* above) with a WE and EIL/ELF-oriented classroom practice perspective and implementation of existing materials with teaching ideas for classroom practice (one or more lessons) in the local context, tailored in terms of age and level of proficiency. In these lesson plans, students' involvement in the retrieval of materials/examples is to be encouraged, as well as the inclusion of examples from the use of English in their everyday local context (see e.g. Corbett, 2010; Lopriore & Vettorel, 2015; Vettorel, 2014).
  (b) Sharing of findings in class discussion, both in presence and in the course online platform (e.g. Moodle), in order to create a shared repository of teaching ideas and lessons.

## References

Corbett, J. (2010) *Intercultural Language Activities* Cambridge: Cambridge University Press.
Lopriore, L. and Vettorel, P. (2015) 'Promoting awareness of Englishes and ELF in the English language classroom. In H. Bowles and A. Cogo (eds) *International Perspectives on ELF-oriented Teaching*. London: Palgrave MacMillan.
Vettorel, P. (2014) Connecting English wor(l)ds and classroom practices. *TEXTUS* XXVII (1), 137–154.

## Contributor

Paola Vettorel is Assistant Professor in the Department of Foreign Languages and Literatures – University of Verona. Her main research interests include ELF and its implications in ELT practices and materials.

# Autoethnographic Inquiry Project

## Goals

(1) Students will develop an awareness of their own preconceptions concerning the teaching and learning of EIL.
(2) Students will negotiate and enact identities as teachers of EIL by critically reflecting on their instructional priorities, values and beliefs.

**Appropriate Courses**: 'English as an International Language: Linguistic and Pedagogical Considerations' or any other language teacher education courses which has an EIL focus.

**Class Time**: This is an out-of-class assignment which entails critical reflection on class discussions and readings. From the first to the last step, this project spans over a semester.

## Procedure

This autoethnographic inquiry project comprises four main steps: data gathering, data analysis, reporting findings and sharing with peers.

(1) *Data gathering.* In this section of the autoethnographic inquiry project, students are going to use four other class assignments as data sources for their project.

  (a) *Initial expectations paper*: They are expected to write a paper in the first week of the semester in which they need to describe what they would like to learn in this course and what contributions it will make to their learning to teach English.

  (b) *Language learning autobiography*: In the second week, they need to submit an autobiographical paper in which they recount their language learning experiences.

  (c) *Critical reading response*: Additionally, each week they need to write a response prior to class meetings which they will revisit after class discussions to delineate their thoughts and feelings about assigned topics. The topics of this EIL course include the following: Englishes around the world, going beyond the native speaker as a benchmark in traditional ELT, teacher and learner identities and the ownership of English, use of L1 in English classes, contextual factors and students' needs, revisiting ELT methods from an EIL perspective, promoting intercultural competence, creating EIL materials and lesson plans, principles of assessment in Teaching English as an International Language (TEIL), developing a curriculum of TEIL.

  (d) *Final reflections paper*: Two weeks before the semester ends, students are expected to write a reflection paper in which they need to discuss how this class has contributed to their professional preparation as teachers of English, whether it has fulfilled their expectations and what questions are left unresolved.

(2) *Data analysis.* Students are expected to carefully read through and analyze those threads of autoethnographic data gleaned from the initial expectations paper, language learning autobiography, revisited critical reading responses and final reflections paper. Through this analysis,

they are asked to investigate and examine their own instructional values, beliefs and priorities in relation to their prior language learning experiences, current self-conceptions and future aspirations as English language teachers. They are encouraged to scrutinize how they enact their identities as teachers of EIL while their personal practical knowledge interacts with the principles of EIL pedagogy.

(3) *Reporting their findings*. The subsequent step is to craft their personal account detailing the findings about their own teacher identity which they are expected to have (re)negotiated and (re)positioned through class readings, discussions and assignments. They are expected to discuss their introspective observations regarding what kind of EIL teachers they are and envision becoming.

(4) *Sharing with peers*. Lastly, students need to present their findings in a class meeting to further externalize and verbalize their teacher identity (re)negotiation and (re)positioning and to kindle class discussions concerning the intersection of their ongoing language teacher learning and identity development.

## Contributor

Bedrettin Yazan is an Assistant Professor at the University of Alabama. His research focuses on EIL, teacher learning and identity development and nonnative English-speaking teachers.

# Index